DEINDUSTRIALISATION AND POPULAR MUSIC

Popular Musics Matter: Social, Political and Cultural Interventions

Series Editors:

Eoin Devereux, Aileen Dillane and Martin J. Power

The Popular Musics Matter: Social, Political and Cultural Interventions series will publish internationally informed edited collections, monographs and textbooks that engage in the critical study of popular music performance (live and recorded), historical and contemporary popular music practitioners and artists, and participants and audiences for whom such musics embody aesthetic, cultural, and, particularly, socio-political values. The series sees music not only as a manifestation of global popular culture but also as a form that profoundly shapes and continually seeks to redefine our understandings of how society operates in a given location and era.

Titles in the Series

DEINDUSTRIALISATION AND POPULAR MUSIC

Punk and 'Post-Punk' in Manchester, Düsseldorf, Torino and Tampere

Giacomo Bottà

ROWMAN & LITTLEFIELD
INTERNATIONAL

London • New York

Published by Rowman & Littlefield International, Ltd.
6 Tinworth Street, London SE11 5AL, United Kingdom
www.rowmaninternational.com

Rowman & Littlefield International, Ltd. is an affiliate of
Rowman & Littlefield
4501 Forbes Boulevard, Suite 200, Lanham, Maryland 20706, USA
With additional offices in Boulder, New York, Toronto (Canada), and London
(UK)
www.rowman.com

British Library Cataloguing in Publication Information
A catalogue record for this book is available from the British Library

ISBN: HB 978-1-78660-737-9

Library of Congress Cataloging-in-Publication Data
Names: Bottà, Giacomo, 1974- author.
Title: Deindustrialisation and popular music : punk and 'post-punk' in Manchester, Düsseldorf,
    Torino and Tampere / Giacomo Bottà.
Description: Lanham : Rowman & Littlefield Publishing Group, 2020. | Series: Popular musics
    matter: social, political and cultural interventions | Includes bibliographical references and
    index. | Summary: "The book offers a new and unique point of view on industrial cities and
    their popular music cultures based on interdisciplinary research and methods"-- Provided by
    publisher.
Identifiers: LCCN 2019057100 (print) | LCCN 2019057101 (ebook) | ISBN 9781786607379
    (cloth) | ISBN 9781786607386 (epub) | ISBN 9781538148273 (pbk)
Subjects: LCSH: Popular music--Social aspects--Europe--History. | Punk rock music--Social as-
    pects--Europe--History. | Post-punk music--Social aspects--Europe--History. | Deindustrial-
    ization--Europe.
Classification: LCC ML3917.E85 B67 2020 (print) | LCC ML3917.E85 (ebook) | DDC 781.66--
    dc23
LC record available at https://lccn.loc.gov/2019057100
LC ebook record available at https://lccn.loc.gov/2019057101

CONTENTS

ACKNOWLEDGEMENTS

The idea for writing this book came during my fellowship as a Von Humboldt Foundation experienced researcher at the Zentrum für Populäre Kultur und Musik of the University of Freiburg, in Germany. I hereby thank Michael Fischer and Nils Grosch for their support during my application and during my stay in Freiburg. I am grateful to Eoin Devereux, Martin J. Power, and Aileen Dillane for several great conferences in Limerick and for accepting this book in the series Popular Musics Matter: Social, Political and Cultural Interventions. Thanks also to all the editorial personnel at Rowman & Littlefield International.

Chapters or sections of this book have been presented as papers at international conferences. The International Association for the Study of Popular Music (IASPM) biennial conferences have been, over the years, the place to discuss my ideas in a friendly, safe, and supportive environment. I hereby thank all IASPM members I met over the years, in particular: Antti-Ville Kärjä, Geoff Stahl, Tony Mitchell, Rosa Reitsamer, Fabian Holt, Johan Fornäs, Franco Fabbri, Alenka Barber-Kersovan, Gonnie Rietveld, Christoph Jacke, Chrizzi Heinen, and Martin Cloonan. Thanks to Paula Guerra and all the KISMIF family in Porto; to Matthew Worley and the Interdisciplinary Network for the Study of Subcultures, Popular Music and Social Change; to Iñigo Sanchez, who invited me to present some of the findings of this research in a keynote speech in Lisbon; and to Leonard Nevarez, whose *Music Urbanism* blog has provided me with inspiration, critical insights, and great music.

Many people helped me while I was spending time in industrial cities. I thank Helge Schreiber, in Oberhausen; Rudi Esch and Fernand Hörner, in Düsseldorf; Heikki Uimonen, Severi Helle, Juho Karisaari, Juho Kaitajärvi-Tiekso, and Lasse Ullvén, in Tampere; and Alberto Vanolo, in Torino. All the people I interviewed in the course of this research—too many to mention—have given precious accounts of their lives and their music making. I hereby thank them all: *lo spirito continua*.

The University of Helsinki has been my main affiliation over the last fifteen years. I thank Anu Korhonen, Anne Haila, and all my colleagues in urban studies at the Faculty of Social Sciences and in European area and cultural studies at the Faculty of Arts.

The Finnish Cultural Foundation funded my research and partially the writing of this book with a full two-year grant.

Love to Tanja, Joel, Anton, and Martta. Cyril Connolly allegedly stated that 'there is no more sombre enemy of good art than the pram in the hall'. I think this is untrue; it just takes a little more time to get things done.

This book is dedicated to G. P. Bottà, my papà, who couldn't see it finished.

INTRODUCTION
Metal on Metal

In the late 1980s, I was an Italian pupil in a two-week school exchange program in Wuppertal, West Germany. Wuppertal is a typical industrial city, where German metallurgical concerns developed and grew across various historical eras until the late 1970s *Strukturwandel* (paradigm change, deindustrialisation). Since the 1970s, these concerns have systematically disappeared, leaving behind a huge amount of empty and vacant industrial-built environment.

One evening during my stay in Wuppertal, I was shyly attending, in my host's home, a party in honour of a family friend artist who made abstract sculptures out of industrial debris. Some of her works were placed in the living room and on the stairs. I was trying my best to decipher what the guests were talking about, and they were mostly chatting about *Tanztheater* or national politics, while smoking and drinking Rhine white wine. At the end of the evening, as the artist was leaving, she decided to give us a small performance; she took out of her bag a small bar of metal and started banging on one of her rebar artworks on the stairs. This went on for minutes. The noise was loud, repetitive, and mesmerising. I didn't understand exactly what was happening, and I was not aware of the fact that not far from there (actually just 30 kilometres from there, in Düsseldorf), Die Krupps' Jürgen Engler was banging on something quite similar onstage. However, I sort of understood that the particular noise of rusty metal on rusty metal had something to do with what surrounded me, with the empty factories, the red brick walls, the rusty iron bridges, the towering chimneys, and the *Schwebebahn* (suspension monorail) I was taking every day to school, as well as with the people who had lived and were living there. I was fascinated by industrial materiality and by the patina of the past that covered industrial architecture; at the same time, I could sense its atmospheric appeal and ability to inspire and enable cultural production in general and excruciating noise in particular.

What I experienced on a staircase in Wuppertal somehow shaped my understanding of what I will call here 'industrial sensibility' and my interest towards sounds, noises, and places, without even mentioning my record collection. In fact, popular music genres such as hardcore punk, house, industrial, 'post-punk', and heavy metal share a common origin in the decaying industrial cities of the late 1970s, in and outside Europe. Music critics and fans alike canonised and understood these genres as cinematic scores for grey, gloomy, depressive industrial environments or for their evocation. It is apparently logical to think of an organic relationship between deindustrialisation and this kind of music production, and to establish it through a reference to decaying industrial cities, industrial noises, and rhythms of the factory.

Later on, already a working adult in 2008, I survived the global financial crisis, although its effects still linger on today in many countries in terms of political instability, the adoption of austerity policies, and the European sovereign-debt crisis. Especially in the beginning of the crisis, several articles and cultural commentaries about a so-called recession culture appeared (Shaw 2009; Senior 2009; Linn 2009). According to these articles, the economy was apparently inspiring a lot of cultural production, ranging from *The Simpsons* episodes to whole new HBO series, and was influencing lifestyle choices, revamping DIY, and making people more civic-minded. These articles envisioned a connection between 'bad times' and a vital and exciting cultural production, although sounds in general and music in particular were somehow missing. Other articles, which also started appearing in connection with the recession, looked at cultural signifiers from the so-called roaring twenties and from the late 1970s deindustrialisation, hinting impatiently at the chances of pop history repeating. Journalists and bloggers welcomed the return of punk fashion (McVeigh 2012) or compiled playlists of past recession songs (Waitt 2009).

The British newspaper *The Guardian* published a piece in 2008 with the title 'Things Really Must Be Bad: AC/DC Are No. 1 Again'. In the article, the author relates the Australian band's appearing in the charts with economic downturn and explains it like this:

> AC/DC's appeal in unpredictable times is straightforward. People crave something uncomplicated and dependable in a time of uncertainty, and rock music has never produced a band so uncomplicated and dependable as AC/DC. . . . Small wonder that people turn to AC/DC in their millions when the world appears on the brink of chaos. Here is escapism into a world untroubled by sub-prime mortgages, record public finance deficits and the baleful state of the FTSE 100, but escapism of the most comfortingly consistent kind. (Petridis 2008)

In times of crisis, music might even be a so-called affordable luxury, just like red lipstick, that is, something simple and at hand to find solace in, thanks to its immediate availability and its simplicity, but also deeply connected to the past; it would have been difficult even in 2008 to see AC/DC as a 'new' band.

Another 2009 article in the same newspaper, entitled 'Artists' Creative Use of Vacant Shops Brings Life to Desolate High Streets', reports the words of an artist:

> "Rather than letting lots of pound shops appear, we are encouraging people to start up businesses," said Firmin. "We know recessions are awful but can be a good time for artists as creative ideas start appearing while otherwise redundant people are sitting at home fiddling and doing creative stuff." (Booth 2009)

Similarly, in 2010 an organiser of raves described how

> in a recession, as we've seen with the dawn of acid house and with New York in the 1970s, anywhere where's there's been a really good underground clubbing scene, you get into buildings. When you get into a building you've got the potential to have raves. Instead of gentrification, you've got empty buildings and construction projects are never finished and that creates a vacuum. If the recession continues then history indicates that the underground illegal club scene tends to thrive. (Townsend 2010)

The AC/DC article's thesis implied that in times of crisis, we aim at something basic and uncomplicated; however, artists in the other two articles undermine this thesis and refer to new and exciting cultural expressions getting born in troubled circumstances.

Journalism offered very simple explanations, linking economic crisis and cultural work in a cause-effect relation. At the same time, the nostalgia towards past recessions and their music worked as a sort of coping mechanism. However, linking unemployment and vacant spaces with creativity and resourcefulness, or even better with hedonism and resistance, is a risky business. It puts the relation between empty spaces and creativity upside down, as if emptiness in itself would evoke ideas and inspiration and not, for instance, depression and desolation. However, these articles also show the impact that deindustrialisation had in framing a certain basic understanding of the 'industrial structure of feeling' (Byrne 2002). It also frames the elective affinity between economic and social distress, on one hand, and cultural production on the other, as a powerful narrative.

Apparently, after being questioned several times about the matter, even music journalist Simon Reynolds felt compelled to write something about it. Deconstructing the simplistic casual relation between bad times and good music through some straightforward logic, he affirms that 'at some point along the way music and the social/economic became uncoupled' (Reynolds 2009), an intuition that he developed further in *Retromania* (2011).

What Reynolds calls 'uncoupling' happened in particular circumstances, an unwanted consequence of deindustrialisation. Since the mid-1970s, this abrupt structural change has erased a vast range of industrial production from European industrial centres, relocating it in less-regulated countries with cheaper workforces or stopping it altogether in the name of economic restructuring. Deindustrialisation has considerably changed the structural forces at the basis of working life and production. Sherry Lee Linkon (2018) describes this form of economic restructuring as a half-life, still affecting US communities, places, and individuals across decades and generations; she denies the post-industrial thesis as a lie, as 'we are not yet "post" anything' and 'people still make things' (Linkon 2018, 5). Several contemporary studies (Emery 2019; Nettleingham 2019; Kohn 2009; Strangleman 2013; Strangleman, Rhodes, and Linkon 2013; Cowie and Heathcott 2003) share this view and examine deindustrialisation as a process that is still unfolding, very much present in working-class life as memory, affect, and in material terms, generation after generation.

In this book, I argue that popular music was a powerful instrument for dramatising the crisis of industrial cities in late 1970s Europe and the subsequent step to post-industrial societies because it was somehow able to anticipate the post-industrial shift and foresee the future fascination for industrial atmosphere and symbolic consumption by adopting industrial 'musicscapes'. During the high time of deindustrialisation, music became a 'vanishing mediator' (Jameson 1973), bringing industrial societies, worldviews, and values towards the post-industrial and disappearing in the process. Music vanished, at least in this role of mediator, once industrial cities tried to move on and embrace the post-industrial promise of a new paradigm. When 'deindustrialisation music' came back, lately, it was assigned a completely different and ancillary function in relation to place.

I am unravelling the articulation of industrial musicscapes and deindustrialisation in the context of European industrial cities by comparing four case studies: Manchester (UK), Düsseldorf (Germany), Torino[1] (Italy), and Tampere (Finland). Music played a slightly different function in each of these cities; it developed and disappeared along slightly out-of-sync temporal lines, roughly between 1976 and 1984 (with a coda until the 1990s in Manchester), and with very different outcomes. Some Manchester musicians, like New Order and Morrissey, achieved global success and careers that today span four decades, while some Torino bands—like Nerorgasmo, for instance—rarely played outside the city borders. However, we find in all the above-mentioned cities a certain 'industrial' music-related dynamism during the time of deindustrialisation, one that left tangible and intangible heritages behind. The four cities have been chosen because they represent different regions of Europe and play different roles in popular music history and canonisation. Moreover, they represent different typologies of industrial cities, ranging from one-company town to commercial hub, from prototypical to peripheral. They are cities I am familiar with, have emotional bonds to, have spent time in for shorter or longer periods of time, and where I can interact in their respective national languages, although with some difficulties due to industrial city slang and accents. Using interviews with musicians and record-label owners and examining artefacts such as fanzines, records, tapes, and posters—all largely but not exclusively related to punk, post-punk, hardcore punk, and electronic/industrial music cultures—I am aiming at understanding the relation among economy, culture, and place under the particular contingency of deindustrialisation. I am more interested about time (late 1970s–early 1980s) and place/theme (industrial city) than about definite music genres. My main aim is to disentangle industrial sounds from industrial places and rebuild their affinity, not from the perspective of cause and effect, with crisis giving birth to 'industrial' music, as in the nostalgia journalism discourses, but rather as articulation, where music was able to anticipate dramatic societal changes and affect the context where it was taking place, both as social practice and as performance. What matters to me is that the relation between place and sound (in this case, popular music) is an articulation and, as such, is arbitrarily constructed but at the same time reflects a particular 'structure of feeling' (Williams 1980) from a social point of view and a 'urban ethos' (Krims 2007) from the spatial one.

SETTING THE SCENE

The spatial and social context where music 'takes place' is not given; it is created via identities, representations, and practices; it reveals aspirations, fears, and individual perceptions of reality; it shows power relations and worldviews. Moreover, this context can be material and tangible, in form of a shared rehearsal space or a club, and at the same time intangible and affective, related to these places' histories, reputations, stories, and atmosphere.

Interviewing individuals who were actively making music in industrial cities under deindustrialisation was challenging on a variety of levels. First of all, it is difficult to overcome the 'punk habitus' that some of them took up immediately when questioned about their past. Diffidence towards researchers and 'adults' (even if the majority of my informants were approximately ten years older than I was) was sometimes difficult to overcome, but my own engagement with music often provided help in constructing a communicative and emotional bond. In addition, it was mostly discussing places and moving across them that provided me the most interesting material for this book. All this revealed to me that punk and 'post-punk' worked in sociological terms as *glocal* forces, able to create bonds across class, national, and sometimes racial divides on a cosmopolitan scale but at the same time maintaining strong local contingencies. It is fascinating to see how industrial city scenes networked and transferred signifying practices, sometimes embedding them into very different local environments. Will Straw has been examining for years the way 'scenes' can be implemented to study tight urban communities and their visibility, especially at night. In this book, I am referring to music-based communities in industrial cities as scenes and preferring 'scenes' to 'subculture', on one hand, and 'music world', on the other.

The so-called Chicago School of sociology first introduced the idea of 'subculture' (Gelder 2007), but its formulation became more consistent within the Centre for Contemporary Cultural Studies (CCCS), based at the University of Birmingham. The CCCS examined subcultures in connection to working-class youth and the 'spectacular' community making that appeared in British cities and towns after the Second World War. The CCCS examined youth urban communities in materialistic terms, as based on rituals and style, that is, the music they listened to, the clothes they wore, the territory they claimed for themselves. Subculture was understood as being in a double articulation, with the working class as a whole and with the dominant class, therefore, always a subset of something more complex and organised (Hall and Jefferson 2003). This positioning was widely criticised in the late 1990s because of its lack of flexibility in addressing highly volatile community making among youths in postmodern and post-industrial times.

'Scene' has found fertile ground in popular music studies since the early 2000s, for instance, with the publication of the edited volumes *Post-Subcultures Reader* (Muggleton and Weinzierl 2003) and *After Subculture* (Bennett and Kahn Harris 2004) and in the extensive work of Andy Bennett (Bennett and Peterson 2004; Bennett 2004). As said already, in the early 1990s Will Straw had begun using the concept in reference to popular music (Straw 1991; 2001). Straw's style is rich in references to public press and public spaces, across cultures and across the whole twentieth and twenty-first centuries, creating historical contingencies and genealogies in relation to urban culture in general and towards nightlife in particular. Moreover, he connects the existence of scenes not only to music making and to the flexibility of postmodern identity building but also to cosmopolitanism, legislations, commerce, local traditions, and to their interaction. According to Straw (2001), a scene expands and contrasts within two extremes in urban cultural analysis. On one hand, scene invites to the analysis of visibly social cityscape, providing the means to dig beneath the spectacular surface to look for its 'grammar' (Blum 2001). On the other, it loosens up social morphology, liberating the study of urban communities and allowing a richer understanding of varieties and mobilities within and across them.

Crossley (2015) has criticised the term *scene* for being too familiar and too loaded to be used in scientific research. He prefers to adopt the term *music worlds* in examining punk and post-punk in Manchester, London, Liverpool, and Sheffield between 1975 and 1980. Crossley justifies his choice by first referring to 'social worlds' (Blumer 1986) and to the fact that they are built on shared collective meanings, concerns, and interests, which enable spaces of interaction. Crossley brings this further by adopting the work of Danto (1964) and Becker (1982), who analysed the social aspects of art making, through the term *art world*. For instance, Becker (1982) saw art first and foremost as an activity carried out by a complex network of people, including audiences, in particular places, following certain conventions, and exploiting certain resources. However, the term *world* can be criticised as being as compromised as *scene* by its common-sense use; furthermore, it creates self-sealed sociological systems, which fit into rigid methodological frameworks but fail to reveal the porous and precarious dimension of their existence and the affects attached to it. In addition to this, the term undermines one of the most significant elements of music making: performance, which 'scene' states clearly, especially when we refer to its secondary meaning as 'stage'.

This book approaches music scenes as embedded not into a class or a world but into the ever-changing, fragile, and porous life of deindustrialising cities and into a complex system of mutual cross-fertilisation. Too often cultural urban research on music has been based on one city only or on a comparison of cities within a single national framework. In the first case, there is a clear risk of relying too much on local historical continuities; in the second, there is a tendency to explore music making as a mere national project. In the four industrial cities I am considering, punk and 'post-punk' were the music genres, became social practices, and built tight scenes, being at the same time both local and embedded into international 'networks of friends'.

Raymond Williams made sense of this temporal and generational commonality with the concept of 'structure of feeling'. In Marxist language, Williams defined a 'structure' to describe 'a particular quality of social experience and relationship, historically distinct from other particular qualities, which gives the sense of a generation or a period' (Williams 1977, 131). Deindustrialisation and its culture can be examined as a structure of feeling because the term has both a material and an affective dimension, apt at making sense of temporalities. Moreover, Williams adopted the concept in reference to lived experiences, combining the social, the generational, and the historical to provide a framework to read and interpret, for instance, literary conventions (Williams 1977).

With this aim in mind, I developed a multilayered analysis of popular music artefacts or 'musicscapes'. Popular music is in fact able to convey meanings in three layers: textscape, soundscape, and landscape. With 'textscape', I am referring to lyrics and song titles; with 'soundscape', to the use of certain sounds, melodies, chords, and rhythms; and with 'landscape', to the use of certain visual imaginaries in record covers, photo shoots, and merchandise.

In this book, I am especially interested in showing how popular music worked with places, and industrial urban spaces in particular. In this specific field of analysis, attention to textscapes will focus on street names, toponimies, landmarks, architectonical features, social stereotypes, local prejudices, reputations, and hegemonies. Under soundscapes, I will concentrate on real or perceived industrial sounds and noises; the use of local slang, accents, and dialects; and of traditional local melodies, rhythms, or harmonies. Landscape will address the pictorial or graphic use of industrial elements.

Krims (2007) used the concept of 'urban ethos' to explain the limits and borders of the spatial discourse in music. Through a limited set of examples, he envisaged the tendency of specific narratives to become *the* representation of the city in general in certain historical periods. Urban ethos doesn't apply to a city in particular, despite being shaped by the fate of certain prototypical ones like New York City and Los Angeles. Krims also identified 'genre systems', gender and race, as factors contributing to the framing of a particular urban ethos, and as all of these factors change as cities themselves change and play host to new kinds of capital accumulation, such differences are always registered as profoundly *historical* facts. They will originate in real, material social relations and the changing spatial strategies by which cities adjust to accumulate capital. But they will then be imagined in representational strategies and sometimes even used to refashion cities themselves. (Krims 2007, 24)

Krims described how popular music representations become very important and can even turn into instruments for planning and branding cities. This is a strategy that has had successful results, for instance, in the case of Liverpool, in the United Kingdom (Cohen 2007a), or Austin, Texas, in the United States (Wynn 2015), and that continuously affects municipal discussions around the world.

'Place' has become a catchword, whose relevance can be at best grasped by the stigma asserted to its contrary, formulated by the French anthropologist Marc Augé with the term *non-lieu* ('not-place').

Industrial cities are places with short or no history at all in traditional European perspective; they are saturated by non-places, ranging from high-rise blocks to malls, from factories to railway stations, from motorway nodes to underpasses.

When I first started analysing popular musicscapes from industrial city scenes, I was amazed by the lack of direct references to places. It took me some time to understand that the urban ethos I was looking *at* was very different from the one I was looking *from*. My fascination for the industrial atmosphere is in fact linked to the consumer perspective of someone living in a post-industrial society and continuously searching for places based on buzz, authenticity, and distinction. As a tourist, I expected the real Manchester (to cite one of the most researched and represented industrial cities) to be simply a reproduction of the represented one, allowing me to recollect and mediatise on Instagram the atmosphere of the black-and-white photos by Anton Corbijn and Kevin Cummins and the sound of Joy Division, the Fall, and the Smiths. What these bands and these photographers, among others, were doing was exactly the opposite: they were running away from Manchester, the deindustrialising city, and visualising otherness by occupying, editing, twisting its spaces through excruciating noise and by 'looking at the light through the pouring rain', as the title of a Kevin Cummins book (2012) suggests.

DRAMATISING THE RHYTHM OF THE FACTORY

The rhythm of the factory has been used to explain a variety of genres, ranging from soul to house music, from industrial to heavy metal. Depending on factors such as the kind of production, the presence of classic Fordist chain work, robotisation of the machinery, and the organisation of work, a factory can produce very different soundscapes, at different levels of volume. The impact of the factory on popular music is very much based on the idea of repetition and serialisation of rhythm, which has a lot to do with our understanding of mechanical work and with its fictionalisation in music and with the increase in the use of electronic sound machinery (such as drum machines and computers) from the 1970s onwards. Partly responsible for this is the German band Kraftwerk, who consistently made use of a certain imaginary, developed long before by the Bauhaus movement or early science fiction in Weimar Republic Germany (e.g., Fritz Lang's *Metropolis*) that was connected to modernity, post-human societies, and robotisation.

In this book, however, it seems more fruitful to determine the connection between popular music and the industrial city under different terms. In fact, the first often provided human, imaginary, and material means for the second to survive. Especially in times of economic crisis and consequent urban decay, music has channelled creative forces and often provided unexpected ways out. I think it is, therefore, important to examine deindustrialisation as a key element in the evolution of the relation between industrial cities and popular music. Industrial cities are to be understood as articulations of space more than as articulations of place; their music is therefore less romantically bound to a certain local pride and more interested in conquering and 'making space' in a variety of cultural expressions. Dick Hebdige talks about punk's ability in 'dramatizing' the crisis (1979, 87), but at the same time he notes that 'it was predicated upon a denial of place' and 'it was blank, expressionless, rootless' (1979, 65). For him, punk lived in the paradox of being local and at the same time of being 'nowhere' really. This is true of much of the punk music produced around 1976–1977 in Great Britain: it was locating itself into a TV drama (or worse, into a soap opera) performing the crisis. This was very much connected to the 'filtering' of punk statements through the music industry, which saw punk as a profitable new music wave to commercialise and standardise into a commodity. For instance, the cover of the first The Clash album (1977) is a black-and-white shot by Kate Simon that was taken outside their rehearsal space. The three members of the band are standing in a narrow concrete alleyway, surrounded by brownstone walls. The path probably leads to an underground parking lot or to the yard of a housing project; it hides them and doesn't reveal anything spatially relevant. Authenticity is ascribed to the Clash via their nonironic facial expression, posture, and clothing, and not via a particular real or imagined locality. It tells of an urban environment that is not yet able to produce anything and that was built with the mere purpose to lodge anonymous urban crowds that had no future or past to long for but just grim, everyday boredom. Central to the picture is not the landscape but the heroism of the band members, standing as urban cowboys in front of glimpses of an anonymous, unfriendly environment, ready to be reproduced in posters for every teenage bedroom in the country.

In my view, punk was able to express its potential only in connection to the activities of scenes in industrial towns and during periods of decline. Always using the British experience as an example, it is in Manchester and Liverpool that punk 'mutated' from a London aesthetic experiment into a powerful instrument to communicate and dramatise urban decline (Cohen 2007a).

It is surprising that what was happening in the North of England and in distressed areas of the United States was later labelled 'post-punk', even if happening chronologically at the same time of what in New York City and London was called 'punk'. In fact, like any other post-something mentioned in this book, 'post-punk' is both a continuation and a radical break from what was simply called 'punk'. I think that a possible key to read this shift has a lot to do with the democratisation of certain cultural practices and the consequences of uneven urban developments. 'Post-punk' bands were usually born in industrial cities and were rarely design-intensive products of a corporate music industry. The step from the Clash to Joy Division or from the Ramones to Black Flag has more to do with the disproportionate impact of the changes in economic regimes affecting bands in Salford differently than in London, and in Hermosa Beach differently than in New York City, than with mere genre-related conventions.

In my view, the notion itself of 'post-punk' should be reexamined. In the seminal *Rip It Up and Start Again*, Simon Reynolds (2006) gives a definition very much based on a certain canon formed by the British media (the New Musical Express in particular) and arising from a certain cultural capital. Recognising the uniqueness of Pere Ubu or Television, praising the work of the Fall and Arto Lindsay contributed enormously in recognising certain artists as part of the cultural history of popular music. Nonetheless, in my view, the English-speaking and canon-based focus limits a lot what 'post-punk', for instance, in continental or Nordic Europe has been and the impact it has had on an enormous range of industrial cities around the world. This book extends the definition of post-punk, for instance, to hardcore punk, proto-techno, electronic body music, and noise experimentations, all sharing a common origin in industrial towns and trying to respond and/or 'dramatise' real urban crises under different geographical, social, and economic circumstances.

BOOK STRUCTURE

In this introduction, I laid out some personal and academic reasons for writing this book. I described my own fascination with industrial cities and the music arising from such environments during deindustrialisation. I also explained why I am referring to music scenes. Aware of the potential extent of this topic and its related expectations, I also narrowed the field of research in time and space.

Chapter 1 defines the industrial city and discusses its history, role in urbanisation, and its crisis in the 1970s. It addresses issues related to urban planning, economic paradigm changes, and the step from industrial to post-industrial society. It also identifies the major discourses surrounding industrial cities, their inhabitants, and deindustrialisation by looking at architectural and urban studies literature; at industrial city representations in film, novels, and art; and at their dystopian associations. Industrial sensibility and atmosphere are a central concept for this chapter, dealing with the creation of a certain kind of cultural fetish for brutalism and decline. The chapter is partly based on a revision and extension of my article, 'Dead Industrial Atmosphere: Popular Music, Cultural Heritage and Industrial Cities', in *Journal of Urban Cultural Studies* 2, no. 1 (2015).

I am aware of the fact that a genre called 'industrial' exists and that it takes its inspiration from the aesthetics of the industry, especially in its most dystopian connotations. However, in my view, this genre represents one possible cultural enactment of the industrial sensibility and should be considered among others. I am presenting an explanation of this choice in chapter 2. That chapter introduces the relationship between the industrial soundscape and music making. It starts this by questioning, via aesthetics and musicological theory, the binary notion of music and noise. It then deals with the industrial soundscape, its history, elements, and regulation within cities. I then describe a genealogy of industrial city music by giving examples and exploring the features of music genres, artists, and pieces that have been directly inspired by or that are understood as being linked to industrial sounds. This is divided into two main branches. One is related to art music and to the way futurism and the Russian avant-garde adopted industrial sounds as aesthetic references. The second branch encompasses popular music, from eighteenth-century industrial folk to Chicago electric blues and Detroit soul and all the way to Kraftwerk and library music.

Chapters 3 to 6 present four case studies.[2] Chapter 3 is partly based on revising and extending my article, 'The City That Was Creative and Did Not Know: Manchester, Pop Music and Cultural Sensibility', in *European Journal of Cultural Studies* 3 (2009): 349–65. It explores Manchester's successful music scene from the late 1970s to the early 1980s, including major bands such as Joy Division, New Order, the Smiths, and the Fall. The formation of a local music scene is analysed through the notion of an urban creative milieu, stating its historical debt to the city's industrial heritage; place images produced by the local popular music scene are examined as visual, aural, and lyrical productions. The chapter also stretches to the late 1980s and early 1990s, examining the consolidation of the local popular music scene through bottom-up and entrepreneurial projects and the regeneration of some areas of Manchester. It also looks at the role of the 'New Left' local authority, its difficulties in recognising the city's creative capital, and its attitude towards the production and consumption of popular music. The conclusions present some general reflections on the Manchester legacy, the city's successful regeneration towards a 'post-industrial creative city', and its significance for a definition of creativity at the urban level.

Chapter 4 is about Düsseldorf and the Ruhr, a polycentric and high-ly dense conurbation, among the biggest in Europe, whose vast indus-trial heritage was celebrated when the Ruhr was named the 2010 Euro-pean Capital of Culture. Düsseldorf lies outside the Ruhr geographical area and has been nicknamed its 'office desk' (*Schreibtisch des Ruhrge-biets*) because many administrative headquarters of the Ruhr's metal-lurgy firms were located in the city. The Ruhr has been a cluster for German hardcore punk and heavy metal, while Düsseldorf has been a hotspot for the development of punk and electronic music. Bands such as Mittagspause and Die Krupps are from Düsseldorf and often used their proximity to the Ruhr as justification for their sound and image. I am considering both the Ruhr and Düsseldorf together because of their proximity and the hybridity of their music scenes. Of great importance to this chapter is the relationship between sounds and materiality, art and architecture.

Chapter 5 examines the *Collettivo Punx Anarchici* ("Anarchist Punk Collective"), active in Torino (Italy) in the early 1980s. The chapter is partly based on a revision and extension of my '*Lo spirito continua*: Torino and the Collettivo Punx Anarchici' (2014). I reveal how the Collettivo was dramatising Torino's decay and social unrest, a conse-quence of the crisis affecting FIAT and the automobile industry. Bands such as Contrazione, Declino, and Negazione were able to 'sound out' urban alienation and decay, creating original, nonprofit, and self-organised forms of musical production. At the same time, they were naively trying to reclaim public space, after the dramatic ending of the *anni di piombo* (the years of lead, a 1970s era of political violence) and the middle-class retreat into the private sphere. Torino is the case with the least bibliographical material, apart from some articles in music magazines and fictionalised memoirs. Interviews and ethnographic ob-servations are therefore more abundant in this chapter than in the others.

Chapter 6 is about Tampere, known in Finland as the country's own Manchester and nicknamed *Tampester* and *Manse*. In the 1980s, bands such as Bastards, Riistetyt, Kohu-63, and Kaaos were playing fast and furious hardcore punk, which one musician described as *känninen saundi* (drunken sound). Their work was mostly based on independent, oppositional and DIY ethics, and some of these bands were the first Finnish bands to tour continental Europe and the United States. I focus specifically on issues such as the relationship between sound and place in the specific context of Tampere as an industrial town. I consider the soft and hard infrastructures that allowed bands to proliferate in Tampere more than in other Finnish centres, and I outline the international networks that made touring and distributing music outside Finland possible. I also consider the soft deindustrialisation happening in the city as a result of social democracy. In conclusion, I look at the legacy of these bands on a local, national and global scale. This chapter is also based on interviews and first-hand observations.

Chapter 7 addresses the ongoing heritage-making of European industrial landscapes, both at the individual/local and at the national/supranational level. It addresses the existence of industrial cities' *lieux de memoir* and examines the leading or ancillary role of popular music within the intangible cultural heritage category. It also problematises the heritage-making of popular music because of the latter's embedded cosmopolitanism. It also considers its risks to a city, including the creation of inequalities and gentrification, and the fetishising of decline.

Chapter 8 revises the main lines of analyses and methods presented in the book to achieve a nuanced and complete understanding of the relationship between sound, space, and place, mostly based on the use of Jameson's concept of the 'vanishing mediator'. This is achieved by a comparison of the four case studies. In addition, it shows how a comparative analysis can overcome limitations based on a one-scene or one-city approach or on the adoption of a superficial 'global' scale.

In the conclusion I discuss the issues arising from examining the popular music cultures of deindustrialising cities. I recap the main arguments I examined in the central chapters. I also reflect on the difficulties of working across nations and languages and offer some ideas about possible continuations and extensions of this research.

This book has some clear temporal and spatial limitations. I am aware that industrial cities are a global phenomenon, and so is popular music. By following contemporary music media, I became aware of the extent and variety of cases still reflecting the elective affinity of industrial settings and cultural production, especially outside Europe, and the continuous influence that the 'industrial paradigm' in music still exerts. As Tony Mitchell puts it, 'identity formation through music is an active, fluid process of production, creation and construction, not a question of

mere reflection of nation state, place, landscape or environment'
(Mitchell, 2009, 187–88).

NOTES

1. I use the Italian *Torino* instead of the English Turin. Both have been
widely used in English texts, including during the 2006 Winter Olympics, when
the municipality decided to consistently use the Italian version of its name.

2. I am using several first-hand interviews in these chapters. All details of
an interview are shown at its first occurrence, in text. Then, subsequent references to the same interview are simply shown as ([surname, if needed], interview, year). The name of the interviewed is shown in full in the first occurrence
and later I adopt just the first name, surname, or nickname, according to the
most common use within the scene and for readers' clarity.

I

THE INDUSTRIAL CITY

Looking at a European industrial city today might be a bit like looking at a Sony Walkman TPS-L2 cassette player. They both bring back memories of a recent past. We all know that they both used to be very popular; they shaped innovative ways of production and consumption for a certain period of time, and they both involved mass production, each one of them looking not dissimilar from others. As many individuals wanted a Walkman, many governments needed a city or an urban region that could produce wealth through industrial production and manufacturing.

With the invention of the CD and its portable player, the Walkman lost its value and turned into technological trash or a cheap, out-of-fashion flea market item. Its colour, shape, and composition suddenly looked shabby, depressing, and a bit dirty, weak in technical qualities and producing a sound that was poor in comparison to the new arrivals.

The same could be said about industrial cities. The post-industrial discourse, together with the transfer of industrial manufacturing premises beyond the West, had the same effect that technological advances had on the Walkman and made industrial cities look anonymous, shabby, depressing, and a bit dirty. During the 1980s, they became places that were waiting to be updated for a new era, where culture—rebranded as creativity—would take the place of the economy, similar to the way laser discs replaced magnetic tapes. Also in capital cities, in centres with mixed work division, and in port towns, former industrial districts were reshaped to lodge new forms of work, in connection to services, information technology, education, and culture, or a combination of them. This process also had social consequences: new inhabitants with new jobs often invaded the most appealing working-class parts of towns, looking for authenticity and picturesque housing with industrial atmosphere. This process was labelled gentrification, and it capitalised on industrial spaces as fetishised commodities.

This happened under different circumstances in the Lower East Side (NYC), in Neukölln (Berlin), in Kallio (Helsinki), and elsewhere, and it continues to happen around the world. But it is not merely gentrification as a sociological phenomenon that interested many former industrial districts around the world. Christopher Mele, in reference to New York's Lower East Side, refers to the tendency of the new inhabitants 'to gesture toward and even mimic the look and feel of the very social elements they threatened to displace' (Mele 2000, vii). This process cannot be described merely as a social and physical upgrade, as a flow of capitals, or as aesthetic sanitation; it implies an aesthetic command, appreciation, and fetish of a certain kind of atmosphere.

With the 1970s economic crisis, industrial cities stopped understanding and imagining their futures as sites of manufacturing and production and preferred to emphasise services and consumption. Industrial cities began marketing themselves as distinctive, cool places where people could both have fun and do business. All material elements that offered a reminder of the industrial past were emphasised, individualised, and aestheticised. However, this did not happen with the same level of success in all 'pure' industrial cities (only Bilbao and Manchester come to mind), many of which often did not experience gentrification and simply became desolate, shrank, or had to rely on state intervention to see premises reconverted so as not to completely lose their real estate value.

The Walkman did not disappear, thanks to a second cycle of fetishisation (McRobbie 1989); it turned into some kind of retromania icon, its picture to be ironically worn on a T-shirt, for instance, or reproduced on protective cases for mobile phones. At the same time, cassettes are still produced and used by specific scenes as an element of differentiation, responding to a logic related to the subcultural capital of certain groups of consumers. The Walkman may well be sought after as a nostalgic fetish of one's own personal history; nowadays a working Sony Walkman TPS-L2 can often attract bids of around five hundred euros on online auction sites, though we can ask ourselves what for. In the same way, the atmospheric and aesthetic ambience of the industrial crisis has never been so sought after in contemporary cultural production. Not only do films celebrate them but subcultures that developed within them are inspiring contemporary fashion and museum exhibitions, and music genres born in them are painstakingly being reproduced. Even the brutalist architecture is still very much present in the popular imaginary, and it is continuously adopted to convey many different meanings throughout popular culture.

The 2008-originated and ongoing economic crisis brought surprisingly real manufacturing into the forefront of economic and political discourse as means for stability and growth. For instance, in the 2012 French political elections, the need to save the national manufacturing industry came to the forefront of electoral campaigns, in relation to the closing down of an *ArcelorMittal* steel mill in the Florage area of northeast France (Leigh 2012). Suddenly, Europe seems to remember that the manufacturing sector is still a relevant element in its core economy. Although the service industry has made up for the losses in hard industry, the ongoing economic crisis puts the development of the last thirty years in perspective.

During its existence, the industrial city challenged city officials, architects, and planners in channelling the needs of an expanding but unstable capitalism into urban planning. Their efforts should have increasingly provided welfare and self-realisation to the citizens, as workers and as consumers. Nonetheless, the industrial city was also realised in strikingly similar ways in noncapitalist societies, like the formerly socialist countries of Eastern Europe and more or less with the same aims.

DEFINITIONS

The industrial city might simply be defined as a city shaped by the highly organised material interaction of capital and labour in manufacturing. This definition is kept so general to include as many centres as possible. There are in fact different kinds of industrial cities: classic ones from the first Industrial Revolution, one-company towns, utopian towns planned via social engineering or philanthropy, highly specialised centres, industrial agglomerations, and even port towns. It is in the nineteenth century, thanks to the so-called first Industrial Revolution, that this urban type expanded throughout England and then on a global scale (Allen 2009).

This huge technological change in manufacturing production became a 'revolution' because of its enormous impact on society, labour, the organisation of local and global economies, and our understanding of time, space and belonging. This is why history and social sciences research focused for a long time on the relation between modernisation and industrialisation.

In urban historical research, there has been a tendency to work on individual industrial cities, with the examples of Manchester and Sheffield, in the European context, and of Detroit and Chicago, in the American context, towering over the rest. Contemporary historical research has begun filling the gaps by referring to industrial cities in global comparative perspective, by extending their stories beyond deindustrialisation, and by focusing on policies of various kinds, ranging from planning to environmental perspectives, from heritage making to cultural representations (Zimmermann 2013). However, the emphasis is very much on contrasting previous narratives of doom to underline positive ongoing developments, ranging from urban recovery to redevelopment, from renewal to tourist appeal. There is also a relevant classic corpus of research focusing on sociological traits (Badham 1986; Drucker 2007); however, the pure spatial dimension of the 'industrial' is sometimes overseen.

The formation of industrial cities is interpreted often as a consequence of a wider process investing technology, economy, work, leisure, culture, human relations, and power. The 'urban' as scale of analysis and as agency in the industrialisation and modernisation process seems to be taken into account only later, in reference to the emergence of the so-called post-industrial cities. In this literature, industrial cities are considered a historically defined type of the urbanisation process under industrialisation. The active role of manufacturing in the history of planning is sometimes overseen in favour of other spatial aspects, such as sprawl, suburbanisation, and segregation. In addition, cultural manifestations of the industrial cities are often seen either as simple/naive expressions of the working class or as intellectual, external, and stereotypical representations. 'Post-industrial cities' is an inclusive and all-encompassing urban type, adaptable for all kinds of cities in the globalised world, as if the 'post-' prefix completely erased the real and material meaning of the adjective 'industrial'. It seems apparent that the shift from 'industrial' to 'post-industrial' radically changed the way we understand the economic, cultural, and spatial functions of cities, and that deindustrialisation not only changed an economic paradigm but originated a brand new way to think about urbanisation in general.

The industrial city rose in connection to the first industrial revolution: economic capital and manufacture production clustered and rationalised in dense areas, close to energy sources such as coal and in proximity to navigable water or railways. This happened sometimes in small market centres, which suddenly rose in population and radically changed their economic function, first at the regional, then at the national, and finally at the global level. This began in the late decades of the eighteenth century, in towns in the North of England such as Manchester and Sheffield (Clark 2009, 133); these centres were, in the beginning, dependent on surrounding rural villages and areas, and only later, thanks to big technological changes and an inflow of capital, did they transform themselves into self-sufficient cities (Hall 1975, 21–30). As such, industrial cities relied on the subdivision of manufacturing, involving also the nonskilled labour of women and children. In 1782, the first large purpose-built cotton-spinning factory using steam power was opened in Manchester (Clark 2009, 149); however, it took several decades before this technology took over similar areas in continental Europe.

The North of England radically transformed into an industrial landscape across the nineteenth century, and similar developments took place on the continent in the Netherlands, Belgium, and Germany. A network of big industrial conurbation, middle-sized specialised towns, port cities and administration centres began developing in the United Kingdom, thanks to political stability and the global imperial market of the Commonwealth. Engels ([1845] 1969) was deeply impressed during his long stay in Manchester, and his *The Condition of the Working Class in England* is still considered a valid analysis of spatial segregation and of the submission of urban design to the interests of nascent industrial capitalism. In addition, young Engels understood that in industrial cities, population accumulates, just like capital itself does, and this explains their exceptional growth (Engels 1969, 42). What capitalism needed in early industrial cities was density of population in walking proximity to factories, so that the journey to and from them wouldn't be too long. Engels revealed the immense inequality that made industrial cities possible, and the way this inequality was material and spatial:

> The town itself is peculiarly built, so that a person may live in it for years, and go in and out daily without coming into contact with a working-people's quarter or even with workers, that is, so long as he confines himself to his business or to pleasure walks. This arises chiefly from the fact, that by unconscious tacit agreement, as well as with outspoken conscious determination, the working-people's quarters are sharply separated from the sections of the city reserved for the middle-class. (Engels 1969, 57)

De Tocqueville ([1835] 1958), in his travel chronicles around England and Ireland, also reported on cities of the North (Manchester, Birmingham) as ruled by industrial production. For instance, on July 2, 1835, he notes:

> The pressures which drive men from the fields into factories seem never to have been so active as now. Commerce flourishes and agriculture is in trouble. We hear in Manchester that crowds of country folk are beginning to arrive there. Wages, low though they seem, are nevertheless an improvement on what they have been getting. (De Tocqueville 1958, 176)

De Tocqueville also penned the famous metaphor of the dirty sewer producing pure gold (De Tocqueville 1958, 175), a vivid image of the huge paradox embedded into early industrial cities, where labour exploitation and capital gain achieved their most dystopian interaction.

Both Engels and De Tocqueville, in fact, focus on the very early and unregulated industrial city, where child labour, long working hours, segregation, and bare exploitation of labour was rampant, and where urban planning and welfare were basically nonexistent (Hall 1975, 22–30).

This classic model was very adaptive; parallel to this, however, a new paradigm in industrial production and economic growth brought new industrial cities in existence.

Simon Gunn (2013) claims that industrial city history can be broadly framed around four periods. The years from 1800 to 1880 encompass the phase of the already named first Industrial Revolution, where the classic industrial cities were born in connection with coal and textiles. Gunn considers the industrial cities born around this period to have been the most versatile in terms of adaptation to technological, architectural, and engineering changes. The phase of the second Industrial Revolution, from 1880 to 1920, is based on the heavy steel and iron industries, the spread of Fordist methods of production, and the first wave of social reforms.

Gunn considers the third period, from 1930 to 1970, as the climax in the industrial city history, with the spread of specially defined industrial zones, mass housing programs, slum clearance, and highway systems with mass motorisation. The period from 1970 to 2010 is one of deindustrialisation, urban fragmentation, and entropy. It sees forces already at stake, both at the end of the nineteenth century and during the interwar period, taking over and affecting the city negatively in terms of loss of inhabitants, economic crisis, and reputation. This periodisation is interesting if we consider it not only in temporal terms but also spatially: the visual signs of these four time frames are layered and sometimes simultaneously present in form of architectures, mindscapes, reputations, discourses, and affect. They create a palimpsest (Bottà 2012) of material, atmospheric, and affective layers, which affects the way we can talk and make sense of the 'industrial'. Moreover, the history of the industrial city in Europe is connected to nation building, labour union struggles, welfare implementation, immigration, technological optimism, and architectonic modernism. It also involves warfare, which has modified several times the geopolitical situation of the European continent and conditioned the development and horizons of supranational, national, and local economies. Last but not least, it also involves a continuous attempt to hide, tame, and sometimes solve the endemic environmental problems connected to the industrial activities, ranging from noise and smell pollution to toxic waste landfills. For instance, *Sheffield: City on the Move* (Coulthard and Coulthard 1972), a documentary about the northern English city, was commissioned by the city's publicity officer and released in 1972. The film starts by introducing what seems a striking innovation: the factory smoke ban, which made the city centre 'smokeless' and clear (Sheffield Libraries Archives and Information 2005). Sheffield factories are said to be producing steel, which is 'still at the heart of the city's heavy industry' and which is 'built into our modern life in countless essential ways' (Coulthard and Coulthard 1972). In the early 1970s, environmental innovations were still understood only in their function of facilitating city life without putting obstacles to the most important element—once again, production. Very clear both in the structure and in the content of the documentary is the self-evident centrality of the heavy industry as able to 'forge' all the other cultural, social, and architectural elements of Sheffield. Like many other cities and regions in Europe, Sheffield organised and understood itself as an industrial city; it was bound to a specific kind of heavy production, which influenced and determined all other aspects of city life, ranging from its social structure to its cultural offerings. In addition, being known as an 'industrial city' since the post-war era seemed to overcome its traditional dystopian image, thanks to the interplay among technology, innovation, and welfare. The dreams, aspirations, struggles, expectations, activities, *Weltanschauung*, and feelings of its citizens were strongly linked to this understanding.

Throughout its history, down to the contemporary global spread of industrial conurbations over the Global South, material production is the main paradigm for the economic growth and spatial development of the industrial city. Paradoxically, an industrial city produces material goods, whose consumption further 'produces' the city. Technological innovations facilitate production, and other functions are secondary. For instance, the first electric lights in Finland (and in the whole of Northern Europe, according to the plaque commemorating this) appeared in the *Plevna* weaving shed of the Finlayson company, located in the centre of Tampere, on March 15, 1882. This innovation allowed more efficient working hours even in the darkest months of the Finnish winter. Following on de Tocqueville's metaphor, it is the flow of gold that maintains and develops the dirty sewer, allowing the gold to continue flowing. This paradox shapes daily and yearly rhythms, planning, transportation, education, and the implementation of policies. For instance, an industrial city relies on swift transportation both of goods and people to and from production areas. This was refined overtime and achieved its technological climax in the construction of complex motorways and in the rise of the car as nearly exclusive regime of mobility, which is still negatively affecting cities today. The industrial city also relies on the education and training of certain professional figures and on their continuous availability, secured especially by continuous immigration from rural areas and from developing countries. Still today, certain materials and architectural styles are typical of industrial cities: functionalism and bare concrete.

Central for industrial cities is the idea of continuous growth and expansion, which is, however, sometimes achieved by political decision-making, which takes place elsewhere, namely, in capital cities (see table 1.1 for a summary of this dichotomy). Across Europe, we can find several examples of a clear dichotomy, if not a tension, between industrial centres and capital cities. Apart from the four examples mentioned in this book, we find similar patterns in Holland, between Amsterdam and Rotterdam; in Sweden, between Stockholm and Goteborg; in France, between Paris and Marseille; and so on, depending often on the size of the country and its history. Rarely have capital cities around the world been pure industrial cities, despite sometimes having had a strong industrial character (like, e.g., Berlin, New York City, or London). This is mostly connected to the fact that power (in political terms) resides physically in capital cities, and industrial cities depend on it. From the point of view of mental maps (Gould and White 1974), capital cities are always central (even if not in strict geographical terms), while industrial cities are in vague peripheries. Cultural institutions that perpetuate knowledge, such as national museums, archives, and universities, are in capitals; while in industrial cities resides technology in terms of research centres and polytechnics. Capital cities also tend to have a stronger 'imageability' (Lynch 1960) and individuality—a stronger brand, based on buzz, colours, and offerings—while industrial cities are bound to monotony and greyness and a more blurry focus. The idea of people immigrating from rural areas and finding quick enrolment into the working class also implies a clear imbalance in terms of social mix of the typical city population. Industrial city inhabitants are considered inferior in terms of manners, behaviours, free time activities, language, and cultural life. Rob Shields (1991, 207–45), for instance, identifies 'the North' in England as an imaginary industrial space on the margin, without a clear jurisdiction, under constant bad weather, and with a highly emotional population that is devoted to football and binge drinking. Shields deconstructs this myth by tracing its origins in intellectual and literary tropes built in the South of England that aim to reestablish via culture London's privilege over the periphery of, for instance, Lancashire and the Midlands.

ECONOMIC CRISIS, DEINDUSTRIALISATION, AND INDUSTRIAL CITIES

The price paid by industrial cities in the step from industrial to post-industrial society has been very high. It has not only implied a huge loss of workforce but it has also revolutionised the balance in inner centres and peripheries, in energy and circulation systems, and in self-images and understandings. Many places shrank or disappeared from the map, many districts suffered segregation or became gentrified, and people became unemployed, were displaced, or developed mental and physical problems. The full impact of a transition to a post-industrial economy can be recognised only in a few centres, and its consistency over time even less.

Michael Moore's first documentary, *Roger and Me* (1988), tells of the closing down of an assembly factory of General Motors in Flint, Michigan, the director's hometown. In one scene, an ex-worker, recovering in a mental hospital, is describing the day he 'cracked' after having been laid off five times in five years. He left the assembly line, got in his car and, driving towards home, he switched on the radio to see if it would cheer him up. The Beach Boys' 'Wouldn't It Be Nice?' was playing, and he tried to sing the lyrics, but he got 'an apple in my throat . . . trying to rationalise with those lyrics, trying to think "wouldn't it be nice", just wasn't working' (Moore 1988). The scene continues with the song scoring a streetscape of empty, run-down single houses filmed from a moving car.

Table I.I.

Capital City	Industrial City
Power	Power-dependant
Centre	Periphery
Education, knowledge	Technology, innovation
Colours	Grey
Buzz	Depression
Wide offerings	Monotony, monofunctional
Culture	Without own culture
Sharp, individual	Atmospheric, suspended
Privileged inhabitants	Rough inhabitants

This is just one of the many moving scenes of the film, where desperation and ironic distance are continuously intertwined, and it shows
much more than an Adorno-inspired critique of popular music in capitalism could tell. This scene reveals the false promises and augmented
romanticism the cultural industry is feeding to people in an effort to
divert them from understanding their real condition. However, it also
implies the idiosyncratic function of popular music as signifier of certain socio-economic contradictions. The Beach Boys could be analysed
as a Fordist band: their songs were carefully assembled by a team of
producers, arrangers, and musicians in an intricate studio work, thanks
to modern technologies and craftsmanship. The band is forever linked
to a time of economic prosperity and optimism, where popular music
became the voice of an apparently careless youth who was, however,
aware of going to live a life of full employment and the joys of a suburban lifestyle. It was not the music produced for people who were losing
their job; it was not music meant for dramatising an urban crisis.

Deindustrialisation and economic crisis have been analysed widely,
for instance, as 'creative destruction' due to a technological change
(Schumpeter 1942) or as a cyclical moment of crisis, embedded in the
nature of capitalism itself (Lipietz 1992). Both theories tend to ignore
cultural expressions and merely see them as reactions to economic,
social, or technological structures. They both rely on the classic Marxist
division into base and superstructure.

These approaches neglect the role played by popular culture in
'dramatising' the crisis and making sense of it and, by doing so, in giving
imaginary or material solutions to it. The aim of this book is to attain a
better understanding of the impact of the crisis on the dreams, aspirations, struggles, expectations, activities, *Weltanschauung*, and feelings
of citizens. On the imaginative level, popular music focused on the
representation of the collapsing industrial space and on its effects on
the individual. On the material level, it began appropriating and transforming space: dense local scenes began developing in many industrial
centres.

This book aims at reformulating the relation between industrial cities and popular music, from homology-ridden narratives of rhythms and
structures to a more multifaceted understanding of intertwining economic regimes and cultural expressions. It also takes into consideration
distinctive sounds and scenes that are able to signify the industrial city

as a socio-economic urban conurbation, and its crisis. Addressing the 'elective affinity' between industrial cities and certain forms of popular music is, therefore, a way to better understand the 1980s urban crisis.

Crisis under capitalism has been explained in various and sometimes discordant ways. Schumpeter's thought has had a great impact, first of all, because it recognised that capitalism is highly unstable due to social and natural changes, but especially for technological reasons. In *Capitalism, Socialism and Democracy* (1942) Schumpeter affirms that technological growth is not steady; it is based on sporadic ideas, which are absorbed and implemented slowly along decades. When they reach the full integration, a 'creative destruction' occurs. The imaginative power of this term has provided much common sense in dealing with the material consequences of the crisis as some kind of 'price to pay', to restore a guiding development. In case of cities, the passage from industrial to post-industrial could be as well examined as a sort of creative destruction. The new organisation of work based on flexibility, growth of the third and fourth sector, the centrality of the information technologies, and specialisation has been described as the main factor behind cities' transformations. Nonetheless, this shift occurred because of a precise political programme, implemented in the United States by Ronald Reagan and in the United Kingdom by Margaret Thatcher, in the name of liberalism (Harvey 2005).

Various thinkers and researchers gathered into the 'Regulation School' also address widely the concept of crisis in capitalism, focusing especially in its being embedded within the system itself. Their concepts of 'regime of accumulation' and 'modes of regulation' help in shedding light on the contextual elements at play during a crisis and during the consequent change in the mode of capital accumulation. Arrighi (1994) explains economic crisis by the contradiction between the goal of capitalist accumulation and the means used to achieve this goal. The author identifies the main feature of capitalism in the late twentieth century in the cyclical tendency to first expand on the material level, thanks to production. When this reaches its limits, capitalism offers a temporary solution by giving way to financial accumulation, which is unsustainable and eventually brings about the reorganisation of the whole global capitalist system. Industrial cities and their development served capitalist expansion at the material level, thanks to continuous production. Capitalism quickly dismissed European industrial cities and preferred to decentralise and move to countries where labour forces could be better exploited, and where there was a lower cost of means of production, while at the same time 'financialising' the crisis.

Looking at the economic history of the twentieth century, it is easy to identify business cycles and their impact. The Great Depression of 1929 towers as the longest downturn, while the economic boom after 1945 was the longest period of expansion. After the first energy crisis of 1973, it is possible to identify an increasing volatility in the proliferation of short crises and of short-term expansions (like the 'dot-com bubble' of the 1990s) around the globe, together with an increase in financialisation. It is therefore possible to identify a huge change, which the Regulation School describes as a shift in the regime of accumulation. From the 1980s onwards, economic instability affected the very nature of the industry in general and of industrial cities in particular, bringing a change in the very urban regime of accumulation. At the time, industrial cities in Europe started tagging themselves as 'post-industrial' or 'post-Fordist', without exactly knowing the modalities and consequences of the 'creative destruction'.

David Harvey in his analysis of the ongoing economic crisis started in 2008 (Harvey 2010) has identified four explanations used in media and common sense: human nature, institutional failures, failure of certain theories, and cultural origins. The first explanation relies on the animal spirit leading to excessive greed and therefore to the collapse of the market; the second looks at the possible reconfigurations that the global market should accomplish in order to work better. The third explanation appeals to the reprise or dismissal of certain theories followed by investors and governments. The fourth identifies specific foreign countries (for instance, Greece or Italy within the European Union) or specific political cultures (the 'Anglo-Saxon disease') as the causes of the crisis. Building on classic Marxist theory, Harvey argues that capitalism is never able to solve its problems; it just moves them around the globe, in areas that are unevenly developed. Cities are, at the same time, the places where flexible accumulation takes place and the most important product of this accumulation. At the height of an economic boom, real estate prices are high, interest rates are rising, and people are buying. Higher costs slow down building new construction; therefore demand and the rate of investments fall, and the whole economy falls into a crisis.

The role of cities in the crisis is therefore double: they are the arenas where the business cycles play out, and at the same time, they face the immediate material consequences of their downturn, namely, urban decay. Cities have been the first victims of any economic crisis, while their upper class and elite only have been the best beneficiaries of financial upswings and developments. Harvey sees the intensification in the frequency of economic crises as a consequence of the historical turn in world economic and political history in 1979 and 1980, when neoliberalism became the dominant discourse (Harvey 2005). There is a common understanding in urban research that industrial cities in Europe and the Western world disappeared to make space for the post-industrial ones. This assumption is based on the quick and still unresolved transfer of production to enormous urban conurbations in countries with cheaper workforces, such as China and India. Of course, this shift transformed and it is still transforming many city centres in Europe and the United States.

INDUSTRIAL CRISIS AS ATMOSPHERE

Nowadays, any European city would find it difficult to define itself as industrial; for instance, Sheffield brands itself as green and innovative, and it describes its industrial past only in terms of history and cultural heritage (Marketing Sheffield 2018). There is a growing conformity in European cities around the idea that capitals, citizens, and tourists should be attracted through spectacular infrastructures and intense cultural life. Not all cities were obliged to completely reshape their economic structure, and some of them, under the innovation surface, are simply continuing to function as industrial centres. Taking into account two cases from this book, in Torino, the FIAT Mirafiori plant in the southern end of the city is still producing, at least partially, real cars, and in Tampere, the Metsä Board Tako paper mill puffs out smoke in the city centre, a few hundred metres from the reconverted 'post-Fordist' factories. This is, of course, not to undermine the fact that the 1970s crisis and subsequent deindustrialising left a big impact on former industrial cities in terms of unemployment, distress, and empty and vacant industrial premises and spaces. Every economic crisis is bound to leave material debris behind. The concept itself of creative destruction implies a material legacy of ruins. This has been particularly true of the 1970s paradigm change, which erased much employment in the industrial sector from Western Europe and transformed industrial cities into decaying, empty, shrinking centres, abandoned by labour forces. This happened at various speeds and in different national contexts across Europe, and the way this was carried out in the United Kingdom is striking in its quick and painful operationalisation. However, the results were similar in terms of built environment: what was once a thriving mechanism of technological production became ruins. Ruins are nothing new in European continental understanding. For instance, anarchist Buenaventura Durruti said in an interview during the Spanish Civil War that

> it is we [the workers] who built these palaces and cities, here in Spain and in America and everywhere. We, the workers. We can build others to take their place. And better ones! We are not in the least afraid of ruins. We are going to inherit the earth. There is not the slightest doubt about that. The bourgeoisie might blast and ruin its own world before it leaves the stage of history. We carry a new world here, in our hearts. . . . That world is growing in this minute. (Van Paassen 1936)

In his utopian abandonment, Durruti understands ruins as a necessity, for the new revolutionary world to rise from them, even if it means destroying what the workers have materially built themselves. Ruins are projected, therefore, into the future, as a signal of the oncoming demise of the bourgeoisie.

Ruins had interested aesthetic and philosophical thought for centuries before Durruti but always in connection to the past. Enlightenment and later Romanticism saw in them an architectural memento mori and a symbol of the irreversibility of time, to be ruminated upon through the lenses of nostalgia (Huyssen 2006). For Georg Simmel (1907), the architectural ruin represented the revenge of nature over the human spirit. Simmel understood ruins in paradoxical dialogism, torn between human spirit and nature, past and present, purpose and chance. According to the German sociologist, built architecture rested upon humanity bending natural matter into precise forms according to its own imagination; on the other hand, a collapsed building, its turning into ruins, is a tragic confirmation of its artificiality. In a ruin, materials regain their true form and return to their natural status; they emanate peacefulness and melt back into the surrounding natural environment, confirming their being something ancient, something of the past.

The attempt to describe and make sense of industrial cities has characterised a great deal of cultural production in the nineteenth and twentieth centuries. For instance, in the British literary context, Charles Dickens's *Hard Times* (1855) takes place between London and Coketown, a fictional northern English city of red bricks, covered in thick smoke. Manchester resident Elisabeth Gaskel also sets two of her novels (*Mary Barton*, 1848, and *North and South*, 1855) in industrial settings of the North, also contrasting industrial cities with the supposedly more civilised South. Descriptions of the early-industrialised towns are from the very beginning based on a comparison with more cultural or refined places. At the same time, authors are always keen in portraying architectural and atmospheric features. These elements didn't change much over the years. There has always been an attempt to understand industrial cities through cultural ones, that is, by comparing landmarks, layers of history, inhabitants, and cultural artefacts.

The 1950s' so-called kitchen-sink films also focus on describing northern industrial cities. These black-and-white portrayals of desolate individual destinies, in surroundings dominated by brick walls, gasworks, and puddles, collaborate in defining the post-war industrial crisis. The same happens with Italian *neorealismo*, which often focuses on the inner migration of unskilled workers from the rural South to the northern industrial metropolises, such as Milan, or to desolate lives at the margins of quickly developing but still ambiguous in-between spaces. These films share a common trait: their portrayals of poverty, social distress, and urban problems come from a privileged standpoint, that in the British new wave film has been codified as 'that long shot of our town from that hill'. According to Andrew Higson (1996), the abused opening shot from above is, in fact, programmatic to the romanticising of working-class lives in industrial settings. *Neorealismo*, on the other hand, focused its view on industrial wastelands and on the undefined spaces, rising between rural surroundings and city outskirts. These vague spaces were used as mirrors for the eradicated individual not able to be modern or traditional, no more rural but not yet proletarian. This is, for instance, the dramatic condition of the protagonists of Pasolini's works such as the film *Accattone* and the novel *Ragazzi di*

Vita. All these works codified industrial landscapes as mirrors for troubled subjectivities, thanks to the use of black and white and to the focus on industrial debris. Rarely do we see in these films active industrial spaces at work; they are more a medium to define a certain sensibility, which goes back a long way. Industrial wastelands become in the postwar European cinema the topos of what Boym calls 'ruinophilia' (Boym 2008).

An interesting aspect, however, is the persistence with which the industrial atmosphere and the 'industrial crisis atmosphere', in particular, continue to haunt our urban mindscape. According to Böhme (1993), atmosphere is a spatial concept that arises neither from the subject nor from the object, although it maintains object-like and subject-like features. Atmosphere is the space allowing objects to articulate their presence; however, it is also sensed in bodily presence by subjects—it is a subject's state of being in space. Böhme's definition of atmosphere makes sense of the modes of relation between object and subject in spatial constellations. It implies, therefore, not only art-related judgemental elements but, as stated by Lehtovuori, 'it foregrounds a two-way relation between people and their environment, where both the social and the material aspect are equally constitutive. People bring with them the social questions: Class, gender, professions, culturally coded practices and social networks, as well as urban economy and policies, enter the analysis' (Lehtovuori 2010, 82).

Lehtovuori describes Helsinki's Makasiinit, former railway warehouses later appropriated as a site of DIY cultural events until their destruction in 2009, with these words:

> Firstly, the rough aesthetics, scars of time, smell of wood and tar and the historic allusions of hand-made bricks, steel trusses and other paraphernalia all contributed to a special atmosphere that attracted users and underlined the value of a different place in the increasingly sanitized city centre. Secondly, the size of the buildings and the railyard, their form reminiscent of a town square, their direction vis-à-vis views and flows, and the fluid, sieve-like spatial organization, originally made to facilitate quick movement of goods through the warehouses, are all specific configurational qualities that explain why the buildings were so well-suited for various events and other temporary uses. The atmospheric and configurational analyses help to understand how, precisely, the material artefact of Makasiinit was

valuable as a 'living' and connected socio-spatial (socio-material) reality. (Lehtovuori 2010, 77–78)

The author never openly claims that the atmosphere of the place can be
classified as 'industrial', but I think that this is a key element in understanding the fascination that the Makasiinit exerted on Helsinki's population. The Makasiinit radiated their own industrial atmosphere in an
augmented way because they were located in the very centre of a capital city known for its culture and for its political role (and not because of
its industry). The fact that the Makasiinit lied a few metres from the
stairs of the Finnish Parliament collaborated further in increasing the
modality of its atmosphere.

Talking about an industrial atmosphere always implies the reverberation of certain perceived or imagined industriousness, brutalism,
roughness, rhythm, murkiness, and noise emanating from street cor-
ners, empty buildings, means of transportations, public squares, en-
counters, faces, appearances, and styles, possibly in all social and material realities. Different cultural traditions and representations created a
huge array of narratives about less educated, louder, dirtier industrial
city inhabitants, and about their attitude. For instance, in the British
context, from Charles Dickens to kitchen-sink films, from the 'Madchester' music scene to *Coronation Street*, the bleak industrial towns of
the North have been celebrated as 'the land of the working class'
(Shields 1991). Even more important is the fact that an industrial city
has little symbolic or branding value, when compared to other urban
centres. Just by pronouncing out loud 'Paris', 'London', 'Helsinki', or
'Oulu', 'Bochum', 'Antwerp', it is very easy to determine the toponymies
that reverberate in our imaginary and the ones that are more anonymous and empty. There is still little place-value connected to industrial
cities because these cities were born without proper connotations outside the world of manufacturing and production. The attempt to shift
their place-value to culture and creativity is fairly new, and the results
have been too unalike to determine their overall success. One of the
reasons behind the impact of the industrial atmosphere could lie in this
indeterminacy as well, with the difficulty in associating it to a place in
particular. The industrial city can therefore be seen first and foremost
as an articulation of space, not of place. The post-industrial city has
been a sometime desperate attempt to bring the notion of place within

this atmosphere and by referring to it as historically funded cultural expression.

MATERIALITIES AND EMERGENT CULTURAL SENSIBILITIES

Marx described the forces involved in economic production as the structure, the real foundation,

> on which arises a legal and political superstructure, and to which correspond definite forms of consciousness. The mode of production of material life conditions the general process of social, political, and intellectual life. It is not the consciousness of men that determines their existence, but their social existence that determines their consciousness. (Marx 1977)

This primacy asserted by Marx to the economic sphere has brought to a variety of attitude towards culture, in terms of its production, consumption, and circulation. For instance, Adorno described how capitalist economic forces shape the cultural industry so that, therefore, culture under capitalism can only produce goods to be consumed. For Williams, however, superstructure cannot be interpreted as a mere reflection. The production of a cultural order is always material; it takes places in space, it determines what we are able to see, to grasp of everyday reality:

> Cultural work and activity are not now, in any ordinary sense, a superstructure: not only because of the depth and thoroughness at which any cultural hegemony is lived, but because cultural tradition and practice are seen as much more than superstructural expressions—reflections, mediations or typifications—of a formed social and economic structure. On the contrary they are among the basic processes of the formation itself and, further, related to a much wider area of reality than the abstractions of 'social' and 'economic' experience. (Williams 1977, 111)

Building on the work of Gramsci, Williams affirmed that even at the cultural level, dominant forces maintain their power by saturating practices, meanings, senses of reality, and values into the cultural hegemony. Hegemony is a whole body of practices and expectations covering the whole of the living experience; it is a lived system of meanings and values, a sense of reality, which is internalised and therefore as profound as anything that Marx would make exclusive to the so-called economic base.

Cultural hegemony is not static, it depends on real social processes of selection and incorporation, and it is perpetuated, for instance, through education, family, training, and class. Dominant culture must be continuously made and remade, especially because it cannot exhaust all forms of being and understandings of reality. There are no main modes of production, dominant societies, and dominant cultures, which can exhaust the full range of human practice, human energy, and human intention.

Continuously there are subaltern forces in the making; these are residual or emergent. These forces are residual when they are expressions of the past, but they are lived as if they were present, such as organised religion or rural living, for instance. They are emergent when they convey new meanings and values, new practices, and new relationships. They can also be alternative or oppositional, with reference to their standing towards society as a whole. Alternative forces are the ones that run side by side with the dominant ones and create a parallel space, while oppositional forces want to change society as a whole and substitute the dominant hegemony. Hegemony's reactions can range from incorporation and attack to overlooking and ignoring, depending on the nature of the subaltern forces. The hegemony consciously and continuously selects and organises cultural practices born outside it.

Art as a form of cultural expression is based on specific activities and relationships of real human beings. According to Williams, it is important to discover the *nature* of a practice and then its *conditions*, not its components:

> What we are actually seeking is the *true practice* which has been alienated to an object, and the true conditions of practice—whether as *literary conventions* or as *social relationships*—which have been alienated to components or mere background. (Williams 1980, 49; emphases are mine)

According to Williams, the base/superstructure dichotomy was overcome in the work of Gramsci by the concept of cultural hegemony.

Cultural hegemony simply corresponds to the reality of social experience in a certain society; it saturates society and constitutes the limits of common sense. Gramsci was therefore able to assert a specific value to culture and, at the same time, to theorise to the possibility of destabilising the dominant hegemony through cultural action.

The bands, scenes, and movements from industrial cities described in this book should be understood as emergent and anti-hegemonic. As we will see, some experiences were oppositional and some were alternative in nature, but they all shared a preoccupation with space.

As noted before, economic crises have a deep impact on the urban environment with regard to decay. Spaces of production might become redundant and therefore emptied and abandoned, ongoing urban developments might be abruptly stopped, whole districts might be left shrinking and decaying by speculators waiting for an upswing, and mortgage-dependant flats and houses might end under foreclosures. The city as a functioning network of transports, energy supplies, and services might experience seizures and blockages. Certain districts might be stigmatised by a major presence of unemployed, and city centres might become the sites for demonstrations and resistance, maybe leading to violence and repression. All European cities have experienced, at least once, some of the above-mentioned real features of an economic crisis in their recent history.

Industrial cities have been particularly stigmatised under economic crisis, and the step towards new economic paradigms has deeply affected their nature. Born as articulations of space, they had to quickly submit to the dominance of place, that is, creating a brand, becoming recognisable, building a history, and assigning a marketable cultural value to themselves. As stated before, in some cases, popular music has been adopted as an instrument to achieve these goals.

What is more interesting for this book is to understand how popular music was affected by these changes in the material dimension of the industrial city, for instance, how urban decay has affected popular music production, consumption, and circulation. Of course, the consequences have been different in relation to national contexts, popular music markets, and other implications. However, one generalising argument could be made through the notion of cultural sensibility, which I defined elsewhere as an individual or collective reaction to certain social or spatial circumstances, which asserts a certain aesthetic or emotional value to a particular place. To offer an example, it is common in every European city to find a former factory turned into a theatre, a media facility, or a restaurant, sometimes with grotesque results. However, there is nothing culturally relevant in an abandoned factory; it is just the expression of a local or global change at the level of capitalist accumulation, a change that affected manufacturing or production. It is cultural sensibility and its spreading from the individual level to the collective that adds a particular symbolic value to the material building and makes it pleasant and inspiring enough to become an art gallery, for instance. There are, of course, very clear logistic elements to it—namely, the size, illumination, and location—nonetheless, its appeal originates in the cultural sensibility of an individual or a few.

What has been previously described as 'industrial crisis atmosphere' is therefore not something given, but it has an origin in a specific socioeconomic context: the 1980s urban crisis and in relation to a specific group of people, which I identify with the post-punk scenes developing in the late 1970s in European and North American industrial cities.

The four cities I will refer to in the following chapters, again, belong to different regions of Europe. They are all secondary centres in their own national settings, but they maintain a strong regional supremacy and, during their industrial history, were central for the globalised movement of different goods.

At different stages, and in different modalities, all four urban conurbations had at least to partly modify their economic paradigm, following deindustrialisation and the 1980s urban crisis. Still, their architectural and planning features still maintain intact many features of their past.

From the late 1970s to the early 1980s in all four cities, popular music became a significant element in youth and cultural activism and leisure time, with the appearance of very active punk and post-punk scenes. Fanzines, bands, tapes, records, festivals, and demonstrations were conceived, produced, and traded within a growing, no-profit and self-organised network. Through interviews with musicians and practitioners, analysis of musical artefacts of the time, memoirs, and documentaries, I will highlight the contribution of anonymous industrial centres in the cultural production of 1980s Europe.

The contemporary economic regime of accumulation has been described as 'flexible'. *Flexibility* is used metaphorically to describe the shift from mass production to the individualisation and target-oriented diversification of what was offered, from more or less secure and uniform working life to precariousness, from manufacture to services, and from concentration to vertical disintegration of large firms through subcontractors. All these steps are used to sustain the idea of a new regime of accumulation, overcoming Fordism as paradigm of production and consumption and Keynesianism as paradigm of economic development (Lash and Urry 1987; Harvey 1989). European deindustrialisation is a consequence of this change. The flexible regime of accumulation was also capable of muting successful subaltern voices, by including them into its project of profit making.

2

A GENEALOGY OF 'INDUSTRIAL CITY MUSIC'

Genealogies of noise tend to associate noise to modernity (Payer 2007; Bijsterveld 2008; Goddard, Halligan, and Spleman 2013; Epstein 2014), as if pre-modern history were a place of silence, sometimes broken by the clashes of armies in warfare. In truth, noise started being a problem in the Middle Ages, and its regulation was carried out extensively, especially in relation to the night time or to festivities. In Turku (Finland) every year on Christmas Eve at noon, the mayor reads *The Declaration of Christmas Peace*; this tradition dates back to the 1300s and advises people to behave peacefully and *quietly* during Christmas time.

It is, however, with modernity and the industrial revolution that noise starts taking its toll on everyday life and becomes a constant preoccupation. From technology to law, from health care to political control, modern institutions have tried to classify, tame, channel, and avoid noise as the unwanted side effect of modernisation. Factory work, political demonstrations, motorised traffic, warfare, and simple human density have increased the level of noise in cities across the twentieth and twenty-first centuries. There are studies indicating that noise might be another component of contemporary urban inequalities, with the urban poor having to cope the most with living environments where noise is increasingly concentrated.

The French classic book *Le Bruit* (Botte and Chocholle 1984), part of the popularising science collection *Que sais-je?*, identifies some general characteristics of noise. These are physical, including intermittence, erraticness, and randomness of acoustic vibrations, but are also relative to their disagreeable effects on the human ears. The authors also refer to the subjective dimension of this last element: what can be indifferent or positive to someone might be really annoying to someone else. According to them, noise has, however, some general features that can be agreed upon. The first one is *intensity*; all sounds, even the most agreeable, become noise if they are too loud. The second is *complexity*, because noise is considered as not having a salient tonal character or a dominant component. However, not all complex sounds can be considered noise. *Brevity* and *high modulations* also belong to noise because it is intermittent and irregular in pitch, frequency, and intensity. Noise originates at the presence of some or all of the above-mentioned features and to the disagreeable experiencing of them. This definition is instrumental to classifying and therefore finding solutions to what the book defines as its most common typologies in our everyday life: traffic and industrial noise. According to Botte and Chocholle, noise is something that can be measured, and its propagation can be tested and somehow limited institutionally; their main interest is providing reflections on how to reduce it and who is paying the most due to its propagation, in social and political terms.

Industrial noise originates with industrialisation and is linked to major inventions, starting with the steam engine and followed by the construction of mines, factories, abattoirs, warehouses, power stations, and vast areas for heavy production.

As seen in chapter 1, an industrial city features the intense presence of visual material with high 'imageability' (Lynch 1960), such as bare materials, like red bricks, bare concrete, and iron; forms that are linear, modular, and pattern-like; colours, like red and grey; and superficial phenomena, like rust and wear. Main architectural elements are chimneys, firewalls, and gasworks.

The visual dimension is a strong signifier of the industrial condition; however, its most debated and regulated features invest other senses, such as smell and sound. Industrial cities can smell of coal, gas, various chemicals used in production; of final products; and of a combination of the above. Modern cities began to tackle vapours and smells from sewers in the nineteenth century, and urban planning started taking into account the origin and entity of certain smells because of their supposed dangerous effects on health. For instance, Alexandre Parent-

Duchâtelet's study on Parisian sewers (1824), motivated both by medical and social purposes, offers an amazing example of the attempt to identify, understand, and classify smells by ethnographic means (Lindner 2004). New York City's Metropolitan Board of Health has tried to limit and control the city's bad smells since 1866. However, common knowledge, superstitions, and beliefs connected to smells, beside smells themselves, continued affecting the perception and reputation of certain districts, especially the ones where industrial production settled (Kiechle 2016). It is only in the early 1970s, nearly a century later, that, as seen in the previous chapter, Sheffield was able to boast smokeless air all over the city, thanks to the Clean Air Act and after decades of attempting to tame this problem.

Along the centuries, regulations also affected industrial soundscapes; however, production by heavy machinery continued making mechanical noise, mostly repetitive, rhythm-like noise, only lately accompanied by swift digital robotic bleeps and bloops. While smells were increasingly controlled and tamed by technology along the years, noise spiraled both in intensity and in sonic palette. Noises represent a sharp and distinctive feature of the industrial city and of its imaginary, and it is only by physically moving heavy production elsewhere that the industrial soundscape can be muted. Funnily enough, it is with music that factories tried to provide an antidote to noise. Music gave only a partial solution to noise pollution in providing working rhythms and maintaining productivity, but it definitely constructed a social feeling on tedious factory floors and a means for resistance among workers (Korczynski 2014, 2007).

Today, it is only cars that provide the lo-fi keynote sound of urban living. Noise can be understood as the main element of the industrial city's material existence and sensorial experience. Noise was also one of the forging elements of the twentieth century. It was a constant interlocutor for music production throughout the century; however, there are two competing narratives in reference to this. The first is connected to the art world of contemporary classical music and to the avant-garde use of noise and found sounds in the context of music composition and of music work. The second is defined by popular culture and by the continuous intermission of mediated sounds in popular music. References to real places, locations, and individual stories have often en-

riched these two narratives, and musicians have justified their production in various ways.

ART MUSIC AND INDUSTRIAL NOISE

I use the concept of art music to refer to classical music production of
the twentieth and twenty-first centuries. Understanding itself solely as
art, this music output has mostly used the industrial world as inspiration
or reflected upon some of its aspects, such as repetition, from the aesthetic point of view. Rarely has an industrial city played a significant
role in the evolution of industry-inspired art music. It is mostly in capital cities and cultural centres that art music flourished in the twentieth
century. A few exceptions can be made: that of Milan, Italy, where
futurist music was first conceived and Darmstadt, Germany, where serial music developed.

   Luigi Russolo published *L'arte dei Rumori* (The Art of Noise) in
1913. Russolo was an Italian futurist painter who wrote this manifesto
of futurist music as a letter to musicologist and musician Balilla Pratella,
who himself had written a text about *musica futurista*. Futurismo be-
longed to the wave of avant-garde art movements that spread around
Europe especially after the First World War and shared with the others
the tendency to redact manifestos. Inspired by a concert of Pratella,
Russolo programmatically referred to the establishment of an art of
noises as a revolution in music, something

> paralleled by the increasing proliferation of machinery sharing in
> human labour. . . . [M]achines create today such a large number of
> varied noises that pure sound, with its littleness and its monotony,
> now fails to arouse any emotion. (Russolo 1967, 5)

This is actually the only direct reference to the industry in the text; in
fact, the author preferred to describe natural, urban, or warfare noises
as the main inspiration for his manifesto and for the new music. However, it shows some interesting ideas, first, in putting machinery and music in parallel evolution and not in causal relation and, second, in noting
the wide variety of noises machines are able to produce. These industrial ideas were, however, overshadowed by the attempt to systematise
noises. The overarching aim for new music was to 'score and regulate

harmonically and rhythmically these most varied noises' (Russolo 1967, 9) and not just to imitate them. Russolo suggested the adoption of noise in the realm of art music, its categorisation within six typologies, and its harmonic and rhythmic subordination and regulation via pitch changing.

Futurism as an art movement was interested in the celebration of power, technology, and speed over more traditional and consolidated art forms and lifestyles. It also had an initial link, thanks to its founder, Filippo Tommaso Marinetti, to Benito Mussolini and to the establishment of the Fascist Party in post–World War I Italy.

The real adoption and celebration of industrial noises in art music production happened in the context of Soviet avant-garde in the years following the October Revolution. Soviet and Eastern European filmmakers, painters, writers, and musicians celebrated the industry as the supreme space for the emancipation of workers and for the realisation of socialism. For instance, Arseny Avraamov wrote and performed the *Symphony of Factory Sirens (Industrial Horns?)* (Simfoniya gudkov, Гудковая симфония) in Baku on November 7, 1922, as a celebration of the fifth anniversary of the October Revolution. This symphony used the whole urban sonic landscape of Baku, including its military fleet, a variety of urban noises, and the sounds from the local factories, together with choirs and shouts, as orchestra; Avraamov conducted the whole from a tower, thanks to the use of flags and following an orchestral script he redacted. A second performance followed a year later, in Moscow.

Alexander Mosolov, another Soviet musician, went even further when he composed *The Iron Foundry* (also known as *Factory: Machine Music*), the first movement of a lost ballet suite entitled *Stal* (steel) in 1926–1927. The composition is based on orchestral sounds layering in repetitive loops and building up to simulate the noise of industrial machinery getting into action. A music critic refers to a live performance at the Liège Festival 1930 in these terms:

> We have the benumbing mesmerism of uniformly repeated mechanical sounds, combined with a kind of lyrical theme, the song of steel, or possibly of man, the ironmaster. (Evans 1930)

In a recording by the Orchestre Symphonique de Paris conducted by Julius Ehrlich from the early 1930s (Orchestre Symphonique de Paris

2013), the piece is indeed dominated by the repetition of hammering metallic noises, which are produced by sheets of steel along conventional orchestral percussions. The avant-garde approached industrial noise by simulating industrial work and heavy machinery with conventional orchestral instruments, with the adoption of found sounds, and with the use of industrial hardware as instruments. Another stylistic element, whose influence can be linked to industrial work, is *Motorik*. This term, which will resurface in popular music criticism in connection to Kraut-rock, initially described the use of ostinato rhythms, for instance, in the work of composers such as Ernst Krenek and Paul Hindemith, although its origin is explained in ambivalent ways. Some critics saw it as a musical strategy already present in the work of Beethoven (Rexroth 2005, 98) and Rossini (Keitel and Neuner 1992, 305). However, some others connected the repetitive rhythm to the glorification of the modern industrial era and to the increasing role that technology played in inspiring art and classical music (Braun 1999, 168). Interestingly, some authors referred to the influence of jazz, where *Motorik* described the continuous excited swing drive, typical of early manifestations of this genre (Mauser 2007, 12; Laf 1954). This second connection is interesting because it demystifies the art music origin of this musical expression and links it to African American culture, possibly turning it into an expression of cultural exploitation.

As a continuous 4/4 drum pattern without breaks, *Motorik* resurfaced in popular music. For instance, Klaus Dinger adopted this drumming style in bands such as Kraftwerk, Neu! and La Düsseldorf and Jaki Liebezeit in nearby Cologne-based Can. For some fans, *Motorik* has become 'the sound of Düsseldorf' (for an overview of this, see Esch 2014 and Stubbs 2014a). It is a rhythm that a listener can sonically associate to motorways, railways, and waterways, which dominate the landscape of this dense and polycentric region at the core of the so-called blue banana. Dinger himself referred to this rhythm as *lange gerade*, long and straight, or as Apache beat, in reference to the repetitive percussion sounds of 'Indians' in Western movies (Dee 1998). British musician and producer Brian Eno calls it Dingerbeat and Neu!beat and considers it one of the three defining drum beats of the 1970s (Stubbs 2014b).

The shift of the term from the realm of classical to the one of popular music, however, lost this semiotic association. Popular music artists ranging from Stereolab to David Bowie, from Arcade Fire to Teksti-TV 666, have used *Motorik* as a referent to a specific 1970s European continental 'Kraut' feel and atmosphere only, denying once more the role that black music played in popular music history.

Often composers of the early twentieth century took inspiration and celebrated industrial and mechanical soundscapes, as already mentioned, through repetition, and this began to influence the understanding of cultural production in general. For instance, Walter Benjamin examined mechanical reproduction as an ambivalent force, which was able to democratise the fruition of art but at the same time deprived it of the 'aura' of uniqueness and authenticity (Benjamin 1963). Krakauer (1996) criticised dancing revue performances as ornament of the masses, where sexless bodies in mass perform the same mechanical moves to please masses of spectators, themselves put in order in tiers. The German thinker understood ornament as having no meaning outside itself and compared it to industrial production, where the aim of production is in production itself and in the generation of profit. However, he also stated that

> the masses organized in these movements come from offices and factories: the formal principle according to which they are molded determines them in reality as well. When significant components of reality become invisible in our world, art must make do with what is left, for an aesthetic presentation is all the more real the less it dispenses with the reality outside the aesthetic sphere. No matter how low one gauges the value of the mass ornament, its degree of reality is still higher than that of artistic productions which cultivate outdated noble sentiments. (Krakauer 1996, 79)

The German author was, therefore, aware of the idiosyncratic function of repetition in contemporary cultural expressions. Even if not referring specifically to sounds, he was able to assign a specific function to it and recognise its ability to make the hidden machinery, which enables our understanding of reality, visible. However, experimenting with the industrial soundscape disappeared quickly from the horizon of art music in the Soviet Union, thanks to the arrival into power of Stalin who preferred more conventional musical expressions bound to socialist realism (Makanowitsky 1965), and elsewhere because art music and its world belong to capital cities and cultural centres (not to industrial

towns) and its aesthetics moved quickly towards pre-industrial and ecological themes, a more globalised and technological urbanity, and the
influence of music of non-European origin, jazz in particular.

POPULAR MUSIC AND INDUSTRIAL NOISE

Classical music originated before the Industrial Revolution, and its performance doesn't rely on electricity: the majority of orchestral instruments are based on natural materials such as wood, brass, and metal,
and on their ability to resonate and vibrate when hit, strum, slid, picked,
or beaten. Concert halls for the performance of classical music are
sometimes highly subsidised, and the employment of a city orchestra
takes a huge part of any cultural budget. The history of popular music,
instead, is itself an industrial one: it is based on recording studios, on
factories pressing vinyl, on trucks distributing them. Most of the instruments involved in performing popular music depend on electricity, are
usually cheap and mass-produced, and are enabled by electric amplification. Its performance usually takes place in commercial spaces, where
revenues also come from the sale of alcohol. Its production is embedded into and responds to the rules of an economic market. The sound
itself of popular music, its being repetitive, noisy, and catchy, can be
easily associated with the noises of mechanisation and industrialisation.
Often popular music lyrics deal with the condition of the individual in
an industrialised society. Industrial cities have also played a huge role as
incubators for bands and have become the authentic settings in photo
shoots, record covers, videos, and oral histories. Also, in narratives developed by musicians and fans, often the connection between a certain
kind of music and a certain industrial environment is used as means to
convey authenticity.

Linking popular music and industrial noise seems, therefore, a very
straightforward business, which is sometimes complicated by the attempt to create continuities between the avant-garde art music of the
beginning of the twentieth century and the popular music produced
especially in the late part of the same century. Only thirty-seven years
passed between *The Iron Foundry* (1927) and Martha and the Vandellas' 'Dancing in the Street' (1964), both adopting steel as percussion
instrument; however, the two compositions cannot be more far apart.

The first is a work by a single author trained in classical music theory and composition and performed by an orchestra in a live classical music setting, such as a concert hall. The second is written, produced, and recorded by several individuals, attributed to the lead singing vocal trio, and credited to authors. It is a hit, mostly played as recording, through radio, jukeboxes, and televisions in private spaces, such as bedrooms and moving cars, or semi-private ones, such as bars and discotheques. In addition, *The Iron Foundry* celebrated the industrial world and elected it as inspiration for creative artistic work. It showed that the October Revolution and the establishment of the Soviet Union were based on a strong synergy between cultural and industrial work in enhancing socialism. 'Dancing in the Street' lyrics are about a wave of joyfulness and optimism taking over the streets of all major US cities through dancing. However, it also reflects a particular moment in US history, where the black population was emancipating itself through the civil rights movement, and some demonstrators saw in the song a sort of call to arms (Smith 1999). Both music compositions share a revolutionary elan, which might also be enhanced by the use of metal percussions; however, they are very different in the way they communicate the social context that produced them. Art music is able to inform us about aesthetic trends and the sudden liberation that artists felt after October 1918; popular music tells about social conditions and collective aspirations of the urban black population in the United States in the early 1960s. Industrial in the first example is an aesthetic choice and a creative paradigm, while in the second it is a social reality and a common denominator for all its imagined and material reality. Popular music builds an 'amplified authenticity' for the industrial world. This ability relies on what I call a musicscape built by lyrics and titles (textscape), by sounds (soundscape) and by images (landscape), which layers meaning and references, increasing the authenticity potential of music. Moreover, it relies on a *degré zero* emotional level, which is mostly connected to the human voice, but also to reverberation, repetition, and the beat.

The history of the industrial city runs parallel to the history of popular music, and the articulations between the two are continuous and generate various understandings of the one and the other, going beyond the mere existence of a genre called 'industrial music'. This genre is nowadays known all over the world, thanks to the popularised and commercialised version by acts like Marilyn Manson, Ministry, and Nine

Inch Nails. Its origins are usually traced back to early 1980s Sheffield, London's Hackney, and (West) Berlin, which gave birth, respectively, to the seminal Clock DVA, Throbbing Gristle, and Einstürzende Neubauten. Its name might simply come from the choice of Throbbing Gristle to create a record label named Industrial Records (Woods 2007); however, it is also self-explanatory because of the genre trademarks: heavy style and repetitive riffs combined with pounding rhythms and the use of heavy machinery noises, evoking the soundscape and visual imagery of a dystopian factory, as in an abattoir, a concentration camp, or a battlefield. In industrial music, the homology between a particular sound and the influence of a particular landscape has been taken for granted by musicians and listeners as something organic, although sometimes it verges on stereotypes, simply providing a distorted and loud illustration of the sounds, which are associated to heavy production. The overt use of noises within a music genre, which is highly defined by artiness and avant-gardism, is already evident in classical music of the twentieth century and cannot be seen as an exclusive certificate of origin to industrial music. Moreover, often the link between industrial music and the industrial world denies the influence of black music as industrial genealogy. Industrial music is often perceived as a white experiment, with a dominant influence from white art music and in reaction to African American elements and styles, such as the blues. Often, straightforward connections between black music and industrial, such as the role Kraftwerk played in the birth of NYC hip-hop and Detroit techno are shown as unidirectional and handled as interesting oddities.

However, in this book I am interested in demonstrating that industrial city music and its genealogy rely on the heterogeneous and cosmopolitan dialogue among music cultures, taking place across racial and national divides. Industrial city music leads us into a subaltern history of popular music, where music making anticipated human displacements and economic paradigm changes.

The success of genres, performers, and scenes first incubated in industrial cities has led to the articulation of this homology in a variety of ways. These can also be understood as discourses, as ways to talk about this homology, each of them with its own set of rules and paradigms. A historical approach would allow me to examine popular music as an evolving cultural system of genres, artists, recording techniques, formats, and audiences. However, this would limit my understanding of a spatial continuum, across popular music cultures, that encompasses individual genres and artists. Industrial city music revolves around a few discourses that are continuously at work in its production and also in its reception. These are:

- *Folk and displacement*: Industrial city music provided coping mechanisms and a common language for workers coming from heterogeneous backgrounds and suddenly displaced into an industrial city.
- *Organisation of work*: Industrial city music organised itself as an articulation of industrial work. The ability to carry out autonomously the whole process of music production, both in capitalist or anti-capitalist stance, confirms the persistence over time of certain manufacturing abilities and work ethics.
- *Repetition and noise*: Industrial city music is based on repetition of patterns and riffs and on the adoption of noise as aesthetic choice.

For instance, 'industrial folk ballads' were a product of British folk music of the nineteenth century; they were working-class songs with industrial themes, in the context of the first two industrial revolutions and of the mass migration to industrial towns. They were popular songs, often of unknown origin, performed by amateur musicians and by workers themselves on the way to work, while performing industrial work and while protesting or striking. They were usually transmitted orally and anonymously. Some of these songs were based on older folk melodies, and 'rural' lyrics were adapted to refer to industrial work, to big industrial disasters, or to the industrial worker condition. Sonically, they are still a product of a pre-industrial world and accompanied by acoustic instruments or sung a cappella; however, song titles and lyrics are deeply connected to the new industrial and urban world and society. They are therefore the product of a displacement. These songs were rediscovered thanks to the work of musicologist Alan Lomax in the United States and Ewan MacColl in the United Kingdom, who started transcribing, archiving, and recording them (MacColl 1954). This gave way and enriched the so-called folk revivals that started across UK and US university clubs from the late 1940s onwards (Mitchell 2007; Brocken 2003). Industrial folk songs were reinterpreted as serious political material, being the pure voice of workers and of their social reality. As MacColl writes in the introduction to the songbook *The Shelter and the Cage*, industrial folk songs

> should be sung to the accompaniment of pneumatic drills and swinging hammers, they should be bawled above the hum of turbines and the clatter of looms for they are songs of toil, anthems of the industrial age. Few of these songs have ever appeared in print before, for they were not made with the eye to quick sales—or to catch the song-plugger's ear but to relieve the intolerable daily grind. (MacColl 1954)

Performers such as MacColl himself, Peggy Seeger, Woody Guthrie, and Pete Seeger recorded a few of these songs and collaborated in reviving their political agency in the context of twentieth-century workers-rights struggles. Also in socialist countries industrial folk ballads were often sung in music festivals and recorded by various artists, in several languages. Folk revival performers were among the few artists from the West who were able to perform inside the Iron Curtain. Today, there are still several artists inspired by the industrial folk ballad tradition, ranging from Billy Bragg to Bruce Springsteen. If we consider the industrial folk ballad in terms of a continuum, we can identify a few elements: use of acoustic instruments, augmented lyrical agency, direct reference to localities and events, white male performer mirroring the stereotyped traditional industry worker, the use of traditional Anglo-Saxon folk melodies and chord sequences, systematic repetition in lyrics, and closeness to socialist ideology.

Chicago blues might be the first electrified industrial music, relying on electricity and at the same time putting it to use in sonically adventurous and experimental ways. In general, blues

> served as an ethnoracial and an ethnospatial epistemology, a repository of collective memory, a source of moral instruction, and a symbol of shared social conditions. Made up of more than mere musical forms, figures and devices, blues music as a social institution played a crucial role in creating ways of knowing and ways of being vital to African American people. It did so, however, in coded and disguised form, largely hidden from the sight and surveillance of those who held political and economic power. (Lipsitz 2007, xix)

In this regard, Chicago blues represents a continuum from the original Delta blues and provided the same kind of coded and disguised social and cultural expression of African Americans. Chicago blues originated from another displacement: the black population from the US South started moving to the big industrial cities of the North, such as Chicago, to work in factories. This happened before and during WWI and again after WWII, when about two hundred thousand African Americans moved to the windy city (Goven 2005). Another important city that attracted a lot of workers from the US South was Detroit. Blues songs celebrated moving to Detroit and working for Mr. Ford, and many musicians were working shifts in automobile factories (Smith 1999).

Hand in hand with the move from a rural to an urban setting, changes in technology and in the consumption of live music had an impact on black music making. Blues on the Mississippi were mostly performed acoustic or with basic amplification by individuals or small groups playing in so-called juke joints, where the black population working in cotton fields went to have a good time. In Chicago this music was performed in electrified combos of guitar, bass, and drums, sometimes with piano and harmonica. Chicago blues didn't only refer in lyrics to freight trains, travelling, nostalgia for the South and the condition of the African American male in lyrics; it also gave way to the first popular and electric sonic translation of the industrial soundscape, by 'cranking it up' and creating distortion via loudness. The electric guitar with metal strings, its valve amplification, and the use of the bottleneck slide technique allowed the control and reproduction of noises and the expansion of the popular music sonic palette, for instance, in the seminal work of Muddy Waters, Jody Williams, Bo Diddley, and Hubert Sumlin. At the same time, repetition (the twelve-bar blues sequence) and the use of rhythmic riffs instead of folk melodies went hand in hand with the repetitive dimension of industrial work and life. Muddy Water's 'Mannish Boy' and 'I'm Your Hoochie Coochie Man' and Bo Diddley's 'I'm a Man' verses are all based on the repetition of a simple, heavy riff, which only after a while resolves into the classic blues structure. The mechanical insistence of this riff recalls the sound of an industrial press, something that many musicians were familiar with from their daytime jobs in Chicago's factories and abattoirs. *Motorik* originated in this mechanical repetition, inspiring art music and later German Krautrock, probably another form of cultural appropriation in popular music.

Bobo Jenkins, who played blues and worked in an automobile factory in Detroit claimed, 'That whirlin' machinery gives me the beat. It's
like hearin' a band playing all day long. Every song I ever wrote that's
any good has come to me standin' on that line' (Smith 1999, 12). Blues
musicians also addressed the harshness of the working conditions, in
songs that were at the same time forms of protest and coping mechanisms, informing others that they were not alone (Smith 1999, 13).

Chicago blues, and Chess Records in particular, also showed the
increasing role played by record labels in creating genres, labels, and
stars within popular music, especially in connection with what we could
define as 'industrial entrepreneurship'. The industrial city gave a chance
to create enterprises devoted to the production and consumption of
popular music and slowly, from black communities and the 'race music'
label, this music took over the rest of the US population and the world.

This is, for instance, the case of the Tamla/Motown record label.
Motown and Motorcity are nicknames for Detroit, the city where Hen-
ry Ford not only founded the automobile industry as we know it but
also expanded and made consistent the modern assembly line and with
that, the industrial organisation of work. The assembly line was, in fact,
already in common usage in relation to meatpacking districts and abattoirs and only later applied to the assemblage of mechanical objects,
such as automobiles (Klüver 2008).

Several car companies clustered in Detroit. This brought about a
steady immigration of skilled and unskilled workers from the South,
many of African American origin just as in the case of Chicago. To the
Tamla/Motown label is often attributed a Fordist-style organisation of
work as concerns recording studios (Quispel 2005). In fact, Berry Gordy
Jr., the label founder, liked to compare Hitsville U.S.A., his headquarters and studio, to a car factory. Gordy himself had worked on the
assembly line and understood how efficiency and mass production
could be applied to hit singles. At Hitsville U.S.A., a group of musicians
known as the Funk Brothers provided the core backup music for various individual artists and vocal groups, assembling hit single after hit
single from 1959 to 1973. The documentary *Standing in the Shadow of
Motown* (Justman 2002) gives voice and face to many of these musicians
and pays tribute to the already departed. Studio work in the analogue
era was laborious and involved the technological expertise and creativity
of musicians, recording engineers, and producers. The straight connec-

tion between Motown and the automobile industry seems, therefore, plausible at the level of 'organisation of work'. Both Motown and Ford experienced a long era of development, both at the creative and economic levels, and industrial growth looked unstoppable. A video of Martha and the Vandellas takes them lip-syncing their way through 'Nowhere to Run' in the Dearborn Assembly Plant in River Rouge for *It's What's Happening, Baby*. The TV show, led by the NYC-based DJ Murray 'The K' Kaufman, aired on CBS-TV on June 20, 1965; gave visibility to many British, African American, and Latinx artists; and was partly produced by the US Office of Economic Opportunity. It is therefore not by chance that in this video we find a perfect match of two Detroit-based industries. Martha and the Vandellas are seen dancing and singing among the workers, making their way through the paint shop. In the assembly line, they are able to step into the backseat of a Ford Mustang while the engine is mounted into the front trunk, and in the last part of the video, once the final fittings are done, the ready car, driven by 'The K' himself, is able to leave the plant. 'Nowhere to Run' is one of the best-known songs by Martha and the Vandellas and, together with 'Dancing in the Street', share the use of industrial machinery to fortify the beat. In this latter case, the producer George Ivy Hunter used a tire iron during the recordings, while snow chains are used for percussion in the former. Both are automobile accessories, readily available to anyone with a car, but their semiotic power in the context of Motown and the above-mentioned industrial synergy cannot be underestimated. Industrial authenticity has a strong material component based around the idea of production. Despite being produced and sold in millions of exemplars along decades, the Ford Mustang still transmits among car fans a strong sense of authenticity by representing a unique piece of design and the best of the 1960s positive attitude and economic upswing. Music in itself is unable to attach the volatile and abstract notion of authentic to something tangible and spatially defined. It achieves this by relying on something extra-musical—something material that is outside music itself. Detroit as a one-company town played this role. The city defined a certain kind of car and a certain kind of music and the way we were able to talk about them in times of economic upswing.

Of course, another strong synergy can be found in the realm of affect. Motown hits of the 1960s convey an optimistic and affirmative attitude towards life, love, and industriousness. These songs express an 'industrial structure of feeling', made of energy and activity, be it in an assembly line, in a civil rights demonstration, on the street, in a car, in a union strike, in a dance hall, in bed, in a recording studio, or in a riot. Motown also plays a key role in defining the so-called Northern Soul culture in the North of England. This music culture started in the 1970s and defines today a musical canon and a dance scene (Raine 2019), which is roughly based around obscure soul and funk music from the United States, including several Tamla/Motown artists. This spatial and temporal continuum can only be explained as articulated in the industrial city and working-class experience and in the industrial structure of feeling, across time, and racial and national divides.

As stated previously, economic crisis and deindustrialisation changed considerably the way these synergies worked; however we can 'feel' a similar industrial entrepreneurship at work, across the Atlantic Ocean, in a German town of North Rhine Westphalia in the early 1970s. Kraftwerk put Düsseldorf on the industry city music map. The band formed there and gained worldwide popularity thanks to hit singles like 'Autobahn', 'Das Model', and 'The Robots'. They maintain a cult status among electronic music fans across the world, having contributed to the birth of genres such as techno, hip-hop, synth pop, and house music. The classic line-up, a quartet of robots/showroom dummies in red shirts and black ties was very much at odd with rock stars of the same era and found attention from fans and critics across the world; in particular in France, in the United States, and in the United Kingdom. Founding members Ralf Hütter and Florian Schneider (born Schneider-Esleben) were born in 1946 and 1947, respectively.

The band has given way to a number of biographies and to an edited academic collection (Albiez and Pattie 2011), always on the border between scientific rigor and fandom. These books detail the band's history and refer to the highly intertextual value of the band's oeuvre, encompassing *musique concrète*, Italian futurism, expressionist German cinema, design and architecture, and post-humanism. Much has been written also about the band's legacy for the establishment of an electronic music continuum across the Atlantic (see, e.g., the introduction to Barr 1998, 1–25). Their discography has been celebrated as a *Gesamtkunstwerk* (total work of art) and exhibited live in influential contemporary art museums such as MOMA (Museum of Modern Art) in New York

City, the Tate Art Museum in London, the Neue Nationalgalerie in Berlin, and the K20 Kunstsammlung in Düsseldorf, with the *1 2 3 4 5 6 7 8* retrospective.

There have been several attempts to straightforwardly link the band's sound and poetics to the city where they formed, rehearsed, and recorded and which is the home of several of the band's members and collaborators today. Many biographies spend pages describing, sometimes erroneously, features of the city on the Rhine: for instance, the significance of *Kraftwerk Lauward* (a power station) for their name choice (the band was initially called 'The Organisation'), the fact that two members of the band lived in close proximity to the Mannesmann-Hochhaus (designed by the father of a band member), and the location of their studio/headquarter in an 'industrial area' of Düsseldorf. However, thematic hints tracing back to Düsseldorf in the band music, what I called the 'textscape', are few and far between and can often be easily dismissed as general references to modern life in urban settings. The sparse lyrics of songs like 'Autobahn', 'Das Model' / 'The Model', 'Neon Licht' / 'Neon Lights', and 'Schaufensterpuppen' / 'Showroom Dummies' connect to Düsseldorf as a city of highways, neon lights, retail fashion, and party, although the city is never overtly mentioned.

My main interest here, however, is not so much in the representational dimension of music as in the way the band adopted certain discursive strategies, effectively connecting themselves to the industrial world and to Germany / Ruhr / Düsseldorf as real or imaginary industrial places. Kraftwerk in fact continuously story-tell themselves and their music, displacing real work through a tongue-in-cheek 'art world' attitude. These stories have sometimes contradicted one another or have been unmasked in band member autobiographies, but they remained consistent over time. The mystification of art production is a typical strategy apt at maintaining an aura of mystery towards inspiration, the creative process, and the artefacts themselves. Creativity is here understood as a complex structure, based on multiple thinking styles and not bound exclusively to a sudden flash of inspiration (Bilton 2013). Kraftwerk chose rationally to move from the initial free-form *kosmische Musik*, so similar to many other German psychedelic bands of the period, such as Can and Tangerine Dream, to an over-the-top minimalism in form, sound, and references. The narratives, labels, and branding strategies they used were consistent with their musical and extra-musical choices.

Germanness, for instance, is both a lens that has been widely used in analysing Kraftwerk oeuvre and one of the labels the band consciously adopted. For instance, Lester Bangs (1995), in his first interview with the band, insists on underlining the band's national origin and using terms such as 'Teutonic' and 'Fatherland' in connection to them. Hütter, responsible for most of the answers, is more than happy to report that

> we want the whole world to know our background. We cannot deny we are from Germany, because the German mentality, which is more advanced, will always be a part of our behaviour. We create out of the German language, the mother language, which is very mechanical, we use as the basic structure of our music. Also the machines, from the industries of Germany. (Bangs 1995)

Hütter's hyperbolic rhetoric is able to fascinate Bangs and the readers alike, in refusing to please the American audience with a simple aligning of the band to the popular music canon. Germanness becomes a strong means to brand the band's unique positioning in pop, and this is achieved by equating the nation with its industrial and technical power. However, from the *Ralf und Florian* LP on, all Kraftwerk albums have double English and German versions in lyrics and titles, for the joy of record collectors but also in response to a clear commercial marketing strategy.

Another strong brand for the band is *industrielle Volksmusik* (industrial folk music). The term appears in various interviews (Bohn 1981; Gill 1997; Hartmann 2003) and has been used in band biographies, in academic articles (Albiez and Pattie 2011; Schütte 2017), and conferences to describe the band's music in an exclusive way.

Musicologist Timor Kneif, tried to define rock music as a whole with the term '*industrielle Volksmusik*' (Kneif 1982, 191). According to Kneif, *Rockmusik* maintains some features of *Volksmusik* in relation, for instance, to informal learning, performative value, and imitative writing practices. However, rock has its own features, too, such as its urban origin, its hegemonic use of English, and the connection with modern life tempo and technology. The paradox of rock music lies in this duality: it is an industrial product of the capitalist and conservative music industry, led by profit maximisation, but it is also a radical expression of young people, therefore it is at the same time *industriell* and *Volksmusik*. Peter Wicke criticised this definition, saying that it can only lead to conceptual misunderstandings (Wicke 1992).

Despite the fact that both Hütter and Scheider were avid readers of musicological literature and attended various courses and conferences, it is impossible to know if they were aware of Kneif's use of the term. Kraftwerk had used it already in 1981, for instance, in an interview in the *New Musical Express* (Bohn 1981), therefore anticipating Kneif by one year. It is, however, possible that Kneif used the term well before the publication of *Rockmusik*.

Kraftwerk biographer Tim Barr calls it '*elektronisch Volksmusik*' (*sic*) and translates it as 'electronic people's music' (Barr 1998). He connects this concept to Stockhausen's music theories; the musician incorporated elements of folklore from various origins in his electronic compositions, for instance, in *Hymnen* and *Telemusik*. Bussy refers to '*industrielle Volkmuzik*' (*sic*) as a label given by critics and adopted by the band to differentiate themselves from the Krautrock bands (Bussy 2001, 68). In both cases, the spelling mistakes are revealing of the exotic and orientalising (or better, Germanising) dimension of these labels. It doesn't seem inappropriate, then, that Buckley decides to rely on English, with 'industrial folk music' (Buckley 2012).

If we examine closely the original German version of the term, which is the most commonly used by the band itself, we can understand better why the band decided to adopt it as a brand for themselves. 'Volksmusik' is in fact very controversial; it can be translated either with 'popular' or with 'folk' music (Morgenstern 2015). It is often associated with German national awakening and to the creation of a common cultural paradigm, founded upon past cultural creations of the 'simple people', the naïve but ethnically pure originators of the German *Heimat*. 'Heimatklänge' (translated in English as 'The Bells of Home') is the title of a song from the *Ralf und Florian* LP (1973). In the naïve LP booklet, the song title is featured in a collage with a girl playing a keyboard and a mountain peak (the *Lorelei*?) in the background. The word is written in pseudo Gothic font and adorned by two alpine flowers. *Volksmusik* is based on *Heimatklänge*, but both *Volk* and *Heimat* are deeply problematic terms in the context of post-war Germany. The band is definitely aware of the controversies connected to using this kind of imagery and to the fact that it bends to the far right or to the left simply by switching emphases. However, they also rely on the camp kitsch-iness these terms evoke, for instance in connection to the so-called *Heimat-Filme* (Von Moltke 2005, 161–62) and to what is considered the authentic *Volksmusik*, like the one, for instance, performed by local 'Düsseldorf bard' Heino (Akbar 2018).

The adjective *industrielle*, industrial, completely estranges the meaning of *Volksmusik*, showing Kraftwerk storytelling ability at its fullest. As seen in Kneif (1982), there is actually very little space for industry in *Volksmusik*, whose themes usually cover countryside and small-town idylls, overly simple melodies, in the context of oral tradition and that implicitly see the industrial world as corrupting. The use of simple melodies in Kraftwerk music has more to do with a high art classical canon, inspired by serial composition, than with a folkloristic one. Both Hütter and Schneider have classical music backgrounds and performed in their youth with beat, jazz, and avant-garde ensembles. The reference to a German *Volksmusik* is therefore implicitly denied by the fact that it is *industriell*. Let's see, for instance, how the band uses the label in these well-known interview snippets:

> We once called our music industrielle Volksmusik. I think this is what we stand for. We're very much involved with environment. Dusseldorf is called 'The Office of the Ruhr' (the heavy industrial belt of Germany)—it is all glass and steel and concrete and blocks. (Bohn 1981, 32)

> Our music has been called 'industrial folk music' . . . that's the way we see it. There's something ethnic to it; it couldn't have come from anywhere else . . . we are from the Düsseldorf scene, from Ein Ruhr scene, which is an industrial area, so our music has more of that edge to it. (Gill 1997)

Hütter links in both interviews the adjective 'industrial' to the *Ruhr* region, one of the historically most industrialised areas of Europe, therefore locating Kraftwerk sound into a particular environment. However, this is emphasised by hyperboles, for instance, in describing the band as part of a 'scene' set in 'Ein (*sic*) Ruhr' or referring to the Düsseldorf nickname, the 'Office of the Ruhr'.

There are some examples of industrial soundscapes in the music of Kraftwerk. An obvious one is 'Metal on Metal', the 'Trans-Europe Express' coda, where the band actually recorded a rhythmic pattern by using metal scraps and bars:

> I would cover our devices in thin steel sheets fitting them with a hammerblow to the surface, and this led to my suggestions to use this harsh sound for the snare drum. We even considered using enormous metal sheets and an oversized sledgehammer to beat out the number on stage. For that reason, we experimented with the most diverse types of metal sheeting in front of microphones in the studio. 'Metal On Metal' therefore became our first industrial song, as they were later called. (Flür 2017)

Another is a middle section of 'Autobahn', where screeching synth noises score the part of the imaginary car journey through the area. However, the Ruhr was not a music hotspot and the scenes, which later developed there in connection to punk and heavy metal, have little to do with Kraftwerk.

Several English-speaking authors and the band itself translated the label as 'industrial folk music', which, as seen here before, responds to the evolution of British folk after the Industrial Revolution and is therefore unable to convey the same meaning as the German original. Moreover, the term has lately resurfaced to describe the music of other bands. For instance, Simon Reynolds uses the term for Pere Ubu (Reynolds 2006, 71) Test Dept, and Einstürzende Neubauten (Reynolds 2006). An article on Pitchfork celebrating Pere Ubu's first album in its fortieth anniversary stated that 'Ubu's self-described "industrial folk" already sounded like it came from some far-off, future land' (Coney 2018). Coney hints at the fact that the band itself came up with that particular label, therefore somehow anticipating Kraftwerk by some years. However, it also proves difficult to find any confirmation of this in the Cleveland band's interviews and works.

The idea of Kraftwerk concealing real work with narratives continues if we take into account the KlingKlang studio. The studio was located in a warehouse, at Mintropstrasse 16, in close proximity to the Düsseldorf railway station. The space first consisted of one big room and served simply as a rehearsal room for the band. It expanded in surrounding spaces and was redesigned several times to host the band's recording studio, office, living room, and storage, until the whole was emptied and relocated in 2009. The railway station is a very busy node for the whole region, with a current turnover of more than 250,000 people a day. The station surroundings, in continental fashion, used to be partly industrial and partly commercial. Some buildings host fast foods, ethnic shops, game parlours, strip clubs, bars and barber shops, which nowadays take over most of the area. Illicit activities also find place around the station, such as drug dealing, for instance. Hütter and Schneider rented out the space in 1970 and later named it after a song from their second LP. KlingKlang is accessible via an inner yard, behind a gate with a shutter. Today, it is empty and a traffic cone (one of the symbols of the band) in the backyard serves as a memorial of its former function.

The first visual appearance of the KlingKlang, still named simply as Kraftwerk Studio in the credits, is on the back cover of *Ralf und Florian* LP (1973). The duo looks at one another behind their 'work stations' of keyboards and electronic effects. Bare, whitewashed brick walls dominate the room, with one side covered by insulating egg boxes. In the front, we can see the two monitors adorned, respectively, with Ralf and Florian neon names. Florian is holding a flute on his lap, and a steel guitar lies on a stand next to him. An old-fashioned lamp lights in the middle, more suitable for the living room of a middle-class family.

This picture is the only one where Kraftwerk is portrayed authentically in their own very private creative setting, surrounded by nearly all the equipment they used live at the time, including speakers and the iconic monitors with the neon signs. In addition, their sitting positions, specular to each other, is similar to the one they adopted live. The configuration of their desks is at odds with popular music canons and responds to another important narrative of the band, the *Musikarbeiter* ('musical worker') one. The band uses this label for the band, adorning their own music making, once again, with 'industrial' qualities. Work in industrial societies was dominated by an ideology of rationality, efficiency, and also a kind of stoicism (Dubin 1987). This found its most hyperbolic expression behind the Iron Curtain in the Stakhanovite movement, while in capitalist societies Fordism was similarly aiming at regulating and maximising profit through production. Using 'music worker' instead of 'musician' was a clear provocation to make Kraftwerk stand out. Moreover, it created again a place-based connotation to the band, which compared itself to other German companies, machines, and technologies and to the above-mentioned regional industrial background.

This narrative had the effect to hide two actual working strategies of the band. First and foremost, creative musical work, based on inspiration, creativity, and playfulness, typical of the music production. This was kept hidden, behind the shuttered gate of the KlingKlang studio. Only a few adpets were left in, at agreed times. Karl Bartos (2017) reveals how complicated it was for him to gain access to rehearsal sessions. The aura of the studio and its activities still brings fans to visit the street and try to make sense of the seedy atmosphere of a railway station surroundings. The band was able to record autonomously at the KlingKlang and were able to get an unusual licensing contract, implying that they delivered to the record company a finished product, a master tape accompanied by a fully designed and credited cover.

Kept from view was also the real physical work of handcraft, mostly carried out by the live percussionist Wolfgang Flür, a trained cabinet-maker and store builder. The band's intuitions in relation to recording, production, and performance required continuous technical efforts. For instance, Flür conceived his drum pad with Schneider (although a US patent on the instrument was registered by Schneider and Hütter; Flür 2017, 53–54). He built the drum controller with a wooden board cut from a local carpentry. Claudia Schneider, Florian's sister and a student of architecture who made celluloid jewels in her free time, provided to Wolfgang a piece of the material from a plastic factory near Moers. This was used to adorn the wooden basis. The metal pads were found in a scrapyard collecting metal industrial waste near the Berger Allee 9, where Flür was living with Emil Schulte and Karl Bartos. He assembled the drums in a cellar that he had transformed into a workshop on the ground floor of the flat. Hütter and Schneider had rented the flat from the Mannesmann company.

These insights reveal the very real and very material agency of the industrial city, where raw metal waste, available in scrapyards around town, became an actor in the development of contemporary electronic music. This reveals the complicated relation between materialities, creativity, and innovation in the context of Fordism and industrial society. It shows how heavy industrial production is not able to use all raw materials: it leaves waste that can be used to contest, subvert, and redefine production itself. Moreover, industrial work cannot exhaust creative endeavours. It might even lead to get people dancing to electrified scraps of metal being beaten with rods.

Dominating the charts next to the synthetic sound of Kraftwerk are glam bands, from Slade to Sweet, from David Bowie to Mott the Hoople. Glam rock spread in the early 1970s, maintaining some features of the 'industrial backbeat' of Chicago blues, for instance, in the so-called stomp and roar. Stomp refers to the steady 4/4 rhythmic pattern of basic rock music, adopted widely in glam, which invites feet to stomp and hands to clap through repetition; it is also widely used in song titles. Roar has to do with distorted guitar riffs. Slade was from the heavily industrialised and slowly declining Black Country region in the North of England. In his book about glam, Reynolds refers to the 'industrial proletariat mindset' of the band and of the way critics and fans understood their appearance, behaviour, and sound within that particular context (Reynolds 2016). We can talk about displacement also in the case of glam, for instance, at the level of cross-dressing and gender fluidity, evident in the use of costumes, high heels, makeup, and long hair.

Typical of this era is also the strong connection between industrial sounds and what is now known as 'library music'. Plenty of radio and television studios provided the chance for musicians and music engineers to experiment with 'weird noises' in connection with providing soundscapes and soundtracks to radio shows; sci-fi, police, or horror movies; and series. Notably and in various decades of the twentieth century, Pierre Schaeffer at the Radiodiffusion Française in Paris, Luciano Berio at the Studio di Fonologia in Milan, and Delia Derbyshire at the BBC Radiophonic Workshop, among many others in various other countries, had an influence on the national popularisation of certain noise effects and later of electronic music (Belgiojoso 2014). However, their focus was much more on real or fictional urban soundscapes. There are only a few examples of full-on, thematic engagement with the industry, for instance, the work of Alessandro Alessandroni on the *Ritmo dell'Industria nr. 2* (1969) and *Industriale* (1976) LPs.

As I will show in the next chapters about individual case studies, deindustrialisation radically changes the way music and industrial cities interact, leading to a temporary demise of music in post-industrial cities.

3

MANCHESTER

Manchester is the first city in the world that can be called industrial. Throughout the centuries, goods were produced in Manchester and in neighbouring manufacturing towns in the North of England and shipped out to the world from the port of Liverpool. Politicians, intellectuals, entrepreneurs, and businesspeople visited Manchester to learn how to plan, build, and run an industrial city, while many local entrepreneurs sailed abroad to develop similar industrial businesses. Cities around the world labelled themselves as Little Manchesters or as the Manchester of their country; Tampere was such a city, as I will reveal later in this book. Streets in other industrial districts were named after the British city, like Rue de Manchester in Molenbeek-Saint-Jean, Brussels.

Concomitantly, two other features framed Manchester as an industrial city prototype. The first is football. With two internationally recognised strong teams, Manchester City (founded in 1894) and Manchester United (founded in 1902), Manchester has developed a strong reputation within this sport and its culture. It served as an example for the founding of teams in other industrial cities around Europe, including the other three under examination in this book, Torino in particular. Football was the Saturday or Sunday entertainment for the anonymous working masses in industrial cities and was instrumental in the development of local pride and dedication to work among people who had been displaced from elsewhere (Goldblatt 2008).

The second phenomenon is music. Especially since 1976, popular music has worked as a creative urban milieu and has acquired international acclaim in continuous interaction with the local social and spatial environment, with memory and with city image.

Just as it was the first city to be called industrial, Manchester was also among the first centres in Europe to experience deindustrialisation. Although economic fluctuations continuously framed the city history and the Second World War also had a strong effect on the city architecture, it is with the 1970s that the paradigm change and economic restructuring affected the city the most and changed its nature forever. The years of deindustrialisation coincide with the success of bands such as Buzzcocks, the Fall, Joy Division, and the Smiths. These bands revealed an uncanny sensibility in the way the 'ugly northern industrial environment' and its crisis could be perceived and represented. A similar cultural sensibility brought the independent music entrepreneur Tony Wilson to develop the independent label Factory Records and later the club venue Haçienda FAC 51, which worked as cultural catalysts in the city's reimagining and partly for the renewal of some of its areas. However, they also revealed the false promises of cultural regeneration.

The relation between the city's reputation and these bands and people is still strong and celebrated every year by new products and events. Fandom for Manchester bands is global and encompasses social, cultural, and political divides. For instance, Morrissey has a consistent and adoring following among Latinx in the United States (Devereux and Hidalgo 2015), while the image featured on the cover of *Unknown Pleasures*, Joy Division's first LP, has been branded, licensed, and pirated on objects of all kinds, ranging from shoes to T-shirts, from mobile phone covers to oven mitts. Nevarez (2013) examines how Joy Division came to sound like Manchester, by looking at how the work of local entrepreneurs, music journalists, photographers, and film and documentary makers framed the band and especially their first album as pure and authentic expression of what the northern city was about. These cultural industry workers adored the band and contextualised the band's sound continuously into an 'illusory object "place"' (Nevarez 2013, 74) that they labelled 'Manchester'. This operation was carried out over the years as a cultural sedimentation (Lindner 2006) and changed its meaning over time, only lately bonding with the neo-liberal strategies of urban redevelopment in a post-industrial city. The band nowadays defines a certain post-industrial aesthetic in connection to gloom, grimness, and greyness but also to 'industrial chic' appeal. Joy Division signify both a certain sound and a certain visual component that seem inextricable from each other and are both at the basis of Manchester 'myth' (Barthes 1957).

This chapter ends in the 1990s, stretching its time frame more widely than any of the other three case studies, revealing how the 'vanishing' of music in post-industrial cities can take different paths and timings. In 1997, at the local level, the experience of the Haçienda FAC 51 and of Factory Records ended and, at a national level, Tony Blair became the first Labour Party prime minister since 1979. In July 1997, the newly elected prime minister invited some cultural and media producers to 10 Downing Street for an election party, among them Noel Gallagher, songwriter and lead guitarist in the Manchester band Oasis, and the band's record label owner, Alan McGee, who at the time was a member of the Creative Industry Taskforce.

In the late 1990s, popular music in Great Britain was turning into Britpop, a pacified and all-encompassing national booster of economic export. Popular music scenes were slowly abandoning local textures and narratives, both on the material and imaginative levels, to gain attention on the global scale. While music vanished from place and turned into data, neo-liberal forces began to focus on cities and on the urban symbolic capital, which was originally accumulated through music.

THE NORTH

Following Shields (1991), we could claim that the image of Manchester has been constructed as a 'place-myth'. It is located in the extreme North of England, therefore in a 'marginal place' that arouses a particular fascination. 'North' has always had working-class and industrial connotations in England, developed in the last centuries by a set of cultural elements, often filtered by fiction, such as films and novels set there.

The writer Charles Dickens used the geographical divide, whereby the North represented always the most desolate, poor, and evil landscape (as in Coketown covered in smoke in the novel *Hard Times*,

1854), a counterpart to London, the site of wealth and civilisation (Shields 1991; Preston 1994; Moretti 1998).

Manchester is often central to these representations of the 'North' because of its historical significance in the development of the whole region. The city has been the first industrial town of the world, carrying the burden of negative connotations that will later designate many other cities at different scales. The concentration of workers in hygienically and socially hazardous environments, the fast rise of an industrial land-scape composed of canals, chimneys, red brick factories, and dormitory quarters corroborated the 'shock' of the first visitors, such as Friedrich Engels, whose stay in the city inspired *Die Lage der arbeitenden Klasse in England* (1969). The book, which describes Manchester as the arche-typal manufacturing town, is nowadays considered one of the first soci-ological accounts of an industrial city (Vicari Haddock 2004, 59) and of its structural inequalities.

The situation of the city worsened with the First World War, which set the seal to the slow downgrading of its wealth. The loss of the Indian market, together with the bad economical conjunctures following the Wall Street crash in 1929, slowed down the mass migration in search of jobs, and unemployment began to affect many districts. From the 1950s on, the small city centre emptied, and many inhabitants moved to the high-rise projects in suburbs and satellite towns. In this period cinema set its eye on the North and the kitchen-sink films, black-and-white dramas set in a vague industrial environment, began romanticising the working-class condition, ascribing to it a particular bohemian aura. In these films, just like in the soap opera *Coronation Street*, which was first broadcast on Granada TV in 1960, the industrial landscape is used as scenery for the 'authentic' stories of dissatisfied, unhappy working-class youth dominated by alienation, unsatisfied greed, and a bitter 'northern' sense of humour.

The end of the 1970s saw the bottom of the slow industrial disman-tlement, when the conservative prime minister Margaret Thatcher came into power. Hillegonda C. Rietveld, in our phone interview on June 5, 2019, had this to say about the times: 'The centre of Manchester was not very much occupied. . . . People were living in the surrounding neighbourhoods and not in the centre, where were empty industrial buildings with plants growing out of the walls.'

Between 1972 and 1984, hundreds of thousands of manufacturing jobs were lost in the Greater Manchester area (Oswalt 2004) and unemployment reached 16 percent in 1986 (Evans, Fraser, and Taylor 1996). British city centres were reorganised, following a model of regeneration based on a free-enterprise approach, the restriction of local government, and the creation of new semi-autonomous bodies outside the control of local government, called quangos (O'Connor 1999, 83). The media coverage of the North emphasised the wreck of city centres and localised in them the 'British crisis' (Shields 1991, 231–44).

A GIG IN THE LESSER FREE TRADE HALL

Novels in the nineteenth century and films and other media in the twentieth century made possible the circulation of certain images of Manchester and the consolidation of its place myth around Great Britain. These representations were often external to the life of local communities and based on the individual point of view of outsiders; places were barely used as settings and stages and didn't contribute directly to the cultural creation. For instance, in the so-called kitchen-sink films, 1950s social realism drama set in industrial cities of the North, it was common to see an initial shot of a dense landscape or rooftops and chimneys from a privileged point of view, 'setting the scene' for the film plot. This has been codified in film studies with the trope of 'that long shot of our town from that hill' (Higson 1996) and constitutes a powerful representation of place that some bands will adopt, either ironically or as medial referent for social realism.

The Manchester popular music scene active from the late 1970s onwards overcomes the internal/external division in cultural production. For the first time, images produced locally acquire a niche in the global market through their circulation. The birth of British punk in 1976 led to attempts to democratise the music industry (Hesmondhalgh 1998) and is essential to the success of Manchester bands (Milestone 1996). Punk first developed DIY strategies connected to production, distribution, and marketing in fashion (T-shirts, pins), music events (gigs), press (fanzines), and musical supports (EPs, cassettes). These elements became easily produced and accessible and relied entirely on the opportunities offered by underground circulation (Reynolds 2006; Savage 1991; Worley 2017).

A clear example of this new cultural attitude and the mythical starting point of the Manchester music scene was the concert given by the infamous London punk band the Sex Pistols, at the Lesser Free Trade Hall on June 4, 1976.

Peter McNeish and Howard Trafford, who would later change their names, in punk fashion, to Pete Shelley and Howard Devoto were two local students of the Bolton Institute of Technology. They either met at the Electronic Music Society of their university and shared a love of Krautrock and computers (Reynolds 2018) or, according to other sources, through an ad for forming a rock band and a love for the Stooges (Robb 2009, 40). After reading a live review of the newly formed Sex Pistols in the music magazine *New Musical Express*, Pete and Howard rented a car and drove to London to see the band play live twice, on February 20 and 21, 1976, while staying with their friend Richard Boon, who was studying at the University of Reading. They were also able to make their way to the infamous SEX shop on the King's Road and talk Malcolm McLaren into bringing the band to Manchester, where they would organise a gig.

The Free Trade Hall, which has sadly been turned into a hotel, was a place of enormous local significance where, among others, Bob Dylan, David Bowie, Patti Smith, and Pink Floyd played. It was built on St. Peter's Field, the place of the Peterloo Massacre, where workers gathered to listen to the speeches of radical reformers and were brutally attacked by the police, on August 16, 1819. The establishment of the Anti-Corn Law League in Manchester also took place symbolically on the field, and the construction of the Free Trade Hall was started as a public building to commemorate the liberalisation of trade in agriculture. The hall changed its function over the years, becoming the rehearsal space for the Hallé Orchestra and the major live music venue in the city. The *Lesser* hall was a smaller room, upstairs from the main venue, used for events of minor importance, and the two students easily rented it for the Sex Pistols gig. The local progressive rock band Solstice, from Bolton, opened for the Sex Pistols, while Buzzcocks, the organisers' band, could not perform, due to the lack of a bassist (one was found on the same night) and a drummer. During the intervals, the just-released Ramones debut album was played (Robb 2009, 48).

According to various sources (Nolan 2006; Albiez 2006), approximately forty to one hundred people attended the gig. About six weeks later, on July 20, the Sex Pistols played again in the same venue, supported by two newly formed local bands (Buzzcocks, and Slaughter and the Dogs) and the crowd had meanwhile multiplied to some hundreds, also thanks to the media attention that the band began to gather. They played again at the Electric Circus twice in December, during the infamous Anarchy tour, where the majority of dates were cancelled.

A dispute is still ongoing about who attended the first, the second, or any of the first two Sex Pistols gigs because of the mythical status that they acquired in local history. The book *I Swear I Was There: The Gig That Changed the World* (Nolan 2006) tries to 'set things straight', although it seems to increase the mystery. It is sure that some members of Joy Division/New Order, Buzzcocks, the Smiths, the Fall, the music journalist Paul Morley, the local cultural entrepreneur and TV journalist Tony Wilson, the producer Martin Hannett, and artist Linder Sterling attended one or both gigs and were inspired by them. Some of these people had already gotten involved in music or were planning to do so, but the synergic significance of the gig should not be reduced. For instance, Peter Hook recollects the gig in his own book about Joy Division, where he portrays it as a proper epiphany, as a 'sudden revelation' of something superior:

> I remember feeling as though I'd been sitting in a darkened room all of my life—comfortable and warm and safe and quiet—then all of a sudden someone had kicked the door in, and it had burst open to let in an intense bright light and this even more intense noise, showing me another world, another life, a way out. I was immediately no longer comfortable and safe, but that didn't matter because it felt great. I felt alive. It was the weirdest sensation. It wasn't just me feeling it, either—we were all like that. We just stood there, stock still, watching the Pistols. Absolutely, utterly, gobsmacked. (Hook 2012, 67–68)

Bernard Sumner, who was with Hook at the gig, tells of a similar reaction:

> Then the Sex Pistols came along and made us feel we were right. Not only that, they showed us that we'd been right all along. Punk was

something giving us a voice for the first time, and that voice was
screaming at the top of its lungs there right in front of me. It justified
our outlook and at the same time made us feel we were worth something after all. (Sumner 2014, 84–85)

Both musicians remember reacting in a similar way: punk music gave
them the sudden feeling of watching a lived social practice unfolding
live on stage, something that could only be felt and understood in terms
of a collective 'we' and that incited to do the same.

The two Free Trade Hall gigs show that the Manchester popular
music in 1976 started working as a creative milieu and that the gigs
were 'sudden revelations' of this collective sensibility. Camagni defines
a creative milieu as a set of complex networks 'of mainly informal social
relationships within a limited geographical area, often determining a
specific external image and a specific internal representation and sense
of belonging, which enhance the local innovative capability through
synergic and collective learning processes' (Camagni 1991, 3). There
are other useful conceptualisations of active urban creative communities, ranging from the idea of 'art world' (Becker 1982) to the one of
'creative class' (Florida 2002). However, 'creative milieu' stresses the
importance of processes of learning. In this case, it is of course possible
to see learning as an informal process, which allowed a small group of
initiators to develop into successful touring acts, still active after forty
years, and which defined what deindustrialisation might sound like.

The two gig organisers could have easily booked a university live-
music hall or club, but it would have not been in the heart of the city.
Choosing a city centre landmark for the gig of an unknown and outra-
geous band from London reveals the subcultural attempt to take over
territory for the young. Both gig organisers shared with many other
scene participants a suburban and/or satellite town origin and they perceived the city centre as a territory to be explored in the search for safe
spaces, hotspots for resistance, and places to learn. Especially at night,
the city transformed into a terra incognita, where boredom and fascination for both decay and urban oddities fuelled the thirst for learning
how to be in public, how to confront people, and how to stand out:

We'd often get yelled at by beer monsters or even accosted by them
as they sneered at our clothes and musical taste.

> It's hard to believe now that punk was viewed with suspicion and
> hostility by the general population, because of the dyed, spiked hair,
> the piercings and the idiosyncratic approach to clothes, the in-yer-
> face attitude. . . . But back then you risked not being allowed on a
> bus if the driver felt you looked too offensive. (Gina Sobers, in Robb
> 2009, 80)

The independent organisation of a gig and the choice of the venue
might also testify to the importance of local labour tradition. This is in
fact not only connected to rallies, strikes, and assemblies but also to the
autonomous shaping of free time and cultural life and to the establishment of dedicated institutions. In fact, a few years before this gig,
Manchester bands began gathering under a common umbrella organisation called Music Force. Run by, among others, Victor Brox, Tosh
Ryan, and Bruce Mitchell, this socialist music agency provided all back-
line and logistics to set up live concerts and was fundamental for the Sex
Pistols gig (see C. P. Lee, in Robb 2009, 46).

The most relevant element of a creative milieu is its ability to imple-
ment innovations and develop new ideas. The gig sparkled in many the
idea to form a band and develop original music, without waiting for a
record deal. Buzzcocks recorded and released *Spiral Scratch*, an EP
without the help of a record label, just a few months after the gig, in
January 1977. They financed the sum to record four songs, press the 7",
and print the cover through friends and relatives; founded their own
DIY record label New Hormones; and distributed their product in
record shops and per post (Savage 1991, 296), selling more than sixteen
thousand, from an initial pressing of one thousand only (Simpson 2017).
Bands began producing, promoting, and circulating music outside the
traditional record company logics, cutting costs, and increasing artist
freedom. Buzzcocks was not the first band to self-produce recorded
music; this was common in those times because of the opportunities
provided by affordable music instruments, recording gear, and record
pressing. However, Buzzcocks was the first band to adopt this practice
as a statement against the London-based music industry, which in the
same months was competing to sign the Sex Pistols for vast sums of
money. Just as in the case of Kraftwerk and their autonomous organisation of musical work, Buzzcocks show how the work ethic of an industrial city can be also translated into a creative endeavour and how a small

financial effort can bring a music industry revolution, if channelled into a learning process.

For instance, Malcolm Garrett, at the time a second-year student in graphic design at Manchester Polytechnic developed a specific font for Buzzcocks' second EP, *Orgasm Addict* (1977), which the band has used throughout their career.

> He'd used the largest sized Compacta Regular Italic Letraset he could find, rubbed down the relevant letters, photographed them, printed them onto bromide paper, sliced them down the middle, stuck them down on board, and inked in the gap in Rotring pen. 'It was a bit tricky, particularly to get the typeface thin enough,' he recalls. But he wasn't quite happy with this early incarnation. 'I felt the spacing around the Zs wasn't quite right, so I modified them,' he recalls. (Davies 2011)

This description gives a clear idea of the labouriousness of working with graphics and of industrial skills, which were taught in industrial-city places of education. Creativity became a common denominator in the Manchester punk and post-punk music scene. A sense of belonging, proximity, and innovation made it possible for musicians to build a milieu in Manchester without needing to move to London, to this day the common procedure for a British band looking for success. Somehow, even in times of deindustrialisation, Manchester continued operating as an industrial city, with some people putting their creative skills at work in altogether new industries.

THE MANCHESTER MUSICSCAPE

Martin Stokes suggests that music is able to define and transform places and identities, thus acquiring part of its 'social meaning'. According to him, performing, listening, or talking about music 'evokes . . . collective memories and present experiences of place with an intensity, power and simplicity unmatched by any other social activity' (Stokes 1997, 3). Popular music implements places in a credibly authentic way, forming new modalities to conceive and perceive them. Territorialisation through popular music occurs (or better: it takes *place*) on three dimensions: textscapes, soundscapes, and landscapes. Lyrics and titles of songs referring to places make up a band's textscape. The use of local music tradition, local vernacular, or typical city noises constitute a band's soundscape. Finally, the landscape consists of all the visual elements (e.g., photo shootings, videos, covers, posters, clothes, stage) referring to the same particular locality or to its previous representations. The mediation of places through three musicscapes turns popular music into a powerful tool for reimagining places and builds alternative images of cities, circulating around the world in millions of copies. The Manchester scene's use of these musicscapes is strikingly similar to the paradigm introduced by post-war Parisian humanist photography. Stuart Hall referred to six elements of this paradigm: *universality* (human emotions), *historicity* (place-time specificity), *quotidienality* (everyday life), *empathy* (complicity with the subject of the representation), *commonality* (mirroring the viewpoint of the working class) and *monochromaticity* (extensive use of black and white) (Hall 1987, 101). These paradigmatic elements of French post-war photography can also be translated into the textual/lyrical and into the sonic dimension. They constitute an important instrument to analyse the way a certain industrial atmosphere was mediatised into music.

For instance, landscapes in much of the music produced in Manchester in the late 1970s are mostly connected to open spaces. Nearly all of the considered bands, from Buzzcocks to Joy Division and the Smiths were pictured, especially at the beginning of their career outside, in open space, posing in front of empty factories or blocks of flats. Chimneys, cobblestone streets, red brick buildings have been part of the Manchester imagery since the descriptions of Friedrich Engels and the novels of Charles Dickens, and they frame these images within 'historicity', asserting them of a temporal dimension. Architectural elements worked as 'authenticity seals' for their local belonging, confirming the narrative that makes everything 'popular', something 'for real', and therefore addressing 'commonality'. In addition, two other considerations could be made. First, showing the empty and decaying temples of capitalism can be linked to the gloom expressed by these bands. They exemplify the emptiness of capitalist society and of industrialism, which can be best grasped as, when money stops running in, unemployment grows and whole districts are left in physical and social decay. Second, it could be read as an ironic overtone. In 1985, the Smiths posed in front of the Salford Lads Club (youth leisure club) for a shot by Stephen

Wright, which appeared in the gatefold of the band's *The Queen Is Dead* LP (1986). The club was opened in the beginning of the twentieth century, to keep the local Salford youth 'off the streets' and educate them to become 'good citizens', standard for many philanthropic initiatives of the time (Lindner 2004). The Smiths posing in front of the club, located at the end of the real 'Coronation Street', opens up a series of questions concerning identity, as the band was increasingly getting media attention for its overt subversion of working-class values while celebrating, at first sight, idleness, criminality, and social indifference. In addition, most of these bands' pictures were black and white (monochromaticity) and portrayed the bands' members wearing conventional, everyday working-class or lower middle-class 'clerk' clothes (black suits, white shirts, ties, cardigans), reaffirming the idea of a perceived commonality. The bands usually were not posing in any explicit way but mostly naively looking into the camera or shyly avoiding it, which are common signifiers of empathy and universality.

With textscape, we refer to the use of localities, toponymies, street names, monuments, and districts, more or less recognisable as such. The references to the quite unmistakable built environment are variously present in songs by these bands (historicity). The Smiths refer to iron bridges, disused railway lines, and cemetery gates. Additionally, the city's districts are more or less openly referred to, in particular the most rundown and disfavoured at the time, like Whalley Range, Cheetham Hill, and Ancoats. The band Joy Division relies less on the direct nomination or representation of the built environment and concentrates much more on its subjective psychological effects. In their lyrics, the built environment is evoked because of its monotony and desolation, structuring a sinister textscape (monochromaticity) that only through circulation goes back to being identified with Manchester by the listeners (Nevarez 2013).

Along other northern centres like Sheffield and Liverpool, Manchester musicscapes codified the connection between a certain kind of music and a certain kind of landscape forever. Simon Reynolds labelled this sound 'post-punk', describing it as follows:

> Rather than rama-lama riffing or bluesy chords, the postpunk pantheon of guitar innovators favored angularity, a clean and brittle spikiness. . . . This more compact, scrawny style of guitar playing didn't fill up every corner of the soundscape, and this allowed the

bass to step forward from its usually inconspicuous, supportive role to become the lead instrumental voice, fulfilling a melodic function even as it pushed the groove. In this respect, postpunk bassists were playing catch-up with the innovations of Sly Stone and James Brown, and learning from contemporary roots reggae and dub. (Reynolds 2006, 36)

The *post-* prefix becomes a temporal divide that seems to define a punk *before* and a post-punk *afterwards*, intrinsically different from the point of view of sound, influences, continuities, political stance, and ideology. However, this divide, if ever perceived in these terms, can be better grasped not in temporal but in spatial terms. Post-punk sound has a spatial dimension connected to reverberation, bass and treble frequency, and repetition, which best expressed the atmosphere and affect of deindustrialisation.

Of course, the post-punk sound is not a monolith but a complex set of musical expressions, and some Manchester bands deviated from it and built a connection with local music tradition, local sound and noises, and the vernacular. For instance, in the Smiths we can hear homages to early North American rock 'n' roll and soul music (which in the United Kingdom is epitomised as *Northern* Soul) genres that were widely played in restaurants, cafés, workers' clubs, and local pubs (commonality) (Robb 2009). The use of certain sound effects (harmonica, synthetic drums) has often been associated with industrial noises (trains, alarms, heavy industry machineries). In addition, the Mancunian accent is easily recognised and sometimes accentuated by the bands' singers, both in performances and interviews, as most notably in the voice and persona of the late Fall singer Mark E. Smith.

Manchester bands communicated place on these three levels. The city's local music scene was able to deconstruct previous media representation and develop a different image of the city, through individual sensibilities and their adherence to a common aesthetic paradigm and worldview. Through circulation, this image reached millions of people, who were able to make it their own, reshape it again, and keep it viable.

THE HAÇIENDA FAC5 I AND THE NORTHERN QUARTER

In the late 1970s, as bands such as Buzzcocks, Joy Division, and the Fall were performing within a local music scene, there was no real urban clustering in connection to popular music. Most of the people involved in music lived in the suburban neighbourhoods or in satellite towns, being of lower middle-class or working-class origins. As in many other cases around the globe, especially in the United States (see Savage 1991, 137, about Pere Ubu and Cleeveland), punk and post-punk local scenes were attracted to the centre by a peculiar fascination for decay, mixed with the availability of spaces, to be used as rehearsal rooms or improvised gig venues. The most known places for live music at the time were pubs, which usually reserved a weekday for live music made by 'young' bands. Outside the pub circuit, there was the Electric Circus on Collyhurst Street, a former cinema and varieté hall in a very dilapidated and poor area. The place became the first punk epicentre, hosting gigs by the Ramones, the Sex Pistols, the Clash, the Slits, and several local punk bands on Sunday nights, but it closed as early as October 1977. The Virgin Records sample *Short Circuit: Live at the Electric Circus* (1978) immortalised a few live recordings from the last two shows with the Fall, John Cooper Clark, Joy Division (at the time still called Warsaw), the Drones, Steel Pulse, and Buzzcocks. Interesting is the presence of Steel Pulse, a reggae band from Birmingham in the sample, testifying to the variety in taste of the Electric Circus crowd and the interracial composition of some of its acts. Paul Worley, in the liner notes of the record, emphasises the shabbiness of the former cinema and of its occupied surroundings, noting also the curiosity that the punk crowd aroused in the local children.

The Squat was another important venue for local bands, located on Devas Street. It was a late-Victorian red brick building that hosted the Manchester College of Music in the university area and was supposed to be demolished to make space for a car park. In the name of heritage preservation and responding to the crisis of affordable housing, a collective of students occupied it in 1973 and turned it into a communal 'art lab' with rehearsal spaces and stage. Music Force could promote gigs there, and it was run as a music club for a few years, until its demolition in 1982 (Manchester Digital Music Archive 2016; Robb 2009). The place provided the stage for the first gigs of Joy Division and the Fall, among many others.

Apart from these individual scene-bound places, there are no hints of a real clustering of the scene or of a real regeneration of districts or areas in connection to music. The music-scene financial situation was poor; city officials tended to ignore popular music because of its irrelevance in the political struggle of the time. The entrepreneurial skills of managers, promoters, record label owners, and musicians themselves were often amateurish. In addition, the manners and aesthetics of bands like Joy Division were taken, erroneously, to be right-wing-related (the singer often wore a brown shirt onstage) or in the case of the Smiths, too overtly queer to cope with the northern working-class tradition.

The situation changed thanks to the consolidation of Factory Records and the opening of the Haçienda FAC 51 (from now on, simply the Haçienda). In addition, starting from the beginning of the 1980s, the Manchester music scene acquired national popularity, which became international by the end of the same decade. Manchester-born and Cambridge-educated Tony Wilson was well-known as a television journalist for the regional channel Granada, where he was able to broadcast the first Sex Pistols television appearance on his *So It Goes* show in 1976. Very curious towards new music and avant-garde and youth subcultures, he started organising a club night called 'The Factory' at the Russell Club in the district of Hulme in 1978 and founded Factory Records the same year. The name Factory recalled the Andy Warhol atelier that was active in New York in the 1960s; in addition, it is obvious in its evocation of Manchester. The independent record label published most of the records of the local music scene, with a few notable exceptions such as the Fall and the Smiths. Wilson signed, along the years, bands like Joy Division, A Certain Ratio, Durutti Column, Quando Quango, New Order, and Happy Mondays. Those bands were free in their artistic choices, and the profit was fairly distributed between artist and label, without label interference in the copyright of the produced material. Each product of the Factory catalogue was given a progressive number, in industrial production style. However, Wilson's exuberance clearly influenced the adoption of names, strategies, and aesthetics derived from avant-garde art movements and political thought, ranging from futurism to situationism, from pop art to post-structuralism.

The Haçienda opened in May 1982 on the corner between Albion Street and Whitworth Street West in a rundown area close to the almost abandoned city centre. The choice was not accidental. As Rietveld said,

> The regeneration plans were already in place before the Haçienda was initiated, and Rob Gretton, the manager of New Order, was in touch with those kind of developments, For example, just around the corner from the Haçienda there was the huge central station that was no longer in use, a beautiful massive station in my mind, but as Manchester went through a downward turn economically, that station was abandoned and later became an exhibition space and concert venue, the G-Mex. This was already in the urban regeneration plans, so finding the space for the Haçienda became part of that new wave of regeneration of that area, which was almost too early. (interview, 2019)

The architect Ben Kelly redesigned the former yacht showroom, maintaining many of the original features of the building, such as the big iron doors, the inner columns, and the outside appearance with red bricks. Its financial existence was based on the co-ownership of Factory Records, Rob Gretton, and New Order, at the time the most successful band of the label.

The success of New Order guaranteed the economic survival of the club and influenced its stylistic choices in the music program. The band sort of discovered dance and electronic music in New York City, and the Haçienda became the first club in Europe to play house music. However, electro and jazz dance were already part of Manchester music culture, thanks to local ethnic minorities and the student crowd. As told by Rietveld,

> In Moss Side lived a mix of black and Irish communities and during the 1980s a lot of the younger generation seemed to be into electro, and also jazz dance. There was also a lot of reggae in the neighbourhood, as well as in Hulme (where also many students lived). Pubs were playing reggae, dub and post-punk, . . . and the reggae dance parties started to shift towards electro for younger people. It is interesting to consider that electro was also part of the third wave . . . what you hear in the early 1980s is really a shift from acoustic instru-

ments to electronic instruments. Still, you cannot really generalise because many bands were still attached to guitar sounds. What I find interesting is that New Order and Happy Mondays, later on, they all listened to dance and house music and techno but they didn't exactly make it, they were still hanging on to band formations with guitars. (interview, 2019; and see Rietveld 2014)

DJs Graeme Park and Mike Pickering started playing house music at the Friday 'Nude' Night at the Haçienda in 1987. The Haçienda gave birth to the first European house music scene, which later developed the practice of rave parties. This scene became infamous as *acid* house because of the involvement of ecstasy. The music press created the term *Madchester*, fusing *Manchester* and *madness*, to designate the local scene and the slow appearance of gang crime and drug trade.

The Haçienda closed once in 1991, under pressure from the Greater Manchester Police. It reopened after three months, but Factory Records went bankrupt in 1992 and the Haçienda had to close definitely in 1997. A private company, Crosby Homes, bought and demolished it. Between 2002 and 2004, an apartment and office complex was completed on the site. Of course, the project maintained the name of the club, in accordance with entrepreneurial strategies, which employ cultural elements as a way to market themselves (Haslam 2000). In addition, the book *The Haçienda: How Not to Run a Club* (Hook 2009) and the film *24 Hour Party People* (Winterbottom 2002) give an anecdotic and semi-realistic portrayal of the Haçienda's history, with the due concessions to myth and sometimes erasing job exploitation and the contribution of women.

Parallel to the Haçienda, and on a different scale, the Northern Quarter also represents an important aspect of the relation between music and urban renewal in Manchester. The name was conceived to designate what used to be a 'leftover' of the unitary city centre plan. Located between Piccadilly Gateway, Ancoats, and Shudehill, the Northern Quarter had been a major shopping area since the nineteenth century, especially along Oldham Street and in the Smithfield Market. It was later devastated by 1960s developments, which culminated with the construction of the Arndale centre, the largest indoor shopping mall of Europe at the time of its construction in the 1970s. The area was rapidly abandoned in the 1970s, left to its own destiny by speculators.

The availability of cheap flats with affordable rents, together with the Enterprise Allowance Scheme (a start-up project for self-employed entrepreneurs) encouraged many musicians and music entrepreneurs to move to the area. Record shops, recording studios, rehearsal rooms, and small alternative shops (such as bookshops, tattoo studios, clothes shops) began to appear in the district, together with flats (Brown, O'Connor, and Cohen 2000). Factory Records itself also opened a bar (The Dry Bar) and a shop (The Area) in the Northern Quarter. The Affleck's Palace opened its premises in a five-storey building, selling street fashion and design in connection to various styles of popular music scenes, such as punk and techno, in about fifty independent stalls.

The entrepreneurs, workers, and inhabitants of the area joined together in the Northern Quarter Association, which tried to put forward the needs and agenda of a 'creative district' in the municipality. From the 1990s on, the Northern Quarter, just like the Haçienda, faced problems in connection with the rise of violence among gangs and the consumption of illicit substances, which the municipality was not ready to control, owing to its 'hands off' policy in connection to the district.

Parallel to the Northern Quarter, the Gay Village (along Canal Street) and China Town also developed, extending further the notion of 'cultural districts' through tolerance, diversity, and ethnicity. Nowadays the municipality formally recognises them all as neighbourhoods.

NIGHTTIME ECONOMY, POPULAR MUSIC AND THE CITY

The era into consideration in this book is more or less the same dominated, on a political national level, by the Conservative Party and in particular by Prime Minister Margaret Thatcher. Thatcher was elected in 1979 and maintained her position until 1990, when John Major succeeded her, before losing his seat in 1997. The conservative policy was concerned with centralisation, neo-liberalism, and the recovery of the British economy through privatisation.

With reference to city policy, Thatcher encouraged collaboration with the private sector, certain of the fact that the physical reshaping of city centres would have an effect on their social dimension as well.

Urban culture was connected mainly to the institutionalised forms of high culture: theatres, ballets, operas, and concert halls, relegating everything else to the duties of low-level officials in connection to leisure. Manchester in the 1970s and early 1980s was one of the most prominent local governments promoting 'municipal socialism', inspired by the labour tradition and by class solidarity. The city was a site of struggle against the Tory government and its policy was connected to basic elements: housing, transportation, and welfare.

From 1984 onwards and most evidently after 1987, the so-called New Urban Left replaced the traditional socialism inside the local Labour Party. This has been explained by the third defeat in the general elections (1987) and by the 'growing awareness of the limitations of what a local authority was able to do in an era of globalisation' (Quilley 1999). There is also a sociological explanation connected to the decline of traditional working-class masculinity due to unemployment and to the increase of ethnic and gender diversification in the labour forces. At the same time, there is also a clear connection to the many 'prodigal sons' rejoining the party who had abandoned it in 1968 (Tickell and Peck 1996; Quilley 1999; Quilley 2000).

The New Left local government in Manchester brought to the city an innovative entrepreneurialism that recalled the deeds of the 'Manchester men' in liberalising the English economy at the beginning of the nineteenth century (Tickell and Peck 1996). This was connected mainly to the reimagining of the city as a whole, after the disastrous deindustrialisation. This reimagining was believed to be central to attract new private investments in the built environment and was seen favourably by Thatcher's central government. The focus of the municipality shifted therefore from social housing and training schemes for the unemployed to big bids in sport (unsuccessful bids for the 1996 and 2000 Olympics, 2002 Commonwealth Games), managerial-led initiatives, and the creation of new tourist attractions.

Thanks to the consultancy of the Institute for Popular Culture at Manchester Polytechnic, the municipality began looking at successful regeneration stories in the United States (Baltimore, Boston, and New York City) and in continental Europe (Barcelona and Amsterdam). A new narrative began influencing the public opinion and city council policy: the 'European city'. Bars and clubs were able to adopt 'more

European' opening hours and licensing laws, following the new philosophy of the 24/7 city. The night-time economy began to be understood as
a paradigm of development and a resource, urban think tank Comedia
published *Out of Hours: A Study of Economic Social and Cultural Life
in Twelve Town Centres in the UK* in 1991, and the 24-Hour City
conference was held at the Manchester Institute for Popular Culture,
Manchester Metropolitan University, in September 1993.

Ironically enough, in the same period, the band Happy Mondays had
a tune called '24-Hour Party People', subtly about ecstasy, the so-called
love drug, able to make people smile and dance, annihilating time and
space, until the early afternoon (typical of the rave scene are the 'after
hours' clubs, open usually from 2:00 a.m. to 10:00 a.m.). 'European'
started referring to everything from 'Spanish licensing hours' to 'cap-
puccino bars' and had a huge impact on the marketing of the city and
on the way not only the municipality but also the citizens saw and
imagined Manchester's post-industrial success.

Quilley (1999) identifies three different assumptions in relation to
the New Left Manchester and questions each of them, as part of a
single script played out by the municipality.

The first is the unproblematic description of the shift from industrial
to post-industrial city, with the latter as a simple next stage in the
capitalist development. Quilley stresses the fact that also in the downfall
of the early 1980s, one-quarter of the conurbation's workforce were still
employed in manufacturing (Quilley 1999, 191–93). We could argue
that popular music seems to be aware of this, referring continuously to
the industrial imagery and heritage of the city and addressing the working class. In addition, the democratic structure of many independent
labels (Factory Records) and organisations (Music Force) and the attitude of most bands questioned capitalism as a whole. However, there
are also interesting articulations, in terms of theory. For instance, as
Rietveld observed,

> There was at first this technologically determined idea of the econo-
> my moving from agriculture to industry, and next to information
> society, a simple concept that was popularised very quickly and has
> also driven policy making. The idea was popularised by people like
> Alvin Toffler in *The Third Wave*, which mentions techno rebels. I
> remember Rob Gretton was reading that book and said, "If you need
> to read one book, this is the one". What New Order got from the

book is that you need to be ahead of new electronic music technology, and so they invested in the latest synthethisers. So there is a theoretical background to what New Order were doing and what also inspired the Haçienda. (interview, 2019)

The second assumption is bound to the belief that in an era of globalisation, cities are competing with each other, and a vibrant branding of a city could make the difference. Under these circumstances, the converting of old factories into offices and apartments and the marketing of Manchester as a place with a high quality of life become priorities (Quilley 1999, 194–97). Popular music can be seen from two different perspectives—one positive and one negative—in relation to this assumption. Popular music represents in fact the *folklore* of the creative class; its presence can confirm the liveability and vibrancy of a place, and its image can be used for local branding. The Haçienda and Manchester bands like the Stone Roses stood on the pages of major lifestyle and music magazines all over the world in the 1990s and were present also in tourist brochures and biddings. On the other hand, the material manifestation of popular music can also be seen as an impediment or a danger. The Northern Quarter's creative potential cannot be recognised immediately as economically profitable, in comparison to the renting or selling of the same premises for the new economy executives and office workers. Popular music (the Madchester scene in particular) was seen as a threat because of its connection to gang violence and drug use. The commission of the *Northern Quarter Regeneration Strategy* in 1995, for example, first overcame the 'hands off' attitude towards the Northern Quarter. Still, the report refers to the mixed use of the area and to the necessity to link its creative potential to the area's 'main commercial core'.

The third assumption is connected to the development of partnerships (with the national government and with the private sector) in the name of growth. This implied the exclusion of conflicts through a cross-class and place-bound attitude. Every step that the local government took was felt and explained as being for the benefit of Manchester as a whole (Quilley 1999, 197–99). Also in this last assumption, popular music plays an antagonist role. Bands and music entrepreneurs (Tony Wilson *in primis*) were aware of the 'pacification' that took place between local and national government in the late 1980s. They understood this as a 'selling out' and therefore were sceptical of any municipal intromission. The local music scene stance for Manchester and local pride was fuelled by global recognition and success, which just needed flexible local planning and licensing. The city was not ready or willing to grant these (Brown, O'Connor, and Cohen 2000).

4

DÜSSELDORF

The Mannesmann-Hochhaus is an eighty-eight-metre-tall skyscraper. Architect Paul Schneider-Esleben designed it in 1958 as the headquarters of the Mannesmann AG industrial conglomerate. Mannesmann AG was founded at the end of the nineteenth century as a producer of innovative metal piping, extending its businesses towards coal, transportation, and eventually mobile telecommunication (Wessel 1990). In the early 2000s, Vodafone telecommunications acquired Mannesmann AG and the building itself. Since 2008, the regional state of North Rhein-Westfalia (NRW) has owned the property (baukunst-nrw 2008) and during the so-called 2015 refugee crisis, one of its floors temporarily lodged refugees (Richters 2015). It currently houses the NRW Ministry for Economy, Innovation, Digitalisation and Energy.

The history and changes in ownership of the building reflect local and global economic shifts, paradigm changes, and deep ruptures in collective dreams, aspirations, and individual destinies. As a shiny, new functionalist headquarters of a metallurgy company, designed by a local star architect, it signified the achievements in wealth, technological growth, and welfare of an industrial society that had to be built from Second World War debris. Chapter 1 describes the structural changes that led Europe towards the unconditional acceptance of the 'post-industrial society' narrative. Some of these changes are evident, for instance, in the Mannesmann-Hochhaus ownership transfer from a heavy industry concern to a global telecommunication one. The so-called refugee crisis also left a mark in the building's history. The current state ownership shows how Germany partly solved problems connected to post-industrial shift and to the vacancy of a huge number of industrial buildings. Some of them were used for institutional purposes, while others became heritage sites and museums (more of this in chapter 7).

The Mannesmann-Hochhaus is also a typical functionalist building from the 1950s, where form follows function and repetition of lines, colours, and materials dominate the structure. Prefab units are assembled into pre-programmed schemes that seem to continue forever. This is a kind of architecture that dominates some parts of the Düsseldorf cityscape. The rhythm of this German city is deeply functionalist: repetitive, mechanical, and functional for production and commerce of the post-war era upswing. The city, however, doesn't wear its industrial connections on its sleeve and prefers to define itself as *Mode-Stadt*, 'fashion city', due to its retail fashion centrality, or as *Schreibtisch des Ruhrgebiets*, 'office desk of the Ruhr'. The Mannesmann skyscraper, as a company headquarters, was connected to factories, offices, and warehouses around the neighbouring Ruhr region, through a dense network of motorways, railways, and waterways, all visible in near proximity to the building. Right in front of this building, parallel to the Rhine and in a very central area, an *Autobahn*, motorway, once ran. The Kraftwerk Lausward, the city's biggest power station, is in close proximity in the neighbouring shipyard area. It seems self-explanatory that bands from this city are called Kraftwerk (power station) or Die Krupps (from the name of another local metallurgy conglomerate) and that these bands developed a synthetic sound based on repetition and technology, to be later labelled 'industrial'.

The articulation of the local industrial realm and of this polycentric and highly networked region works its way into music in a multitude of sometimes interconnected and sometimes isolated paths. It also involves a plethora of scenes, genres, labels, clubs, and bands, which spread out and network in the whole NRW. It is in fact very important to think about Düsseldorf as a city, which is embedded by industrial production into a network of urban centres across a very dense metropolitan region that, in turn, involves the so-called Ruhr Valley to the north and the city of Cologne to the south.

Not all bands and projects considered in this chapter were 100 percent from Düsseldorf; however, its geographical and, as we will see, cultural significance for the whole NRW played a determining role. In particular, the presence of the *Altstadt* ("old town district") carries an enormous significance for the whole region and for its night-time entertainment. This small district is enclosed by the Rhine to the east and by the Heinrich-Heine-Allee to the west. Its history dates back to medieval times; it houses the city municipal office, the Kunstakademie ("art academy") and several other buildings of significance from various eras of German history. Moreover, it is the main site for the Düsseldorf carnival, one of the most known festivities of this kind in Germany (along with a rivalling one that takes place in Cologne). From the 1960s onwards, in connection to the carnival, an array of clubs, bars, discotheques, and restaurants developed in the area. Soon the area began to be celebrated in songs, such as 'Ich will in die Altstadt' (I want to go to the *Altstadt*) and 'Wo bleibt unser Altbier?' (where is our *Altbier?*), both written by Hans Ludwig Lonsdorfer at the end of the 1970s. These songs were presented and sung collectively in carnival *Sitzungen*, that is, 'theatrical variety-show event[s], with music, comic speeches and sketches, dance troupes, and various additional Carnival-related entertainments' (Abbott 2014) and during the carnival Monday parade. They also corroborated the branding of Düsseldorf *Altstadt* as a party mile, where binging and the carnivalesque atmosphere could be enjoyed and re-created every weekend, with the corollary presence of aggression and violence, due to the presence of 'scallies, Hooligan-types and rockers', as described by Ralf Dörper, of Die Krupps, in my interview (in German, author's translation) with him, June 15, 2018, in Düsseldorf.

Still today, the *Altstadt* is *the* site for nocturnal partying, known over the whole region. People flock to the area to celebrate 'girls' nights' and bachelor parties and, more generally, just to have a good time. Strikingly enough, this environment also provided the primordial soup where punk could first proliferate in Germany.

The city tucks away metaphorically its industrial connections behind the *Schreibtisch* brand; likewise, the *Altstadt*, its 'lower' entertainment area, is hidden spatially behind a luxurious mile: the Königsallee, simply called Kö by the locals. This street is dominated by luxury and exhibition, in a continuous succession of fashion boutiques, casually parked Lamborghinis, tailor shops, and high-end arcades. It seems that Düsseldorf lives on ambiguities. Kraftwerk themselves, the city's most famous music legacy, adopted the industrial world in paradoxical ways, hiding real industrial practices behind storytelling, as shown in chapter 2.

It is only by linking the city's economic, geographical, and cultural existence to the neighbouring Ruhr and to Cologne that we can fully understand its cultural output during the late 1970s and early 1980s. An interesting take on this issue is the edited volume *Echt! Pop-Protokolle aus dem Ruhrgebiet* (Springer, Steinbrink, and Werthschulte 2008). *Echt!* reveals the plethora of DIY cultural work taking place in the dense Ruhr industrial valley across the late twentieth century, revealing unexpected talents, deep political commitment, and weird aesthetics. This is achieved by reconstructing, through oral histories, the role that individual artists, obscure clubs, or small publishers played in this German province. In connection to punk, the book editors were able to interview artists Klaus Tesching and Jürgen Kramer. They were born in Gladbeck and Gelsenkirchen, respectively, were students of Joseph Beuys at the Kunstakademie (art school) in 1970s Düsseldorf, and developed their careers in the region, across institutional and non-institutional practices and deeply inspired by punk. It seems very difficult to fully disconnect the Ruhr from Düsseldorf and vice versa, as they are both part of the same polycentric, metropolitan region. Taking a slow one-hour L-shaped journey on a local train from Düsseldorf to Dortmund means crossing the whole Ruhr region and some of its main municipalities—Duisburg, Müllheim, Essen, and Bochum—with the feeling of never really going anywhere. The landscape is consistent in its repetition of factories, chimneys, concrete bunkers, malls, neon lights, and parking lots—an immense industrial adventure park. Scattered around the surroundings are other middle-sized cities and towns, such as Solingen, Oberhausen, and Wuppertal, for instance, that also contributed spaces, people, and ideas to the Düsseldorf scene. The relation to Cologne might be more complicated by city rivalry, which dates back to medieval times and has its best-known expressions in football, beer, and carnival; however, seminal Krautrock combo Can, which provided guidance and inspiration to several bands—such as S.Y.P.H. and Die Krupps, for instance—and several individuals active in the Düsseldorf punk scene actually came from Cologne.

X-9200: PUNK IN DÜSSELDORF

While Kraftwerk attained world success and normal citizens were learning new carnival songs about local beers, a grassroots music scene was
quickly developing in the centre of Düsseldorf. This scene, active between the late 1970s and early 1980s, had a very public dimension,
enacted punk locally, and enabled the formation of bands that later
gained national or global recognition, such as Die Krupps, D.A.F., and
Die Toten Hosen, among others.

I am once again going to use the term *scene* in non-essentialising
ways to refer both to the networking community of people who share a
common interest, and to the places, locations, and situations where this
networking happens (see "Introduction").

Popular music cultures and their scenes are very precarious social
worlds, lasting for a few months to a few years before dissolving, cross-
pollinating, or evolving into other entities. Scenes are not self-sealed
and delimited by clear borders. They evolve and change abruptly,
thanks to technological advances, economic shifts, or generational
changes. Although self-recognition is a significant element in a scene,
we should not forget the role that certain individualities, pre-existing
groups, and side interests might play. In addition, certain scenes and
the affects attached to them can sometimes only be reconstructed and
understood a posteriori, after their disappearance. The punk music
scene in Düsseldorf can only be understood in close connection to the
art world. As we will see, it was in the Ratinger Hof where untrained
and unsigned punks, with limited education and working-class backgrounds discovered 'art', while trained artists with gallery exhibitions
were experimenting with streetwise lifestyles and bad-taste aesthetics.
However, the Ratinger Hof experience also shows the impossibility of
overcoming the intrinsic difference between the art world and popular
music scenes under other than temporary and local circumstances.

The art scene in Düsseldorf is alive today due to the presence of the
Kunstakademie, a consolidated higher institution of art education
founded in 1773 as the Academy of Painting, Sculpture and Architecture of the Electorate of the Palatinate. The long list of its alumni and
teachers include several celebrated artists such as Bernd and Hilla
Becher, Joseph Beuys, and Gerhard Richter. The academy also plays a
big role in city life, for instance, with its ritualistic student exhibition

shows, where wealthy citizens go on the hunt for new art works and artists to support and act as patrons for. The controversial status of Joseph Beuys during his professorship (1961–1972) definitely contributes to the aura of this place. The German performance art initiator sometimes performed or assisted multimedia shows involving musicians in some Düsseldorf clubs and in the Kunstakademie itself (Esch 2014, 25, 27), especially in the late 1960s.

Art students were the first punk fans; some were featured in early band formations and designed record covers and gig poster artwork. For instance, Markus Oehlen, now an established international artist, was the Ratinger Hof resident DJ and played minimal drums in Mittagspause.

Ratinger Hof, a bar/club on the Ratingerstrasse, in the *Altstadt*, was the main point of reference for this hybrid community. Squeezed into a mile of other beer parlours and restaurants and in walking distance from the Kunstakademie, the Ratinger Hof was a watering hole for artists, hippies, and intellectuals, thanks to Carmen Knoebel and Ingrid Kohlhöfer, who had been running it since 1974. The two entrepreneurs were widely known in local art circles and galleries and were married to rising stars of German art, both named Imi (Knoebel and Kohlhöfer, respectively). The bar quickly established itself as a hangout for a small group of artists, intellectuals, and rockers.

The Ratinger Hof is, for instance, visible in a short film by Muscha and Trini Trimpop, entitled *Blitzkrieg Bop* (Muscha and Trimpop 1977). Both directors were music enthusiasts who later joined seminal bands Charley's Girls and KFC, respectively. The primitive motion picture, filmed in 1977 in Super-8 format, shows a male protagonist waking up in a shabby flat and getting ready for his 'street hustle' by applying mascara and dressing up in black leather. His car ride, sometimes in the company of girls and another guy, leads him to the Jolly Joker, a pool and flipper hall at the main railway station; to an *Imbiß*, a street food stall on the Harkortstrasse; and eventually into the Ratinger Hof. The film's score is a playlist of proto-punk US songs of the time, including the Ramones' track that gives the title to the film, the Stooges' 'Gimme Danger', and Mink DeVille's 'Spanish Stroll'. The protagonist's allure and attitude are clearly modelled on the New York City punk/glam music scene, on its 1950s nostalgia, and on a certain 'urban jungle' aesthetics, which was available, for instance, in Scorsese works of the time, such as *Taxi Driver* (1976), and later developed also in Jim Jarmusch's debut, *Permanent Vacation* (1980). It is very clear that this initial Ratinger Hof scene of artists, film makers and music enthusiasts was looking towards the exciting cultural melting pot of New York City and of the Lower East Side especially. This changed when youth magazines such as *Bravo* started reporting on the punk explosion in the United Kingdom.

A punk scene in Düsseldorf specifically and Germany in general was first and foremost an imaginary space in the head of Franz Bielmeier, from Neukirchen, and Ramon Louis, from Cologne, who in March 1977 distributed in the *Altstadt* record shops the first issue of their fanzine, *The Ostrich*. Among reviews of obscure Lou Reed, Stooges, and Patti Smith bootleg tapes and interviews copied and pasted from English music magazines, we can find a mention of the, at the time, more or less fictive band Charley's Girls. The band never released anything during its existence, but according to the fanzine, it was supposedly working on a live LP entitled *Tiger Morse*, which could be obtained from the 'Europe's Only Charley's Girls Fan Club', whose address is, unsurprisingly, (still) Bielmeier's. Both the fanzine and the band name are references to songs by Lou Reed, who is also celebrated in the gender-bending nom de plume adopted by Bielmeier: Mary Lou Monroe. Looking at the subsequent issues of the fanzine, eight in total between March 1977 and the autumn of 1978, it is interesting to track the slow establishment of a network, enabled by postal contacts, telephone calls, and, later, meetings in person in the *Altstadt*. In this sense, issue number three represents the most accomplished, with the first contributions by Peter Hein, who sometimes used his nom de plume, Janie J. Jones, interviews with Cologne-based and short-lived the Stenguns, and a live report and interview with local band Male.

Mary Lou Monroe also pens a short and reflective column entitled 'Punk in Germany?' where he writes, 'Well, people, it cannot go on like this. What we need is a kind of club, I mean, something like a German CBGB's or something. but who is ready to transform their middle-class bar into a punk dungeon?' (Bielmeier 1978; translated by the author). Mary Lou was probably not yet aware of the fact that Carmen Knoebel had recently visited CBGB's in New York City, witnessed the gig of James Chance and the Contortions opening for the Ramones, and decided to turn the Ratinger Hof into the Düsseldorf equivalent of the

Lower East Side punk dungeon. Carmen renovated the place in the beginning of 1977, with the collaboration of her husband, artist Imi Knoebel, whom she also managed. Inspired by the neon art of Dan Flavin, the bar became a club, a sparsely furnished open space with whitewashed walls and bare neon lights, the perfect showroom for a new generation of young people, trademarked by a strong visual and sonic agency (Dreyer and Wenzel 2018). Slowly, the young publishers of *The Ostrich*, who were writing fanzines, buying records, and starting bands, began to hang out in these safe premises and attract the curiosity of artists, especially because of their clothes and attitude. Punk as a music genre and as street credibility overcame art, as the common denominator of the bar clientele. Ralf (Die Krupps) explains,

> It was very much determined by the presence of Carmen Knoebel that there were artists going to Ratinger Hof. That was almost a coincidence; they were all old at the moment. These punk bands were all very young; they were all still in school. At the time a three-year difference was already a world apart. And the artists, they were all over thirty years old, if not even older. There were just a few direct connections, for instance, with young artists such as Markus Oehlen playing with Mittagspause, but the main link to the art scene was indirectly by Art Attack/Der Plan moving to Düsseldorf. Der Plan [an electronic band], that is, Art Attack [their label], was originally a gallery and indeed a gallery in Wuppertal. That means they were in the art scene right from the start, especially Moritz, and when they came to Düsseldorf, there was the plan from the beginning to link with real artists. (interview, 2018)

The Ratinger Hof is central to the accounts, memories, and biographies of a huge number of bands, visual artists, and film makers from Düsseldorf and the Ruhr, and photographer Richard Gleim, also known as ar/gee gleim, provides a rich visual documentation of the place (Gleim 2016).

In our interview (February 6, 2018, in Düsseldorf), former Östro 430 band member Olivia Tawiah describes the place like this, while looking at a photograph:

> This was the stage, yes, it was so long and narrow there, so narrow and so small, this was the bar where you could order, the bar and this was the entry . . . here's where you would sit down, there were small

tables and the pool table, they were there but not for long, people sat on them and here at the end were the toilets, in front of the stage and all these graffiti!

Let's not talk about the toilets, they were terrible . . . and all the others . . . I remember that there were. . . . We were . . . In all pubs we went they kept an eye on us, they were checking where we went because people were writing on the walls all around the city, the buses were covered in them, it was before spraying, it was all Edding. Edding [a felt marker brand] made their best deals back then. (original in Italian; author's translation)

Interestingly, the graffiti doesn't show band logos, which North American bands such as Black Flag and the Dead Kennedys were already using and that Die Krupps, for instance, adopted from the Krupp concern later on. Hip-hop inspired tags and stencils spread in Düsseldorf later, around 1981 and 1982, coinciding with Ja Ja's debut album, produced by Kurt Dahlke (also known as Pyrolator, a member of Der Plan and Fehlfarben), which contained the programmatic 'Graffiti Artists International'. The walls worked more like a medium where the bands' slogans and lyrics might have been created and developed. Said Peter Braatz (also known as Harry Rag), of S.Y.P.H., 'I went in and said "I also have a band, S.Y.P.H." "Wow, great!", "We also have a song Zurück zur Beton" and I sang the song to the people, without music, just sang, and I wrote the lyrics on the wall, so that everybody could read them, for about one year everybody thought we were a real band' (Schwabe 2016).

The neon lighting of the club took no prisoners: everybody was constantly on show, both on and under the minimal stage, turning the whole club into a performance space and erasing the 'fourth wall' between audience and musicians. Moreover, the presence of at least one TV screen, on a mounted rack on the ceiling, invited multimedia sensing and free-form associations among broadcasted images and the live or recorded music on air. Of course, several iconic objects of a traditional Düsseldorf beer parlour remained visible: the bar with taps, the round beer mats that the club sometimes used as tickets or flyers, and the big neon sign of an Altbier brand, which adorned the low façade of the building in pure tacky *Altstadt* architectonic fashion.

In full contrast to the secluded Kraftwerk work logic described in chapter 3, the Ratinger Hof scene was very public. Bands met, organized, rehearsed, were photographed, and developed in public within the narrow premises of the Ratinger Hof and its cellar, where some bands such as Charley's Girls/Mittagspause, early D.A.F., and, for a short period, ZK rehearsed. For them, authenticity was something that had to be lived rather than told, with all the existential crises and narrow-mindedness that this might bring. Furthermore, the developing independent music press of fanzines and later magazines contributed to the establishment of this scene, by providing references to band names, practice sessions, and meeting places to external audiences at the regional and later national level.

Not only the Ratinger Hof but the whole *Altstadt* provided a performance and communication space for this scene. Braatz, that is, Harry Rag described it to me this way in a June 14, 2018, phone interview:

> In Düsseldorf there is an old town, the Altstadt, and in the old town there were a lot of shops for records, if you wanted to buy records, you went there and you get all the super stuff and once in 1977 in the summertime I went there and you could get a newspaper called *The Ostrich* that was actually a fanzine, I bought this and I was completely fascinated and I liked it and I got in contact with these guys of the fanzine and it was a musician from the band Mittagspause and at the time they were still called Charley's Girls, which was the pre-group of Mittagspause and we became very good friends and half a year later my band was S.Y.P.H. and from then on for the next three years we made a lot of concerts together, we came into the scene.

Moreover, it was in the old town that the members of Male, the first German punk band to produce an LP, recognised the appearance of other punks and realised the potential of appearance, language, and, of course, spitting, for shocking the silent majority. According to Bielmeier (Teipel 2011, 34), their first hang out was a red brick wall behind an office block, in front of the Ührige brewery—a hidden spot, though still in the middle of the old town.

Another important spot for the scene was the record store Rock On, which opened in an arcade on the Schadowstrasse:

You could also find the big punk records in the other record shops, something like the Clash you got in any record shop. But the small independent labels, like Buzzcocks or the stuff of Stiff, like the Damned, you got it from abroad or then only in Rock On . . . so this how the scene came to be. And what is even more important, Rock On financed the LP by Male. They let the band rehearse in the shop and paid the recording studio and published the record. (Ralf/Die Krupps, interview, 2018)

As stated before, Düsseldorf doesn't immediately fit into the industrial city stereotype of smoking chimneys and red brick walls and prefers to identify itself through its centrality in retail fashion, services, and administration or through its wealth, exhibited along the Kö. This self-image also works as a differentiation mechanism vis-à-vis the 'real' industrial cities scattered around the Ruhr region, such as Essen, Marl, or Oberhausen. Fashion was an important discriminant also among punks. As Olivia (of Östro 430) explains,

It was an emulation of what was going on in London *mit Pernol gewaschen*, let's say so. We all tried to get the right boots, someone got them sent from London, just like the bondage trousers, all these things that you could get if you were rich; it was a bit, with *Gänsefüßchen*, punk for rich kids. The ones without money improvised, we started cutting shirt and trousers, trying to copy the others, it was a very creative time. (interview, 2018)

Kraftwerk found themselves at ease among the word of discotheques, glamour, models, tailored suits, and mannequins; punks experienced this world in a more confrontational way, and the fashion world was always perceived as unauthentic. Linking themselves to the industrial world represented for punks an authentic unambiguous reality of noise, struggle and locality. Said Pyrolator, of Der Plan, 'I was at the time very much intrigued by the industrial romanticism. . . . In Wuppertal there were many empty factories. And I went gladly into old industrial areas, where the machines still were. It was like discovering industrial areas as adventure playgrounds' (Teipel 2001, 89)

RODENKIRCHEN IS BURNING

Sounds was a German popular music monthly magazine, published
from 1966 to 1983. In the March 1978 issue, rock critic Alfred Hilsberg
wrote a punk feature entitled 'Rodenkirchen Is Burning'. Hilsberg later
extended his music endeavours in a record label, ZickZack, based in
Hamburg. The *Sounds* article is structured as a psycho-geography of
punk on German soil, focusing on new and obscure bands from Hamburg, Berlin, and the 'Ruhr': 'Typical scenery for the T.V. Eyes and
other punks, under the grey sky of the Ruhr. Between coal shacks and
coking plants, the preconditions for a punk movement seem to have
been created: the future of young people in the jungle of this industrial
wasteland is uncertain. Societal conflicts, from renewal projects to steel
crises, should, like the crisis-ridden United Kingdom, be a cause for a
movement that opposes "rational relations"' (Hilsberg 1978).

The 'Ruhr' that Hilsberg is addressing encompasses bands from
Düsseldorf (Male, Charley's Girls) and Cologne (T.V. Eyes), which,
although in close proximity to the area, should not be used to represent
it. However, the rhetorical device is clearly used to associate what the
journalist calls 'preconditions for a punk movement' to the sound produced by these bands and to their aggressive and frustrated attitude.
Clearly, at least in the very beginning, there was no such thing as an
externally defined 'Düsseldorf scene' but something more like a network of spread out 'pockets of punk' encompassing the whole NRW.
The Ratinger Hof for instance is presented in the article simply as a
club with a 'waiting room atmosphere'. Also, the gig accounts refer
mostly to the first disastrous and farcically comical attempts, like the
infamous Male and Charley's Girls school party gig in Rodenkirchen. It
is only with the Carsch-Haus Festival (June 3–4, 1978) that the first real
celebration of the scene in Düsseldorf took place. The festival show-
cased bands such as Male, from Düsseldorf; Charley's Girls, from
Düsseldorf/Cologne; S.Y.P.H., from Solingen; Neat (with Ralf Zeiger-
mann) and 110, from Dortmund. Carsch-Haus was an historical commercial building in the centre of Düsseldorf, which during the 1970s
was dismantled and its façade meticulously rebuilt for a new building a
few metres away because of the extension of the metro system. At the
time, the cellar of the building could be used temporarily for events
(Ralf/Die Krupps, interview, 2018). The gig brought bands and individ-

uals together. S.Y.P.H., for instance, had its debut at the festival; Harry Rag said,

> Carsch-Haus was the first and the last punk festival in Düsseldorf, there was the birth of S.Y.P.H., it was the first time we played live ever . . . after maybe three months of rehearsal? And in these three months maybe each week once or twice . . . it was joy, it was a life experience and then the friends were standing around they were audience so it was always a start, but very refreshing and it gives you some kind of power because you feel like wow I can do something, I am not just a consumer, I can do something for myself. (interview, 2018)

Another significant aspect for the development of Düsseldorf centrality as music city is the economic power attained by Ratinger Hof's Carmen Knoebel. Thanks to the success of her husband Imi in the art world, she was able to invite international bands, such as local favourite Wire and Pere Ubu, but also XTC, Tuxedomoon, Scritti Politti, Slits, and Raincoats, to play at the Ratinger Hof. She also invested in the record label Pure Freude, which she started with Peter Braatz. Later, Carmen opened a proper record shop, although active only for a couple of years, also called Pure Freude, in the suburban address Derendorferstrasse 55, and was able to close licensing contracts with, for instance, Rough Trade.

I ONLY WANT TO DANCE TO CONCRETE

The band S.Y.P.H. formed in Solingen. Peter Braatz (his alt-name, Harry Rag, was from a song by the Kinks) started the band with Uwe Jahnke and Thomas Schwebel in Solingen, but it is in Ratinger Hof and in Düsseldorf that they found their home. Harry Rag said, 'We were always coming from Solingen, so we had our rehearsal room in Solingen at the time and we were already eighteen years old and we had cars and driving licence and so it was just half an hour to go from my town to Düsseldorf in the centre, or with the train' (interview, 2018).

From their earliest recordings onwards, the band developed a unique sound partly influenced by punk, ska, and new wave but also experimented with found sounds, improvisation, and lo-fi visuals

(Braatz is currently involved in the film industry). The two best-known songs of S.Y.P.H. are, interestingly enough, the first they wrote: 'Industrie-Mädchen' (industry girl, first featured on side A of the 7" Viel Feind Viel Ehr, 1979, and in another version on their eponymous debut album, 1980) and 'Zurück zur Beton' (back to concrete, from their debut album). 'Industrie-Mädchen' appears on the 7"as a proto-ska upbeat number and on the LP in a punk-inspired version, with a distorted guitar and a more aggressive attitude. The simple love song is set against an industrial landscape of refineries, good stations, nuclear power plants, backyard apartments, and electrical substations, with a refrain simply stating, 'I like her'. The industry girl of the title is mentioned in the song just in the third person and there are no specific indications of who she is and where the love story happens. Place is built in the song by a patchwork of landmarks, which semiotically link themselves to the overall concept of 'industry' and create the improbable backdrop for the love story. In many ways, a similar strategy is adopted in Ewan Mac-Coll's 'Dirty Old Town', as a prototype of industry city music from the industrial folk era. Braatz explains that the song's author, Thomas Schwebel, was inspired by Buzzcocks, Devo, and Pere Ubu in describing an industrial wasteland, with a teenager and his romantic problems in the middle (Teipel 2001, 89–90). From the point of view of the soundscape, the song appears in S.Y.P.H.'s official recordings in two different versions. A clean ska guitar riff emphasising the upbeat opens the 7" version, the drums follow in simple, repetitive 4/4 with no fills, and the bass tries some Jamaican-influenced lines, while a melodica plays some fills in the distance. In the LP version a fuzz guitar riff dominates, and the tempo is faster, with drum and bass on a simple, nearly martial 2/4 punk rhythm.

Both versions are dominated by aggressive vocals, similar to other Ratinger Hof bands of this era, with clearly spelled out lyrics in German. There is little reference to anything industrial in the sound of these songs. Maybe the repetitive, minimal beat of both could be associated to the rhythm of the factory, although they are most likely due to the naive musical abilities of the band and to influential bands from abroad. As Harry Rag put it, 'The concept was to put the industrial noise and the industrial reality into music, that means the rhythms of the guitar and the rhythms of the sequencers and so was very mechanic; we were trying to make this *bum-tchi-bum-tchi-bum-tchi-bum-tchi* very mechanically influenced, let's say, a lot by Wire, from England, and Devo, from America' (interview, 2018). Deeper connections to industrial as a music genre are to be found in more experimental songs like 'Klammheimlich' (which closes the 7"), thanks to the contribution of Ralf Dörper (later in Die Krupps) on synthesizer, and found material.

'Zurück zum Beton' (back to concrete) opens the LP with a monotonous clean guitar playing one simple major chord in an emphatic 1950s strum over some simple lyrics referring to nature and to turning into an animal. The tempo then speeds up into the brutal one-chord refrain, repeating over and over again, 'Back to concrete, back to the metro, back to concrete', while during the two-chords verse the singer shouts that he wants to dance in concrete. This is, once again, a humorous and punky *détournement*:

> We had a lot of big industries around us but basically let's say the influence of this industry thing was also because of the American bands for example Devo, Pere Ubu which came from Akron and they were singing about industry as a dream and in my case I was writing all the lyrics and in my very first song I turned around the old philosophy by Rousseau which was saying basically back to the nature and this was also what all the people in 1970s and 1960s all this peace movement, anti-*Atomkraft* movement, with the hippies, they were saying back to nature and as punks we wanted to turn it around and I made a song called 'back to concrete' . . . and that was a little bit like a joke because basically I was not against nature but I was, we were a little bit using industry as a symbol for the modern times, which is destroying the humanity, so it was a theme and we had it also in several songs. (Harry Rag, interview, 2018)

Zurück zur Natur (back to nature), as stated for instance by Jean-Jacques Rousseau, appealed to various German art and philosophical anti-urban movements and ideologies, which saw nature as the place of Germanness against cosmopolitan and toxic urbanity. S.Y.P.H. state exactly the opposite and glorify concrete as symbol of ugly urban life in an industrial brutalist city, putting punk in its place. Concrete is the bare symbol of a certain kind of architectonic style, later referred to as brutalism in the United Kingdom (from the French *béton brut*, bare concrete, as in naked surface made of concrete) and which is the most widely used building material in twentieth-century industrial cities.

Instrumentation, chord changes, and melody in these songs are extremely minimal and naive, nearly childish; the lyrics are based on simple, straightforward sentences and delivered with urgency, while the instruments try to keep up with it. As such, these songs pave the way for further developments in the so-called *Neue Deutsche Welle* (new German wave; see Hornberger 2011). The band later collaborated with Can's bass player Holger Czukay, who produced *Pst*, their second LP. By doing so, they shifted from Ratinger Hof/Düsseldorf reality punk towards Can/Cologne Krautrock, free-form and experimental music, a shift of a few kilometres in space, which built continuity across an apparent musical divide. Said Harry Rag,

> I thought that improvised music is more punk than punk, which is just loud and following the structures, following structures is basically the same structure of rock 'n' roll or beat, partly even pop, but improvisation music is something you don't play on radio, you don't know what happens at the concert, the concert is always a unique event and that's this kind of improvisation we followed then. . . . The second and the third records were coming from the inner space of studio of Can and they were influenced by Can and Holger Czukay and they were partly instrumental even so this was then, let's say, Krautrock but I was not looking at Krautrock but also . . . for me it was still punk, because at the beginning of punk in England you had big variations I mean there was from Pistols and Clash to Cabaret Voltaire and Throbbing Gristle and even singer-songwriters with acoustic guitars and electronic groups, you had a big variety, punk was always very, very rich and big variety and this led to this to find our own way . . . we were let's say a hedonistic band, which always wanted to have joy and excess of course, that means whenever we rehearsed something we never . . . we didn't have fun learning songs by heart, we just played around with the instruments and then found something new and in the end when we found something new again then the rehearsal was great, we tried to put that also on stage and the result was that all punk fans didn't like us anymore because they thought, What is this music? Where are the punk songs? We lost the audience we also lost the record sales. (interview, 2018)

Leaving S.Y.P.H. after the first LP, Thomas Schwebel joined a new formation called Mittagspause (lunch break) with members of Charley's Girls, including the singer Peter Hein (a.k.a. Janie Jones), Franz Bielmeier (a.k.a. Mary Lou Monroe) on guitar, and Markus Oehlen on drums. The band developed a pretty unique repetitive sound based on simple guitar riffs, minimal drumming, and no bass. An equalised guitar played by Bielmeier provided the bass frequencies in their recordings, while the other guitar was always on a high treble pitch. The step from Charley's Girls—a fictional band developed in *The Ostrich* fanzine and later turned real, though with an ever-changing line-up—to Mittagspause, with steady members, is very much a professionalising one. Many songs were maintained and developed, including the cover of 1965 *schlager* hit 'Marmor, Stein und Eisen bricht', by Drafi Deutscher. The song figures among the best-known German hits of the 1960s, and it is still widely played in various events by live bands or in DJ sets; there are also several techno and dance music versions of it. The hit represents another important dimension of industrial cities, which is the carnivalesque and 'low' forms of entertainment, targeting the working class. Düsseldorf carnival and the *Altstadt* are clear symbols of this attitude, attracting over decades people from the surrounding industrial region to celebrate holidays and weekends in the name of alcoholic excess. The Ratinger Hof's small, initial circle of individuals and bands established themselves as gatekeepers, referring to everybody else as 'carnival punk'. Mittagspause used 'Marmor, Stein und Eisen bricht' as ironic homage to the *Altstadt*, where Ratinger Hof was itself located. Getting the ironic overtone was as discriminant between the ones 'in the scene' and the ones who were just in it for its carnivalesque expression. The cover song evolved overtime; Charley's Girls played it live in a punk version (Bielmeier 2014) and then turned it into some kind of minimalist Brecht-Weil cabaret song (Bielmeier 2013), which was kept also after the name change (Mittagspause 1982). The band later used a set-up tape recording, mixing the original version with electronic noise (at least according to Fetisch, in Teipel 2001, 114).

MUSICSCAPES FOR THE DIGITAL INDUSTRIAL REVOLUTION

Charley's Girls and later Mittagspause were experimenting with data cassettes that Peter Hein stole from the trash at his Xerox workplace. These cassettes were used as data storage for electronic typewriters and represented a completely new industrial noise based around digitalisation, automation, and data processing. When played in normal tape recorders, they produced screeching sounds, featured, for instance, at the beginning of 'Testbild' (from their eponymous double EP set, 1979). According to Oehlen, sometimes they let those tapes run in the background throughout entire gigs (Teipel 2001, 147). This new industrial sound was just a side result of digital memory storage made through a binary system and stored on tapes. This technology was at the core of the so-called third industrial revolution or digital revolution and the rise of the post-industrial society. Schaefer (1977) refers to the post-industrial soundscape and describes it as embedded into the 'industrial revolution', focusing especially on the noises of factories, trains, engines, and into the 'electric revolution', focusing on the schizophonia of telephones, radios, and Muzak. In 1977, he was not aware of the rise of digitalisation and of the apparent silence that electric cars, Oyster travel cards, personal computers, and robotisation brought about. Mittagspause cassette noises give a voice to a 'silent' storage system for noiseless electronic typewriters and somehow deconstruct the idea of the 'silent' digital revolution. It is only in later Düsseldorf formations, such as D.A.F. and Die Krupps, that digitalisation would also translate into music making, thanks to the adoption of synthesisers and sequencers. Due to his daily job at Xerox, Hein got deeply inspired by digital work, his lyrics often carrying obscure references to it, such as 'Intelnet' and 'X9200'. Intelnet was the telephone network at Xerox and X9200 the code of a copy machine model, which used to be printed on red tape. Hein used to cut and glue pieces of the tape with the code on people, walls, and instruments, turning it into an absurd and Dadaesque slogan for the whole scene (Teipel 2001, 76, 78, 96). Hein also refers to adopting *Industriemusik* ('music of the industry' or 'industry music') as the band's concept, programmatically covering S.Y.P.H.'s 'Industrie-Mädchen' and later recording it with Felhfarben (although as 'Große Liebe', 1981), playing live a long instrumental called 'Industrial Rabotni' and calling a tour 'Industrie total, zurück zum Maschinensaal' (total industry, back to the machine room) (Hein, in Esch 2014, 293).

Dissatisfied with punk as expressive tool, other Düsseldorf musicians were also looking into the industrial world and the fascinating concept of 'industry music' for inspiration. Jürgen Engler and Bernward Malaka, Male singer and bass player, started thinking about the *Stahlwerksinfo-*

nie (steel works symphony) as a music track inspired by the soundscape of an active factory in early 1980, and to "Die Krupps" as a name for the new project. Krupp, just like Thyssen and Mannesmann, was a local industrial dynasty from Essen, devoted to metallurgy. At the same time, Engler had formed Die Lemminge with Ralf Dörper, an electronic duo who will later put out an experimental 7" 'Lorelei/Im Himmel' on *Pure Freude*.

The earliest recording of 'Stahlwerksinfonie', later published and referred to as *Ur-Werk*, features only Malaka on bass, Engler on guitar, and Frank Köllges, a recruited jazz drummer, and lasts 23:42. The song, just like the recorded versions, opens with a steady bass playing the open lowest string of the instrument and a simple steady 2/4 drum pattern, with guitar working continuously at free forms and noise. The real recorded 'Stahlwerksinfonie' appears in two 'halves', A and B. The A version is fast and martial, with screeching noises provided by guitar and sax, some effects, and synthetic sounds. Version B is more groovy in rhythm and at the same time more 'industrial' by using screams and metal-on-metal percussions from the beginning on. Going through the song credits is like looking at the Düsseldorf scene/Ratinger Hof usual suspects: apart from Die Krupps themselves, Peter Hein, who had recently left music, produces the songs and plays some percussions and Eva Gößling (Mania D and Blässe) plays saxophone. It has been already noted that Can, despite being from the rival city of Cologne and representing the 'old' Krautrock sound, were an inspiration for some of these bands, and it is therefore simply logical that Die Krupps decided to record these seminal sessions in the famous Inner Space studio of the band, with Can technician René Tinner. The song was later mixed at Conny Plank's studio. Strikingly, the song is more reminiscent of Can and Krautrock than of any other seminal industrial music and has a progressive and symphonic dimension, which will be quickly put aside by the band, in favour of a more direct attitude. For instance, 'Wahre Arbeit Wahrer Lohn' (recorded in June 1981 and first released as a 12") is based around a simple and fast sequencer line, accompanied with real instruments (bass, drums) fighting to keep up with it, while Engler martially delivers lyrics in German. The lyrics themselves reflect on the body-machine duality, equating oil with sweat, muscles with machines, dirt and filth with real work, pain and blame with real salary. The industrial soundscape is present in the song thanks to a whistle and the steelophon, a sort of xylophone assembled with pieces of scrap metal and pipes. Both provide rhythmic patterns, which vary the repetitive sequenced line and invite to dance. This song, together with coeval ones by D.A.F. and Nitzer Ebb, for instance, established the so-called EBM (electronic body music), a 'floor-orientated derivative of industrial music' (Dicker 2018). Even if pointing in name and image to the old days of the metallurgic industry, the sound of Die Krupps points to another direction and calls for the digital revolution and for a new understanding of body-machine connections based on technology and automation. In the early 1980s, the idea of a 'real' job with a 'real' salary was slowly disappearing, giving way to creative and immaterial work and to the slow precarisation of work into the so-called gig economy. Die Krupps were dealing with the faster pace of digitalisation, with new patterns of consumption, and with the new role that the body would play in them.

ENDS AND NEW BEGINNINGS

The establishment of 'third generation' bands by members of the Ratinger Hof scene led to the first major label contracts, to break-ups, and to the demise of the original scene. The Kunstakademie students went back to figurative art or performance, revealing once again the gap between music scenes, subcultures, and the art world. The Ratinger Hof had already changed ownership in 1980, and several of the original local independent labels went bankrupt. Major labels dictated changes in look, style, and line-ups of several bands. A more traditional understanding of gender shaped who would become a pop star and who decided to abandon music making altogether, as described by Olivia Tawiah (who had gone from playing bass with Östro 430 to the freshly EMI-signed Fehlfarben):

> At that time we had those thirty-six gigs and there I realised that basically my function and also Sylvia's [Sylvia Schütze played trumpet] was more . . . it was that time when there were various bands with go-go girls, these things, and so I had to say no, I don't do the go-go girl for Fehlfarben, it is stupid, no! No! Enough. And then came the invitation to Rockpalast that was great, if you go to Rockpalast you made it and I said after all these thirty-six concerts, a won-

derful experience, this road-movie living for two months together with all these people . . . it was beautiful but then at the same time realising that I have never really been part of the thing, I said no, I do not want to see me in thirty years in a Rockpalast movie doing the *Tanzmariechien* no, not me, and on these things I have an absolute consistency, and there I did like Monika Kellermann at that other time, I said do your Rockpalast alone, they were very angry and I said no, I do not come, and that was it. (interview, 2018)

However, punk music, having become more direct, harsh, and hard-core, began spreading across the real industrial wastelands of the Ruhr. For instance, Helge Schreiber (gig organiser for Network of Friends and Filthy Few singer) gives an interesting portrayal of punk in NRW after the Ratinger Hof, by referring, for instance, to the so-called *Punk Treffen*:

> These punk meetings often took place in Duisburg, where punks from all over the Ruhr met, but also punks from the surrounding rural communities. First we met at the main station in Duisburg and stayed there as long as the railway security or the police did not throw us out. If we were thrown out, which actually happened every time, we ran towards Duisburg city centre, to the big fountain direct-ly in front of the Karstadt shopping centre. Sometimes up to 200 punks were at the meetings in Duisburg, which took place mainly in the early to mid-1980s.

> The distances to the other cities are only very small, so from Obe-rhausen for example it is only 15 km to Duisburg, 20 km to Essen, 10 km to Bottrop and 15 km to Mülheim. The cities have grown so much in the last century that today you can barely recognize the city limits, as the buildings blend seamlessly into one another. Since the distances were not too big, we went to other punk meetings. The punk meeting was not about concerts, but pure meetings during the day. Hang out, drink, have fun and spread chaos. There were always smaller meetings in cities such as Wuppertal, Essen, Bottrop, Dort-mund, Mülheim, Gelsenkirchen, Bochum, etc., where you drove. These meetings were usually announced by flyers or by word of mouth. (email correspondence, September 3, 2012)

What differentiated this later, Ruhr-based hardcore punk scene from the Düsseldorf one was the more open, radical political dimension, the harsher music, the DIY and autonomous production, and the cosmopolitan attitude that brought bands and scenes to network at the European and global scale. This will be taken more into account in chapters 5 and 6, about Torino and Tampere, where similar scenes were established.

5

TORINO

Torino was the first capital of Italy, an industrial city, a migration sanctuary, a divided city, a centre of capitalist power, and a city wounded by fascism and terrorism. But most of all, it has been the city of FIAT and therefore a one-company town.

Torino lies in the northeast of Italy and is the administrative capital of the Piedmont region. Historically, it was the first capital of unified Italy because it was the capital of the House of Savoia and the Savoia king under whose guidance the Risorgimento, the Italian unification process, took place and was ultimately accomplished in 1861. In 1865, Italy's capital passed to Florence and in 1871 to Rome. It is self-explanatory that the capital moved to Rome, both in historical and geographical terms.

During the nineteenth century, Torino was modernised into a capital: investors financed the construction of palaces, squares, and districts to lodge the royal family, administrators, ministers, embassies, secretaries and departments. Long-roofed pavements (*portici*) were built to provide shelters during the king's *passeggiate*. Equestrian monuments were erected around the city to signify power and wealth.

After the Italian government left Torino, the city needed new means of economic stability and development. A few years after losing capital-city status, in 1899, a group of noblemen, financiers, and landowners, including Giovanni Agnelli, established FIAT, *Fabbrica Italiana Automobili Torino*. Agnelli took over the ownership of the company and established himself as a major industrialist in Italy. In 1906 and 1912 he visited the Ford plant in Detroit, and between 1916 and 1922 the architect Giacomo Matté Trucco built the Lingotto in an open area in the southern fringes of Torino. The five-storey factory followed the functional rules of Taylorism, with each floor accomplishing a full cycle of production, ending with a spectacular test track at the top of the building (Levra 2001).

Torino, together with Milan (Foot 2001) and a few smaller centres, became the place where Italian industrialism and entrepreneurship developed. At the same time, the workers movement started its long fight for the improvement of working and living conditions in Torino, with Antonio Gramsci as the best-known intellectual participating and studying this process.

During the fascist regime, FIAT built a second industrial complex, even more to the south of the city: Mirafiori. FIAT workers were among the fiercest opponents to the regime, and several strikes were conducted in Mirafiori, especially in 1943.

During the economic boom after the Second World War, FIAT developed into one of the major industrial concerns in Italy, employing skilled and unskilled labour. FIAT attracted herds of citizens from the south and from the east of the country to Torino, deeply affecting its urban development and the composition of its population. In 1951 the population of the city was approximately 720,000, and ten years later it reached one million (Tranfaglia 1999). This vertiginous increase is a typical trend of a booming industrial city and occurred in various centres in Europe, but rarely did it happen so late in history. This sudden migration brought the city almost to pre-modern conditions: many immigrants were lodged in huts, shelters, and military barracks on the fringes of the FIAT Mirafiori and Lingotto factories. Many simply alternated sleeping in the same bed, according to the factory shifts, in overcrowded and poorly suited attics in the city centre, or they slept on benches in railway stations.

The municipality was forced to quickly solve this overcrowding and provide decent housing for the workers and their families in close proximity to the factories. From the 1960s on, workers were moved to mono-functional blocks of flats, set along rows of single houses built in peripheral wasteland, especially in the southern part of the city, even before asphalted roads could be completed or facilities and shops could settle. Several of my informants grew up in these districts. For instance,

Nerorgasmo's Simone Cinotto, in a phone interview on September 17, 2015, referred to his family history and to the acquisition of a single-family house:

> It was a great shock when my dad said, 'Well, there are some single houses in cooperatives, they don't cost much, we get one, I want to have an house' . . . he brought us in this very remote place, in a district called Mirafiori Nord, that didn't even exist at the time, it was like in the Celentano song ['*Il ragazzo della Via Gluck*', a song about fast urbanisation in Milan], there was this huge block, with a Roma camp facing it . . . there were very lower middle-class people getting their own house for the first time and then there was plenty of social housing on the other side of the main street, with these guys that punched us up, they were really daft, they were displaced from the derelict housing in the centre and they were moved there. . . . I only wanted to run away. (original in Italian; author's translation)

Although living conditions improved considerably in these modern flats, social problems, vandalism, and unrest appeared. What Simone recounted from his childhood happened only a few years after the release of Luchino Visconti's film *Rocco e i Suoi Fratelli* (1960) and Pier Paolo Pasolini's *Accattone* (1961) and the novel *Ragazzi di Vita* (1955) focused on the living conditions in the peripheries of Milan and of Rome, respectively. Both Visconti and Pasolini, in different ways and from different ideological perspectives, saw the quick step from rural to urban and from south to north, as a process that destroyed the sense of human solidarity and the values and rituals attached to the old rural world. Quick urbanisation and the creation of social housing in empty areas, in in-between spaces, which were neither urban nor rural, were also perceived as alienating and as increasing the feeling of eradication. However, the aesthetic emphasis on these aspects and on these particular environments also corroborated their romanticisation and the projections of the directors' desires, fears, and inner worlds.

Nevertheless, in Torino, people from the southern regions of the country had to deal with racist attitudes, and coming from rural areas, they had to adapt hastily to the big-city life of anonymity and coldness. The city developed a sort of dualism between middle-class and working-class areas, with citizens often living parallel lives. In particular, the area surrounding Mirafiori became slowly stigmatised; streets like Via

Artom or Via Millelire were known even outside the city, thanks to the echoes in the media that vandalism, petty crime, and drug consumption were causing (Foot 2001, 138).

YEARS OF LEAD

In 1968 and 1969, concomitant with student revolts, some of the workers started politicising; strikes and demonstrations increased. The unions became powerful interlocutors in reclaiming workers' rights. This politicisation was radicalised in the 1970s, often leading to violence and terrorism. Torino became one of the main stages of Italian *Anni di Piombo* (years of lead). The 1970s, especially from 1977 to 1979, were among the most violent years the city had ever experienced. Left-wing terrorist groups such as the Brigate Rosse and Prima Linea settled in Torino. The Brigate Rosse's first actions were in Milan, but it is in Torino that they founded their executive committee. Judges, journalists, politicians, policemen, classified as class enemies, were executed in bars, on the streets, at bus stops, and in other public places. Normal citizens died, caught in violent confrontations between police and political terrorists. Special laws were passed to increase police rights to search and arrest. Throughout the end of the 1970s, political groups demonstrated on weekends in the centre, claiming their own right to the city, inspired by the work of French radical thinkers such as Henri Lefebvre. Often these demonstrations ended in confrontations with political enemies and the police; riots were common, where Molotov cocktails, tear gas, weapons, and wooden sticks were used. The perception of danger in those years changed massively in the city, and many citizens retreated into the privacy of their homes or gathered in citizens associations. The fact that a big wave of arrests took place also corroborated the feeling of a city under siege. Moreover, Torino's tribunal was chosen as the site for the first trial against the Brigate Rosse, which started in May 1976 and lasted until 1978. The army was often called to monitor areas surrounding justice halls and prisons, while terrorists went loose and attacked lawyers, journalists, and other 'enemies of the people'.

The global automobile industry and oil crises also meant an increase in unemployment. On September 8, 1980, FIAT announced that it was laying off 14,469 workers and putting 24,000 in *cassa integrazione* (a wage-guarantee, redundancy-pay fund); on September 10, 1980, a major strike began, with the support of students, intellectuals, and the *Partito Comunista Italiano* (PCI, Italian Communist Party). On October 14, 1980, a planned assembly of white-collar workers turned into a demonstration through the streets of the centre of Torino, protesting against the blue-collar workers. It will go down in history as the *Marcia dei Quarantamila* (March of the Forty Thousand), although the real number of participants is disputed. On October 15, the strike ended, without any agreement among the opposing parties. In the following years workers were obliged to retire early, leave their job in exchange of a 'golden handshake' or be put on redundant funds for years. There were 149 suicides officially registered among those who couldn't bear the moral stigma of being non-workers in a city where a work ethic was everything. Heroin also began to affect poorer districts and other areas, including some areas of the centre, with the corollary of criminality typical of its consumers.

The monumental *Storia di Torino* reveals some of the major features of these conflict-ridden times. A major contributor to the work, Nicola Tranfaglia, notes that from 1973 to 1981 there were more than a thousand violent attacks and confrontations and twenty-four victims of terrorism (Tranfaglia 1999, 43).

The author also reveals some local specificities within the years of lead:

> Among Italian cities, Turin, is, not by chance, one of the most hit by the terrorists offensive, because it has been the site of a long and hard industrial conflict, where extra-parliamentary groups played, in the 1970s, an important role, and also because it is the site of the biggest private company in Italy, a decisive piece of the economic and political power system of the peninsula. The wounds opening in those years in the city's fabric are serious and have left painful scars: it will take time before they can at least partly heal. (Tranfaglia 1999, 44)

In addition, many terrorists were able to stay visible and menacing:

> The city is shocked and increasingly scared by the series of ambushes, murders and wounding, also because murderers seem to

escape being arrested and many of them—witnesses will confirm this—wander the city or its surroundings as if they do not fear arrest. (Tranfaglia 1999, 836)

The city of Torino, just like Italy as a whole, survived the years of lead through an effective strategy for isolating terrorism; at the same time, secret services and the police were allowed to use sometimes illegal and anti-humanitarian methods, and special laws, such as the *41bis*, a particularly hard prison regime, were passed.

FIAT survived the automobile crisis of the early 1980s only thanks to major cuts in human capital and to the substitution of Fordist production with a more flexible and automatised organisation of work (Lerner 2010). The Lingotto factory plant closed; it had been built according to Fordist strategies of production and was therefore physically unsuitable for the needs of the new flexible organisation of work. Many other small and medium factories, working in connection to FIAT (the so called *indotto*) had to close, and manufacturing clusters, scattered around the city, became dilapidated.

Nonetheless, today the city of Torino is still partly functioning as an industrial city. Visiting the gigantic Mirafiori plant gives a sense of real and uncompromising industrialism. The plant materially producing only one car model, but it is one of the headquarters for the Fiat Chrysler Automobiles (FCA) group, and several former buildings have been reconverted to host new economical or educational concerns.

The radicalisation of youth movements, students and workers, the strong police repression, the madness of terrorism, the economic crisis and deindustrialisation all left scars in the urban tissues, in the mental stability of many, and in the perception of safety and danger in the public space.

CENTRI D'INCONTRO

Diego Novelli, a journalist for the left-wing newspaper *L'Unità*, was elected mayor of Torino after the *Partito Comunista Italiano* and *Partito Socialista Italiano* won the elections in June 1975, and he maintained his position over a decade. His administration wanted, on the one hand, to maintain a peaceful coexistence with the industrial concerns and, on the other, to stop real estate speculation and to solve the problems that citizens were facing in their everyday life, ranging from housing to transportation (Tranfaglia 1999, 831).

Novelli brought new and positive vitality into the city youth and local activism as well. This was effective for fighting radicalisation, criminality, and social isolation (De Sario 2009). Novelli was operating with a clear leftist approach, trying as much as possible to provide the same services, facilities, opportunities, and activities to all inhabitants, without spatial discrimination, but also not focusing on individual or subcultural needs. For instance, he developed the so-called *centri d'incontro* (meeting centres), district-based social centres, run by social cooperatives, where young and older people found spaces to practice hobbies or play recreational activities, ranging from music to theatre, from sport to handicraft. Often, these centres had a rehearsal space for bands. Together with the *Punti Verdi* (green hotspots) and the *Estate Ragazzi* (youth summer), these actions were very much connected to a socialist welfare view on citizen well-being, probably inspired by similar experiences in both Germanies and in other socialist and Nordic countries. At the same time, they were implemented to fight political radicalisation, keep young people busy with 'healthy' activities, and maintain a degree of solidarity and cooperation among citizen of all ages and social groups. As we will see, one of these *centri d'incontro* became the place where the punk music scene could develop.

PUNK POLITICS

The Düsseldorf punk scene could not be fully understood if not in connection to the city's art scene, as seen in the previous chapter; Torino, on the other hand, would be impossible to understand, without considering its strong legacy from the confused political season known in Italian history as the *Movimento del 77*. This complex political movement, positioned on the extreme Left, developed in Italy with various local contingencies and ramifications, in the mid- to late 1970s. The *Movimento* was an expression of a new understanding of political life that focused on individual needs and subjectivities, more than on collective, organised action (Bottà and Quercetti 2019), and that was influenced by the French radical and post-structuralist thought. For instance, squatting began to be practised, partly as a solution to real estate speculation and partly as anti-patriarchal and anti-authoritarian cohabiting. The so-called proletarian shopping and urban rioting were also common practice. However, terrorism and political violence took its toll on the *Movimento*, which dispersed and was dismantled in the early 1980s. The so-called *Riflusso* left many individuals to search for something else. For some, it was heroin; for some, ecological activism; and for some, punk.

For instance, Mara Caberlin, from Contrazione, in a phone interview in Italian on April 22, 2011, told me about being drawn towards punk in these terms:

> In the beginning I wasn't a punk, I came from the 1977 movement, I was really into something else, but slowly, if I wanted to communicate . . . no one was doing anything at the time, I thought, well it's time to do something, and I sort of started folding my sleeves, I was never interested in the Sex Pistols, I was of course into that kind of disruption, that kind of communication. (author's translation)

Also, Stefano Giaccone, of Franti, in a telephone interview in Italian on March 24, 2011, referred to the early 1980s as 'very difficult years for Torino and also for Italy; they were the years of the big arrests, of the so-called end of politics. I came from the extreme Left, but I was not involved in too ugly stories by choice but also for luck, because you also needed luck in those years,' (author's translation). Stefano also referred to a 'generational bridge, which was also a practical and a musical one, between us, coming from the *Circoli del Proletariato* and from *Movimento del 77* down to what in 1982–1983 would be the first punk collectives in Italy and the first squats' (interview, 2011).

These accounts show the excitement in discovering punk as 'alternative cultural space', which 'served as a medium for agency; it stirred people to act. It could, moreover, be used in different ways' (Worley 2017, 46–47). Punk in Torino became for some a political medium and a continuation, with other means, of *Movimento del 77* action:

> The square was not working anymore, in the square you got beaten up, you got arrested, the usual channels, for instance leaflets, seemed worn out, nothing was working anymore, radios were already institutionalising themselves and so . . . trying to put the contents we be-

lieved in into a cultural activity we found ourselves side by side with
some people, younger people, different from many point of views,
but similar in method, doing things starting from yourself, from your
condition, and trying to run the things you live with your own hands
and conveying political contents. One thing that really impressed me
of punks was that often lyrics were like leaflets, what we used to
shout in demonstrations, that then turned mostly into football
hymns, or all what we used to write in leaflets, these guys so much
younger than us, often ten years younger, they were shouting from a
stage and sometimes in a very provocative way. (Picciuolo 1994)

This older group of people got in contact with a younger generation,
still involved in higher or technical education, whose idea of music
making was much more connected to defying boredom or shocking the
average citizens.

For instance, Roberto 'Tax' Farano, of Negazione, said in a phone
interview in Italian on March 12, 2011,

[the year] 1982 for me means approaching music, because something
was burning inside and you wanted to do something else than what
you saw around you, people were bored, they did nothing or they
were taking drugs heavily or were completely used to nothing-
ness. . . . I remember in 1980, at fourteen years old, I saw the
Ramones for the first time, and I started listening to music in a
certain way and then at sixteen, in 1982, I was already playing in a
band, Quinto Braccio [fifth row, the special prison row for political
prisoners], so quite active. (author's translation)

Youngsters were discovering the liberating potential of power chords
and feedback, as shown for instance in *I Ragazzi del Mucchio*, a fictional portrayal of those years by Silvio Bernelli, of Declino (Bernelli 2009).
Yet Torino was going through a radical process of deindustrialisation
that some of the youths consciously or unconsciously felt. In a May 12,
2011, interview in Italian, in Torino, Antonio De Rossi, from Contrazione, told me,

It was a crisis, a sort of city implosion, I thought this had a lot to do
with us, in a bit of a rhabdomancy, in a bit of an artistic way, it was
not something that a bunch of fifteen-year-olds can theorise concep-

tually; it was something felt and done through our bodies, our lives, our music. (author's translation)

Contrazione was among the most political bands of this era and at the same time created continuities with the past, both in terms of political action and in cultural articulations of the economic crisis.

VOGLIAMO UN POSTO! LOOKING FOR A PLACE

Transcribing the interviews with my informants in Torino, it became very clear that the scene had an obsession, if not a real fetish, for a *posto*, a place. Even one of the earliest A4 posters, announcing a punk gig 'against urban desperation', carries the sentence *'vogliamo un posto!'* (we want a place). A place meant a safe space, run autonomously in DIY fashion, where bands could rehearse and play and where political actions could be organised and carried out, ranging from organising boycotts to printing out record sleeves.

If the *Movimento del 77* was interested in reclaiming the city centre and subverting the capitalist mechanisms behind its planning and life, in public, the punk scene was more interested in looking for a secluded and safe space at the margins.

The earliest meeting point for punk-interested youth was Bar Roberto, a shabby bar on Via Po, near the university, frequented by a mix of students, fashion victims, and heroin addicts. Piazza Statuto was the public space where various subcultural groups met. Mods, for instance, had their own place in the square; later on, heavy metal fans started gathering there.

Punks had also their own 'turf', noted Nerorgasmo's Simone:

> Piazza Statuto is basically a corner of the centre [which is a rectangle delimited by four main roads], and on a side of the square, where you find the taxis, there is a small piece of land with two benches and some trees, and we spent hours there, whole days sitting on the benches. (interview, 2015)

The square lends itself naturally as a meeting point because it is a node for several modes of transportation—trams and buses, for instance—

from the more peripheral areas in particular. The bus itself became for some punks a performance space. Simone continues,

> Torino was the greyest and most conformist city in Europe, I think it was the same in Milano and Bologna, but here you felt it more, there was this hood of bad luck, blue-collar/white-collar city and there was nothing much, we were a disruptive presence. The bus and the tram were our theatre because you are enclosed in a small space, people cannot run, cannot leave, cannot avoid looking at you. (interview, 2015)

Another central place was the Rock&Folk record shop, which played an important role. Declino's Silvio Bernelli described it, in an interview in Italian on May 11, 2011, in Torino:

> It was a fantastic shop because the owner once confessed to me that he bought at least one copy of any independent record coming out in the United States, from the most experimental to hardcore punk or new folk or whatever genre, and this has led to the fact that in Torino you find fantastic record collections . . . and this has been very important also for the local radio scene, which created the best national radio disc jockeys, like Alberto Campo, Renato Striglia, Paolone Ferrari. (author's translation)

These places represented the typical youth territories; hanging out outside a bar or a record shop, sitting on a bench or in a tram are very much central to the performativity of punk and to the symbolic territorialisation of any subculture.

A real *posto*, seditious and secluded enough, was found through the mediation of the *Movimento del 77* survivors with the members of a small anarchist circle on Via Ravenna, close to the Porta Nuova railway station:

> In '82 Via Ravenna started, thanks to the people Sergio [singer of Quinto Braccio and Contrazione] and I knew; we were in the scene, it gave some kind of warranty, although anarchists don't need warranties, but we were eager to make things happen and we needed a place. (Mara/Contrazione, interview, 2011)

Basically, a small circle of anarchists understood punks as comrades because of the circled *A*s worn on their sleeves, and allowed them to meet on their own premises. The small group of anarchist punks decided to call themselves and organise initiatives under the moniker 'Collettivo Punx Anarchici'. 'Punx' with an *X* instead of 'punks' was chosen to differentiate themselves from the others. For instance, Negazione's Tax referred to the fact that 'there was another group that was more nihilist and goliardic that considered us too boring and too serious and not punk enough in their own sense' (phone interview, 2011).

Simone, of Nerorgasmo, a member of the so-called nihilist or fun punks, admitted with a certain regret that

> we were really allergic to serious politics, even if not party-related or whatever, we were really allergic to this kind of discourses, we were . . . we were very bound to the street, to shocking the average citizen. Doing politics means having meetings, a place to meet in a dimension that . . . I have absolutely nothing against that, going back I would have done it differently, because you learn more through that than to hang around like a dimwit, but I noticed that only later. (interview, 2015)

The people participating in the Via Ravenna weekly meetings ranged, according to Negazione's Marco Mathieu, 'from twenty to fifty people, sometimes even more' (phone interview, February 19, 2011, in Italian, translated by the author) and activities ranged from boycotting the Municipal Transportation Agency in name of free public transports, to gigs. Continued Marco, 'There were all these elements that could be gathered under political militancy, but it was not only that, musical scene, but it was not only that, urban subculture, but it was not only that, because it was a mix of all of the above' (interview, 2011). Of course, the relation between the older generation, which had gone through the years of lead, and the new generation, which was more interested in musical expression, was sometimes problematic, and Via Ravenna was also a place where conflicts rose. Said Tax,

> Already inside that group of people, when we had to organise a gig, there were huge discussions about the fact that a gig is useless, we have to organise something where we deepen our position—I am talking about the older ones—me and the others, we were more like

yes, right, we are here with our circled *As* and everything but we also want to have fun, get drunk, and play distorted fast music and scream this rage we have, but also have a laugh. (interview, 2011)

The second relevant place for the scene is the *centro d'incontro* in the peripheral district of Vanchiglia, Via Lungo Dora Colletta 51. I already referred to the institution of district-based social centres, run by cooperatives under the mandate of Diego Novelli. Nearly all anarchist punk bands started rehearsing in that particular *centro*. One the educators/operators in Vanchiglia was Sergio, singer of Quinto Braccio and Contrazione, and slowly his presence convinced bands to rehearse there.

As Gianpiero Capra, of Contrazione, recalled in a phone interview on March 18, 2011,

> One of us was an educator/operator there, there was an opening, the chance to have total permission to do things. That brought us out of the discos, a very important step. The space consisted of a rehearsal space, a room two-by-two metres square, with a drum kit and a mini PA. Il Collettivo, Il Declino, early Negazione, and early Contrazione rehearsed there . . . and a place to have gigs, a big room. I think there were five or six gigs there, a very important one with MDC from San Francisco. . . . It was a good thing, at the time we were trying not to compromise and theoretically we shouldn't have been there because it was run by the municipality, but it was a smart compromise allowing us to spend time together, to go from zero to one, when you go from zero to one it is better than nothing, from there we moved to much more extemporary situations until 1987, when El Paso was squatted.

Moreover, Tax reported, the place 'was also a meeting place on Saturday afternoon, you just went there or in the park next to it, *La Piola* and you drank some wine, things like that' (interview, 2011).

Marzio 'Mungo' Bertotti, of Declino, in an interview in Italian (Torino, May 13, 2011), also described how Vanchiglia represented an incredible creativity incubator, where music making was a social, collective, nearly democratic action, based on immediate feedback and response:

All songs on Declino records, of Negazione until their second EP, were born in a context with about ten to fifteen people present in the rehearsal space and they were not only listening to the songs, they could start laughing or pogo dancing or jumping and the songs were songs that not only you and the band liked; that was a socialising moment. (author's translation)

The Collettivo Punx Anarchici organised several gigs in Vanchiglia, each with a particular subject reported as a title on the posters and with a line-up of several bands and no headliners; leaflets with political messages were printed and distributed on the occasion of the gig to clarify and gain awareness for the political message. Not only the punk crowd attended the gigs; many other youngsters in Torino were looking for something to do. Silvio Bernelli told me,

Collettivo started organising these gigs and they were crowded, in the city there was nothing going on, no one knew the bands that were playing, they were teenagers, but we were still going on stage in front of four, five, six hundred people. At this famous gig, I don't remember, I think in February 1983, with MDC, a band from San Francisco, there were nearly a thousand people there, I can say it with conviction because it was me who took care of the accounting and I remember that dividing the final sum for the price of the ticket I got exactly 720—which means that 720 people paid the full price, so let's say that approximately eight hundred to nine hundred people had been there. (interview, 2011)

This gig was seen for many as a turning point; the American band was fast and furious and provided to the local youth new means to express anger and at the same time determination in musical choices. However, Vanchiglia also hosted non-DIY shows and a poster that resurfaced online reveals how a 1984 *Fuga da Vanchiglia* (1984 escape from Vanchiglia) three-day festival included heavy metal, reggae and new wave bands along with something called *video discoteca* and comedy film projections, revealing how the *centro d'incontro* was not exclusively in punk hands.

TORINOISE: COLLECTIVE RECORDED MUSIC

Initially, the music of the Collettivo circulated on compilation cassettes, copied at home, with black-and-white photocopied inlay cards. For instance, Nasty, a key initial figure in Torino punk released the tape *Torinoise* in 1981 in connection with his fanzine *Ansia*. The tape included DIY/homemade recordings and punk bands such as Ivan Siberia, Fiori del Male, No-Strani, Rough, Blue Vomit, Negative Vibrations, Chain Kids, and Nuclear Code. The fanzine *Disforia* released *Torino 198X* (1983), which included tracks from Blue Vomit, Kollettivo, Declino, C.B.A., Quinto Braccio, Kina Punk, and D.D.T.; and *L'Incubo Continua* (1983), with songs by Kollettivo, Cracked Hirn, Obiezione, Hyxteria, Negazione, Crash Box, Underage, and Olivop. The majority of *Torino 198X* recording happened in the Vanchiglia rehearsal room where they could only fit the band and their instruments, 'all cramped, and you can hear it in the recording, it is all uaaah, huge feedback, where there should be stops, there is feedback' (Simone/Nerorgasmo, interview, 2015).

It is, however, with the publication of Declino's EP in 1983 that the *Collettivo* achieves the production of its first (and last) collective effort. The informal group self-financed and produced the EP with the earnings from gigs and created a label *Contro Produzione Dischi* for the occasion. Oliver, of the band Kollettivo, helped with the mixing and the recording. Sergio Tosato, of Quinto Braccio, drew the cover, representing a very simple streetscape dominated by the coldness of what looks like functionalistic architecture, while in the middle of the street a burning white flag hangs on a broken pole. On the back of the cover there is a message signed by Punx Anarchici Torino, while on the inner sleeve there is a long statement signed by the band, and the lyrics.

The final product combines a 7" vinyl record with a thick booklet that articulates the political context for the music production. Crass was the first band to conceive the record as a multimedia product, where messages were not only conveyed by the music, the tracklist, and the cover but also by accompanying texts, pictures, prints, graphics, useful addresses, and contacts. This is, of course, not new: classical and jazz records often contain texts with historic and biographical portraits, comments by highly respected critics, and technical tips to the listener; nonetheless the aims of punk meta-elements were not to accompany the music but to justify and ground its production into a more complex and networked alternative and independent system.

SOUNDS LIKE TORINO

A music scene chronicles and negotiates itself through conflict, imitation, self-regulation, and creation in particular places. Places define a scene, and it is in them that a scene gathers regularly and where it recognises itself as a scene; however, sometimes we mistake the places in themselves as scenes (Straw 2001, 1991). This is what makes Via Ravenna and Vanchiglia so central to this chapter and in informants' narrations. However, far more important in terms of a music scene is determining the existence and the definition of a certain sound associated with it. As I have already stated in the introduction, the idea of a sound, and specifically of an industrial sound, is something that extends beyond the mere aural dimension and includes, along with sounds, images, lyrics, narratives about these, and the emotional dimension, the affect connected to them (see the introduction and chapter 1). In the interviews, I detected two main discourses, which sometimes meet and sometimes are kept separated in relation to the soundscape. The first is an affective one and defines the sound of Torino as dominated by desperation and sadness. For instance, Contrazione's Antonio tells how

> the ones from Turin were deeply depressed, in a crazy way . . . this idea of no future, here maybe truer than elsewhere, coincided with a total crisis of the urban industrial system, of a life model and *Weltanschauung*, upon which Torino had built its fortune and its development throughout the twentieth century. (interview, 2011)

Mara, of Contrazione, refers to a 'huge rage and a huge will to get out . . . because we were young and we could not live like that, we had to explode, get out and let others understand what we wanted' (interview, 2011). Her bandmate Gianpiero refers to the same gloomy emotional dimension:

> Talking about sound, there was something sadder, yes, sadder, I wouldn't say more depressive, but more desperate than the others. The scene in Tuscany was nasty but also sunnier, the Milanese scene

was very hard but also not taking it too seriously, the scene in Torino was really desperate, it was real desperation, if you want a more recent comparison Nirvana are more similar to something from Torino, you can feel Cobain's desperation, it was that thing, in that moment. (interview, 2011)

This desperation is partly explained through the real presence of deindustrialisation, partly connected to musical choices. For instance, Antonio, also a bandmate, programmatically wrote songs, looking at intervals of 4th dim, because 'they were as strident as possible' (interview, 2011), while Gianpiero associates this sound to Negazione's Tax 'playing only two strings at a time as chords, so a very low sound, without the higher strings, very hard, very gloomy and very compact' (interview, 2011). Tax himself also thinks in terms of noise, although he reads it as an involuntary one:

> Feedback makes me think of Torino . . . you had a guitar that sucked, the cable too, you plugged into an amp used already by ten other bands and what did you want to do? You wanted to smash everything, so you pulled up the volume and you had feedback. (interview, 2011)

Only a couple of them refer to the articulation of real industrial city sounds, which might be the second main discourse. For instance, Marco, of Negazione, talked to me about a 'translation of the factory rhythm in something liberating, but also very dark' (2011). In reference to Negazione's hit single 'Tutti Pazzi', Simone, of Nerorgasmo, says,

> I wouldn't have been able to say it like this at the time, but it was really the sound of the tram on the tracks, of the warehouse, of the bus starting up before leaving the terminal in this wasteland covered in snow in January . . . on the first day snow was white, but on the second it was already black, there was this black coat that looked painted with tar, and I had to walk my way home from the terminal and there was this snow, plus the danger of being attacked by the chavs that lived around there and let's say that my music reproduced all of this. (interview, 2015)

Declino's Silvio, on the other hand, says,

> I don't think that there is a sound, but there is an attitude behind the
> sound that could be the fact that being born and growing up in a city
> so full of disadvantages and so difficult obliged you to do your best.
> (interview, 2011)

Others also emphasise the technical skills of Torino bands and the origi-
nality of certain individual musicians. It is sure that there is nothing
related to a certain recording studio, like the MLS in Tampere, to the
work of a producer, like Martin Hannett in Manchester, or to certain
design-based aesthetics, as in the case of Factory Records in Manchester or Der Ratinger Hof in Düsseldorf. Everything seems to work on
the simple level of affect and emotional response to a certain industrial
and urban environment. This gives us the chance to examine the definition of the Torino sound more in relation to its actual musicscape than
in relation to its articulation with extramusical elements.

For instance, sadness and doom saturate the textscape of Torino.
Words like *tristezza* (sadness), *amaro* (bitter), *incubo* (nightmare),
morte (death), *nero* (black), *disperazione* (desperation), *nausea, chiuso*
(shut), *repressione* (repression), *angoscia* (angst), *ansia* (anxiety), *op-
pressione* (oppression) and *pazzia* (madness) occur in several song titles, across bands and recordings. The use of this terminology is reminiscent in some cases of the *Movimento del 77* slogans and imaginary
and is therefore political in nature; however, it also shows how deep
deindustrialisation had gone:

> The city grew like a wildfire, it took up hundreds of thousands of
> people in a very short time and got to the 1970s still full of energy, I
> remember this city with a huge energy, there was such violence . . . ,
> there was political fight, in each district there was this vital violence
> that was incredible in the 1970s; then terrorism appears, heroin ap-
> pears, and all that mechanism that from the economic upswing gets
> to the 1970s suddenly in two, three years, decades . . . all the pieces
> fall apart . . . like an implosion. I didn't conceptualise this thing, it
> was too close, but we felt it strongly in our lives. (Antonio/Contrazi-
> one, interview, 2011)

Very unusual for music produced in this era is the presence of songs
directly addressing Torino. This, for instance, did not happen in Manchester and Tampere. Declino talked about the city as 'not so middle
class and not so working class / once royal now decadent' where people

'feel derided / for their broken dreams to pile up money / but the robot doesn't rebel and start dreaming once again'.[1] Negazione wants to 'overthrow the pride for your cars' and 'destroy the happiness of your Sundays'.[2]

Still, Negazione on *Mucchio Selvaggio*, a split cassette with Declino, develops a song on the basis of real local crime news. 'Omicida 357 Magnum' tells of a road rage episode turning into a gun murder; the tense guitar riffs of Tax and the voice of Zazzo interpreting the cold, journalistic prose of the real article and developing a mini cinematic epos of metropolitan anger. Contrazione's lyrics were a mix of *Movimento del 77* political slogans, social realism, and expressionism. For instance, 'Metropoli' starts with an expressionist anthropomorphism, the metropolis squirming because of state violence, repression, and computers and a narrating I, fed up with having no future. 'A Sud di Torino' (to the south of Torino) starts with a spoken word: 'FIAT Lingotto . . . A district built around a factory. The factory closed; a sleeping district remains; a ghetto built for their survival not for yours'[3] (Contrazione 2006).

From the point of view of the landscape, the visual dimension, bands tend to work with the little they had, in DIY fashion, through collages, simple hand drawings and stencilled fonts. Iconic is, for instance, the cover of Negazione's first EP, *Tutti Pazzi* (1984). The cover is dominated by a black-and-white picture of a punk sitting on the ground next to a trash bin. The trash bin is a typical piece of Italian functionalist urban design, minimalist and cheap in build, adopted in several Italian cities in the 1970s. Blue Vomit also featured the same object, although with someone with their head in it, for one of their posters. The punk, in the iconic black leather jacket and Chuck Taylor shoes, leans his head in his arms, expressing sadness or madness. Behind him, just partly visible, a parked car subconsciously brings back the notion of the one-company town.

Tax recalled,

> I think, it was me who took that picture, and I remember that we went to the south of the city, to Lingotto, close to where Zazzo was living, there are other pictures where we are searching for a place like that, we wanted to homage, I don't know if you know Minor Threat, with him with the head like that, it is a bit the idea of desperation, the classic theme of you, desperate, with a million different

things in your head and willing to change the world and the rest of
the world hates you. (interview, 2011)

MUSIC AS *PUBLIZITÄT* FROM BELOW

The 'public' should be always understood in its spatial dimension. Following Jürgen Habermas's classic definition of *Öffentlichkeit*, 'public
realm' relates to the discursive action of civil society legitimising the
state (Habermas, Lennox, and Lennox 1974). In addition, it is commonly accepted that the negotiation of identities and shared meanings always happens in public. Also, the term has legal and economic connotations, as shown by the ongoing debates surrounding economic crises,
public expenditures, and state bankruptcies around Europe. Nonetheless, it is *on the street* that all these features of the public materialise,
coexist, and come together.

Public and private unfold themselves and should always be understood in space. As Doreen Massey (1984) points out, social relations are
always spatial; space and 'the social' are inextricable from each other.
Whenever we are talking about private and public, we are talking about
ways to define both social and spatial relations.

One of the main criticisms of the work of Habermas is connected to
the fact that a bourgeois public sphere has existed thanks to the sup-
pression/erasure of whatever was felt as threatening, different, or not
valuable, including categories such as women, the poor, the ethnic or
religious other (see, for instance, Fraser 1990, about gender). Not even
in the idealised setting of the Italian Renaissance piazza or classic Ath-
ens agora do we find a public sphere, which is 'a realm of our social life
in which something approaching public opinion can be formed' and
where 'access is guaranteed to all citizens' (Habermas, Lennox, and
Lennox 1974, 73). The notion itself of 'access' to the public realm has a
huge number of connotations, for instance, we can talk about it in
relation to education, physical ability, capital, ethnicity, sexual orientation, religion, gender, and age.

Also, privacy and the private realm, in opposition to that which is
public, has at least two very strong bourgeois connotations: it is inextri-
cably linked, on the one hand, to the gendered feminine domestic

sphere of the everyday (Felski 1999) and, on the other, to private property and greed, as brilliantly shown originally by David Harvey (2003).

The erosion of the public realm is a significant topic in contemporary urban studies, especially in research about surveillance and social control (Koskela 2010, 2006), and about social justice and the 'right to the city' (Mitchell 2003). Moreover, actions we are used to perform in public space, such as gathering, discussing, and socialising, are increasingly taking place in ambiguous real (malls and department stores) and virtual (social media) spaces, while our private sphere is continuously eroded by social media.

Torino in the 1980s was systematically organised as a Fordist city subordinated to industrial production. Public and private were clearly delimited. Private were home, the working place (factory), and the places of consumption (shops). Public were the places of leisure and encounter (parks, squares), places of transit (streets), and the institutions (churches, schools, hospitals, prisons). Deindustrialisation put this canonised distribution of public and private into question. The Collettivo Punx Anarchici rearticulated the private, vacant industrial spaces into public ones, both materially (by gathering in them) and at the imaginary level (by using them in pictures, lyrics, and sounds). However, they also occupied public spaces and made them 'private', winning them as subcultural territories. Their main aim was, however, the creation of a *posto*, as a 'counter-public realm from below' situated in music itself.

For instance, Maurizio Blatto, from the Backdoor record shop, reveals the feel of Torino as dominated by the presence of the *Avvocato* (lawyer), the nickname used to refer to Gianni Agnelli, at the time president of FIAT. The following is from a May 11, 2011, interview in Italian, in Torino:

> There was this real, true feeling that the Agnelli family owned the city; the *Avvocato* went home every evening by helicopter and you saw the helicopter, and the old ones, but also the young ones, were saying, 'There he goes, the *Avvocato*'. It was a clear sign, he governed you from above, you saw him flying by, and he was above you, and you could imagine that each rebellion there might have been, it could only have been directed towards the factory, towards FIAT. (author's translation)

These words show the complexity of the city's social relations and the cultural hegemony exerted by FIAT. In addition, it shows its nearly grotesque spatial articulation, where power is physically present, both visually and sonically, above you.

Another informant, Contrazione's Antonio, stated,

> I have working-class origins and it is not a joke, it is not common sense, that stuff was really like that, it was built on work shifts: 6:00 a.m., 2:00 p.m., and 10:00 p.m., the city was built around those rhythms. Sunday was the only day that these poor souls were able to do their things . . . that thing was a machine, and it was working really like a machine. (interview, 2011)

Interestingly, the economic capital cut through private and public: the city as a public realm was submitted to the power of a private company, which determined its whole rhythm and structure and pervaded its space. When this 'city as a machine' cracked, there were consequences for this hegemonic articulation of public and private. We could argue, for instance, that at the level of the private realm, the city experienced a shrinking of spaces of the industry, decay, and an increase of vacant lots and empty private properties. At the public level, the presence of un-employed people on the streets increased, together with strikes, dem-onstrations, and political conflicts.

Public space, especially in the centre, began to be affected negative-ly by this tension; people became more secluded and less eager to spend time in public spaces, as revealed by Gianpiero, also of Contrazi-one:

> Torino was straight into FIAT with the first tram in the morning, everything closed at 7:30 p.m., at 7:30 p.m. it was curfew, it was a very 1970s kind of feeling, when people really feared going out in those times . . . I lived on Via Turati, at Porta Nuova, in a student dormitory, and when I met my punk friends and then took the tram at 11:00 p.m. back to the dormitory, there was no one else on the tram, it was very strange. . . . You lived and breathed FIAT. (inter-view, 2011)

More and more people closed themselves into the private sphere. John Foot (2001), in his work about Milan, reveals how television became increasingly important, addressing the 1980s in particular. The sociologist Alberto Abruzzese explains the rise of the television set as ersatz for a public realm:

> The real step forward is in the 1980s, with the mixed system Rai-Fininvest. And here it is important to understand one thing: we are a country without a metropolis. This is the main difference with France, with England and with the other developed countries. The metropolis is a huge laboratory of social struggles and desires; it is a space, which is deeply soaked in communication, in visual culture and in visibility, a space which has not been experienced by Italians. We never had Paris, London, New York. . . . Television has been for a long time the new square. (Antonelli 2006)

Abruzzese put forward the idea of a re-framing of the public sphere into the private dimension, explaining it only in terms of the lack of the metropolitan. In my opinion, we could also connect it to the above-mentioned increasing insecurity in public places. The case of Torino shows how violent political confrontations, state control, a difficult integration of labour force from the south into the urban texture, and the concentration of workers into peripheral spaces, all collaborated in making television so powerful as a fake means of *Publizität* and gave way to the invasive power of commercial television and to the early construction of Berlusconi's media power monopoly.

Despite that, this new cultural hegemony of the television and this reframing of the public into the private couldn't, of course, 'exhaust the full range of human practice, human energy, human *intention*' (Williams 1977, 125).

For instance, the cover of Negazione's second EP, *Condannati a Morte nel Vostro Quieto Vivere* (condemned to death in your quiet life) is a drawing by Dumbo, who collaborated with various punk bands in the early 1980s. The picture shows a man sitting on a couch in his slippers, pointing a gun to his head and lifting his hand to hide himself, as if captured by the lens of a camera. In front of him there is a big television, and in the background, there is an entrance door. The setting is quite sparse, in a functionalistic way, reproducing the living room of many Italian families, with the television set as its dominating element. The EP title is reproduced on the wall, together with the band name in its recognisable fonts.

Criticism of television and of a lifestyle dominated by it is a trope of punk and hardcore punk music all around the world (see, for instance, 'TV Party', on the Black Flag LP *Damaged*). Its connotations within Torino are even more relevant because of the above-mentioned Italian-specific role television plays, and also because Italian public television broadcaster RAI was actually founded in the city in 1924 as URI (Unione Radiofonica Italiana).

This example reveals how the punk music scene in Torino was involved in creating what Negt defines as

> a proletarian public sphere, a public from below. The masses won't let themselves be regulated anymore; they don't let themselves be told that they are not angry. Rather, they engage in fusions, they form connections. In that sense, counter public for us is a process of igniting solidarity among people who might otherwise have very different ideas, about the question of foreigners, for example. And in that sense counter public is always its own process of learning, which sometimes may even have deadly consequences when, for example, something that could be seized is endangered by spontaneous unrest. I would like to emphasize the process character. The bourgeois public sphere in contrast is something like a pre-given foil. So the newspapers, the media are in this case the pregiven screen, which filter these experiences and often do not render them. (Krause 2006)

According to Negt and Kluge, it is exactly in 'historical fissures' that 'proletarian publicity' can originate and, since it is not a ruling public sphere, 'it has to be reconstructed from such rifts, marginal cases, isolated initiatives' (Negt and Kluge 1993, xliii).

A similar theorisation of counter-public sphere can be explored further by referring to subcultural research. In fact, the study of subcultures has always focused on territorialities and on public and private as porous definitions. The Chicago School, for instance, in its 'ecological' bias, showed an interesting use of map-based analysis when focusing on the distribution of immigrants, gangs, or hoboes in Chicago and elsewhere.

The Centre for Contemporary Cultural Studies in Birmingham also echoes the Chicago School insistence on territory; however, it tends to assign it a more positive role. According to Hall and Jefferson, subcultures 'win space for the young—cultural space in the neighbourhood and institutions, real time for leisure and recreation, actual room on the street or street corner. They serve to mark out and appropriate 'territory' in the localities' (Hall and Jefferson 2003, 45).

There is here a new understanding of the city. There is no longer a willingness to 'take over the centre', as in Lefebvre's writings about the right to the city, in the 1968 student movement, and in the more or less violent wave of demonstrations of the late 1970s. There is an attempt to take over and claim residual spaces as their own, something that is very difficult to describe with public/private dichotomies.

In some texts and declarations of these bands, it is possible at least to see an intuition of this process of 'making music a counterpublic realm', as here, for instance:

> Our attempt is to not get used to desperation and greyness, but to use the sounds, colours and life of a metropolis, coming everyday into our mind, as an incentive to build a ground for our life and our fight. Fight for the present, against heroin, nuclear energy or themes like informatics and telematics (that from possible moments for wider cultural divulgation will become instrumental to the aims of an increasingly technocratic society), with the conscience of living in an urban landscape like Turin, which shows every day, in increasingly tangible fashion, the symptoms of a progressive decomposition. CONTRAZIONE are for a music, which is not only a punch in the face, but also a moment of projection of our conscience. (Contrazione 1983)

At least in the beginning of the *Collettivo*'s activities, popular music becomes something else: it is no more a commodity, its value is not based on commercial strategy, it is not privately owned through copyright policies, which are constantly resisted by the bands, and it is distributed fairly through a democratic, non-commercial circuit.

Also in the context of live music, the barrier between band and public is definitely broken. Pictures from gigs show bands constantly surrounded and invaded by the audience, which is slam dancing, building the so-called human piles, doing sing-along and substituting the singer in refrains.

Content-wise there is also the attempt to deal with the historical fissures related to Torino as an industrial city in crisis, which will change at least partly its economic paradigm.

By taking into account the role of popular music production within the *Collettivo*, it is possible to determine how the practice of sounding out noise became the real public space. Crisis was an engine of change; it made people aware of possible innovative ways to articulate publicity from below and to question the cultural hegemony of the bourgeois public realm through cultural practice.

What the Collettivo Punx Anarchici Torino was articulating was a new oppositional and emergent perception and use of urban space, which was expressing itself in the sonic dimension through noise; through bodily practices such as pogo, human piles, stage diving; by squatting residual industrial space; by networking with other industrial cities; and creatively with fanzines, graffiti, leaflets, and manifestos. All this provided new definitions and rearticulations of private, public, commercial, antagonist, industrial, and vacant spaces.

NOTES

1. *Mortale tristezza in questa città / poco borghese e poco operaia / un tempo reale ora decadente si sente derisa / per i sogni svaniti di ammucchiare denaro / ma il robot non si oppone e riprende a sognare* (Declino, 'Mortale Tristezza'). Lyrics are reproduced with the permission of the band and are not subject to copyright.

2. *Noi rovesceremo l'orgoglio delle vostre automobili / noi distruggeremo la felicità delle vostre domeniche* (Negazione, 'Noi'). Lyrics are reproduced with the permission of the band and are not subject to copyright.

3. *FIAT Lingotto . . . Un quartiere costruito intorno a una fabbrica. Chiusa la fabbrica; rimane un quartiere dormitorio: Un ghetto costruito per la LORO sopravvivenza, non per la tua . . .* (Contrazione, 'A Sud di Torino'). Lyrics are reproduced with the permission of the band and are not subject to copyright.

6

TAMPERE

Känninen saundi, drunken sound, this is how Arto 'Lättä' Hyytiäinen, of Kohu 63, and Timo 'Lahti' Tammelin, of Bastards, describe the sound of their own city:

> *Lättä*: I would describe it as drunken sound, drunken mayhem.
> *Lahti*: We didn't play sober around here. . . . Not too artsy kind of stuff, well-played but not too focused on the irrelevant things.[1]

The two punk veterans, active in music since the late 1970s, put two interesting aspects on the table: on the one hand, the significance of intoxication, which I will explore later in this chapter; on the other, directness and rawness, which once again reaffirms one of the main industrial discourses considered in this book. The sound of Tampere is solid and deprived of any artiness, an uncompromised expression of anger, something that relies on craftsmanship but that at the same time avoids embellishments.

The city is known around the world, in hardcore punk and alternative music circles, for giving birth to extremely raw-sounding bands. In Brazil there is a curious and continuous following of punk music from Finland, which dates back to the mid-1980s and to some postal exchange of compilations on cassette (Ullvén 2016). This boreal fascination arising in the tropics was celebrated, for instance, by Max Cavalera, of heavy-metal band Sepultura, who sported a Kaos T-shirt in the video of 'Arise' (*Arise*, 1991), the single that consecrated the Brazilian band to world success. Wearing the T-shirt of an obscure band from

Tampere functioned to create a bond with the Brazilian hardcore punk scene, thereby enhancing the band's authenticity among independent circles in the face of a major label deal. Some bands from Tampere started touring Brazil in the 2000s after surprising confirmations of their underground fame in social media (Ullvén 2016).

Thurston Moore, guitar player and singer in the US noise band Sonic Youth, performed at the Helsinki Festive Weeks, a highbrow music festival, with Yoko Ono in August 2013. On that occasion, a journalist from the Finnish magazine *Suomen Kuvalehti* asked him if he knew about bands from Helsinki and about his feelings of being in Helsinki. He responded, 'Helsinki has always been my favourite, because at the beginning of the 1980s, hardcore bands really disarmed me. I wrote letters with the singer of Kaaos and also loved the 7" singles of Terveet Kädet and Bastards' (Numminen 2013).

Oddly enough, none of the bands mentioned by Moore are from cultural capital Helsinki: Terveet Kädet is from Tornio, while Bastards and Kaaos are from Tampere. It seems that Finnish hardcore punk has a particular reputation in underground circles, and Tampere plays a central role in it, especially for giving birth to the majority of bands involved in this particular scene.

As already seen in chapter 5, hardcore punk is stylistically both a simplification and intensification of punk, appearing in the late 1970s and early 1980s, concomitant with the so-called post-punk and also in many ways addressing deindustrialisation sonically and in terms of affect. Hardcore punk lyrics are mostly shouted instead of sung, guitar riffs are repetitive and fast, drumming is fast and based on tempos such as the so-called D-beat, and the general sound is harsh and compact. Often, reverb is abundantly used on drums and voice, asserting a sort of apocalyptic nuance to the mix. Lyrics are related to politics, anarchism, pacifism, state control, repression, and political and social unrest, inspired by world politics and the deindustrialisation of the 1980s. Bands such as Black Flag in the United States and Discharge in the United Kingdom originated this kind of sound, which spread especially in industrial cities around the world, such as shown previously by the case of Torino.

In early 1980s Tampere, the punk scene set the right environment for the development of some uncompromising hardcore punk bands, such as Kohu-63, Bastards, Riistetyt, Tampere SS, and Kaaos; however,

none of these bands were able to exit small, DIY punk circles within
Finland while sometimes being celebrated abroad. While previous
punk bands from Tampere quickly dismantled after the first punk wave,
or professionalised into commercial acts still active today, hardcore
punk bands followed tragicomical destinies, which mostly started and
ended in the Finnish industrial city by staying true to their initial rawness and spontaneity.

TAMPESTER/MANSE

Today, Tampere is the third largest municipality and second largest
metropolitan region of Finland and for a long time, parallel and in
rivalry with Turku, has played the role of 'second city' to the capital,
Helsinki. At the same time, it has always been the most important
industrial conurbation in the Nordic country, especially in relation to
textile and paper industries, and the largest inland municipality across
Scandinavia. Scottish businessman James Finlayson set his eyes on the
small village on the rapids of the Tammerkoski River in August 1819
and found in the natural environment a perfect site to open a textile
factory. The most successful textile company of the country still carries
his name.

   Also, thanks to state subsidies, during the first half of the nineteenth
century, the first modern factory building and the first paper machine
of the whole country, and the first electric light in all of Scandinavia
appeared in Tampere, showing that technological and industrial ad-
vancement has always been at the forefront in the development of the
small Nordic nation (Hietala and Kaarninen 2005). Swedish-speaking
Finnish author Zacharias Topelius first wrote in a footnote to his *A
Journey in Finland* that 'when Finlayson returned to Scotland in 1836,
the term "Manchester of Finland" had already begun to be used for
Tampere' (Topelius [1873] 2013). The nickname 'Manchester of Finland' has been carried with honour by the city throughout the centuries;
one of the city football teams, founded in 1998, is humorously called
Tampere United. Over the years the name has also been distorted in
the Finnish language as *Tampester* or *Tampesteri* and, most notably,
Manse. *Manse* is used colloquially in Finnish to refer to the city but
apparently is not commonly used in local dialect. There are only two

floor-ball teams, named, respectively, Manse United and Manse City in the city, and some local businesses use it as well, but local city branding practices stick to Tampere. The English place-name has been transformed into a Finnish-sounding nickname that has little to do with the official name of the city. Both 'Manchester of Finland' in Topelius's writings and the domestication into Manse seem to imply a labelling from above originating in the power site of the capital. This tension with the capital city, typical of any industrial city, has more sinister historical developments in Finland, especially in relation to its civil war, which erupted in the country in 1918, a year after it declared independence. During this war, Tampere acted as a fierce defender of the socialist red side, against the whites who eventually won and pacified the country. Thanks to its industrial connotations, Tampere has always been a city leaning politically towards the Left, and this is not just confirmed by its hosting the first Lenin Museum based outside the Soviet Union. The nickname Manse could therefore also be connected to the high turnover of workers moving to Tampere from surrounding rural areas and to their apologetic view of the big industrial town dominated by smoking chimneys.

MANSEROCK: CARNIVAL IN DULL-CITY

The most common use of the term *Manse* is in the compound noun Manserock. This label was first used in Finnish music in the summer of 1975, advertising a common tour of Tampere-based Coïtus Int. and Alwari Tuohitorvi. The label might have been a humorous attempt to attract attention to the two acts, and it might have been used before. In 1981, Juice Leskinen (the former singer of Coïtus Int.) published a song with the same title, stating cryptically that Manserock is a boy. Music critics used to refer to new rock bands with Finnish lyrics through terms such as *Härmärock* (which was preferred for bands from the provinces and rural areas) and *Suomirock* (Finland rock or Fennorock) (Skaniakos 2010).

Today, both *Suomirock* and Manserock are common labels to refer to mainstream popular music, sung in Finnish and produced in the period between the early 1970s and the late 1980s; however, the two point at different discourses. *Suomirock* stresses the nationalist role that popular culture took up in Finland, as in many European countries in the 1970s, and that represented a 'new wave' from the generational, ideological, and aesthetic point of view, where popular culture became an instrument for national cohesion and generational memory building. *Suomirock* works in many ways like *Neue Deutsche Welle* in labelling the sonic 'structure of feeling' of the late 1970s and early 1980s and in providing a national and linguistic frame of reference. In many ways, this label can also be understood as populist in nature because it seems to imply a univocal and coherent national-popular voice, the true spirit of national culture in that particular place and time.

Manserock, on the other hand, put a locality in the forefront and created a divide between the bands that were born or sought success in Tampere and the ones that were from elsewhere. The term assigns a certain aura to bands from this particular city; being from the 'Manchester of Finland' provided authenticity both in industrial and in popular music terms, as the northern English town can be associated with both.

There are several coexisting reasons for the centrality of Tampere in the development of a new wave of popular music, sung in Finnish, in the early 1970s. Some are to be found outside music, for instance, in the development of a student community after the foundation of a city university in 1960, which brought about the opening of student clubs and dormitories and the appearance of cafés and record and book shops. The city has also been traditionally associated with theatre, and there is a significant presence of well-known stages, companies, actors, and directors, but also technicians and light and sound engineers. The national television channel YLE 2 also has its premises in Tampere, turning the city into a significant media hub outside the capital region.

Music-wise, Epe's Music Shop and later Poko Records no doubt played a significant role. In 1972, Kari 'Epe' Helenius opened a record shop targeting the new generation of fellow music fans and popular culture enthusiasts with a unique, at the time, selection of imported records, especially from the United Kingdom and the United States. Aware of the fact that Tampere students alone could not bring in enough profits, he also started a mail order business (Aunola 2009). In the same year, Waldemar Wallenius produced the first issues of rock magazine *Musa*. In 1975, after some disagreements with the publisher, he left and created *Soundi*, which is currently the last surviving popular music magazine on paper in Finnish.

It is very difficult to find any reference to Tampere in the Manse-rock imaginary; early bands addressed Finnish youth as a whole in the name of what can be defined as an exhibited 'carnevalistic folklore' (Bakhtin 1984). Bakhtin referred both to carnival as primordial ritual and to carnivalistic literature as a genre with its own features. According to him, carnival has no distinction between spectators and performer; it rejects ordinary structures, hierarchies, and classes; and it enhances free and familiar contact among people. This determines the birth of misalliances and allows the blasphemies and profanities. Genre-wise, the carnivalistic introduces themes 'in a zone of immediate and even crudely familiar contact with living contemporaries' . . . 'the heroes of myth and the historical figures of the past are deliberately and emphatically contemporized' (Bakhtin 1984, 241). In addition, the carnivalistic doesn't rely on legend but on experience and free invention, rejecting stylistic unity.

Books and articles about Finnish popular music often describe Juice Leskinen as the central figure in Manserock. Juice moved to Tampere to study English translation in 1970 from the Savo rural region and formed the band Juice Leskinen y Los Coïtus Interruptus, later re-named Coïtus Int., with Mikko Alatalo, Max Möller, and Harri Rinne. Especially during this early Manserock era, carnivalism dominates Juice's lyrics: songs are naïve and familiar, but at the same time they use a tongue-in-cheek, postmodern attitude towards popular culture, singing about film stars, historical figures, American bands, characters from the Bible, and comic book heroes in common unassuming language, Juice's voice is mixed in front, and the lyrics are easy to understand. At the same time, references to obscure villages and small towns of the north, far away from the capital region and from Tampere, created a Finnish imaginary rural topography. The sound of the band is simple in comparison to contemporary progressive rock bands. Some tracks are pure 1960s rock and roll, others quote doo-wop or surf music, some are closer to acoustic folk music, and others to musical pieces. The mismatch between rock as a fairly recent import and these topographic references is humorous and it is a clear carnivalistic strategy encouraging laughter. Profanity can be also spotted in references to sex (in the band's name for instance, which had to be shortened from the initial

Coïtus Interruptus) and to alcohol consumption. In addition, Juice had a very common, nearly nerdy look, with long, thinning hair, plain clothes, and big glasses, sometimes sporting a bowler hat. Later Manserock bands from Tampere developed further along these lines, playing guitar-led rock and roll, always pulling out a humorous number and sporting simple everyday looks.

Manserock somehow expressed stability, optimism, and welfare, in a country that quickly modernised from its rural and agricultural beginnings. Tampere was, in the 1970s, a fully functioning industrial city with a dull routine of production. In addition, Finnish alcohol policy was based on monopoly and on strict regulations concerning licensing and serving in bars and pubs. However, some liberalisation took place thanks to the 1969 Alcohol Act, which expanded the presence of monopoly shops in rural areas and licensing in restaurants, allowed retail shops to sell medium beer (4,5 percent alcohol), and lowered the drinking age from twenty-one to eighteen (Beauchamp 1981).

Manserock provided, through carnivalistic folklore, an instrument to cope with industrialisation and urbanisation and an element of oddity into a highly regulated industrial everyday. True, it also did it by maintaining strong masculine structures, with all-male bands and lyrics that were often objectifying women. Finland was only slightly suffering from deindustrialisation, economic downturn, or radical restructuring in its employment policies, despite the global effects of the oil crises; in addition, there were few traces of political unrest in the neutral country and nothing that might have been called terrorism. The country will be seriously affected by an economic downturn much later, after the collapse of the Eastern Bloc.

PUNK IN FINLAND, PART ONE

The Finnish youth discovered and enacted punk as a cultural expression thanks to media exposure on TV and in music magazines. In and around Tampere, punk inspired the formation of several school bands. Some of these bands lasted the time of a gig or never left the rehearsal space; others such as Eppu Normaali (actually from Ylöjärvi, a neighbouring town) and Popeda are still active and among the most successful Finnish bands of all time. Bands such as Karanteeni, Kolla Kestää, and

Sensuuri produced only a few singles and albums and are today considered among the forefathers of Finnish punk. All the above-mentioned bands shared, apart from a few exceptions, a middle-class/student background and were able either to turn music making into a profession or to redirect their careers into other paths after some time onstage. Punk represented for them an exciting cosmopolitan fashion and music style from the United Kingdom that they enacted locally and that some of them got in contact with directly, thanks to language courses and holidays (personal interview with Jukka Junttila, November 11, 2011). A turning point for many of them happened when the Ramones played Tampere on May 17, 1977, at the Teknillinen Opisto, the technical school. The technical school provided education to a new generation of industrial workers and, at the same time, thanks to welfare educational policies, also offered spaces for student associations and so-called leisure activities. Eppu Normaali, whose members were present at the event, performed one of their first gigs one day later, at the local high school of their nearby hometown, Ylöjärvi.

These early punk bands all shared what is here defined as a carnivalistic approach, together with a taste for melodies and a keen interest in the rock music canon, which put them in direct contact with the Manserock originators. This made it easy for Finnish mainstream popular music to absorb them back, somehow neutralising the rebellious, amateurish, and spontaneous spirit of punk.

References to local industrial landmarks or toponimies are also basically absent here. As Ratsia, originally from Central Finland, put it in their punk hit-single 'Lontoon Skidit' (1979), they sing about London kids having nothing to do 'but do they know what it is like in Pihtipudas?' These straightforward lyrics, on top of a Clash-influenced combat rock riff, define thoroughly the role that early punk played in Finland. On the one hand, it was an efficient medium to express apathy or boredom and describe the lack of possibilities for self-expression in Finnish rural areas. Pihtipudas is today a municipality of four thousand inhabitants, and the band was surely aware of the oddness involved in name-dropping it. On the other hand, there is a clear attempt to enter into intertextual dialogue with British bands, where *boredom* worked both as lyrical trope and as *blasé* urban stance. As shown before, early Manserock had already experimented with domestication and with intertextual dialogue; both are strategies that provided a 'soft' national framework to cosmopolitan cultural tendencies.

All the early punk bands mentioned above were signed to the same new independent record label from Tampere: Poko Records. Epe Helenius, owner of Epe's Music Shop, decided to start the label, and this didn't come as a surprise, in 1977. Helenius told me in a November 16, 2011, interview in Tampere that

> all the young punks came to our store, because it was the only place where they could get punk music, and I got to know the musicians through the shop, and the musicians were complaining that they have a band but no recording equipment, and I thought, Why not? I can start a label! The UK companies that I was looking at were Beggars Banquet and Rough Trade; they were shops and then they started a label. I did the same: I first had a shop, then started a label from the backroom of the shop, I started the label.

Epe was able to legally and financially start the shop and later the label thanks to the assets of his family in the textile printing industry. For instance, Unitor oy, the shop parent company, present also on the early label logo, was a previously inactive company belonging to his father and to other close shareholders (Aunola 2009, 111–14). Years before deindustrialisation hit the city and its economic paradigm, the Helenius family had already experimented in switching company purposes towards the creative industries.

Epe recounts how he selected the artists exclusively on the basis of his own taste in music:

> They brought me a demo cassette; if the demo sounded good, I found out when they played live and went to see them, and if I liked what I saw and heard then I signed them. I went for the bands I liked, I am a sixties guy, meaning that I am very song-oriented, the actual songs meant a lot to me, most of the bands, not all, but most of the bands that I signed, whether they were rockabilly bands or punk bands, were good songwriters. That was important for me: personality and song-writing skills. (interview, 2011)

At the same time, he was aware that creating a Tampere-only or genre-based label would be too narrow-minded, and he looked for artists outside local circles and across different genres, including rockabilly, doo-wop, and later heavy metal. However, the stability and longevity of his label, in comparison to other independent labels across Europe, were connected to long, faithful relations with successful bands such as Eppu Normaali and Popeda and on relying on the nearly exclusive collaboration with a local recording studio: *MSL* in Ylöjärvi, about ten kilometres away from the centre of Tampere. Mika Sundqvist, bass player of early Manserock glam band Alwari Tuohitorvi, and Simo Lukkanen founded the studio in a wooden single house in 1978 and provided the ideal creative setting for Poko bands to develop and experiment. Poko Records had initially relied on a studio in Lahti: the Microvox, run by Pekka Nurmikallio.

Epe also strongly believes that the industrial city heritage as such was not the main denominator for the success of music from Tampere. He said it had more to do with the fact that

> we wanted to build a scene that was independent from Helsinki, and so we needed all kind of operators, we could sign bands, put the bands on the road, and have the bands in the media without having to go to Helsinki, that was a big thing for us. (interview, 2011)

In these early punk years, Tampere youth were also able to establish the first DIY-run punk club in Finland, Safety Pins Fun Club. The club started when a group of pupils from the Tampere Lyseo high school, also known as *Rellu*, started a fan club for their short-lived band Safety Pins. In many ways, it was a fairly similar initiative to the Charley's Girls Fan Club set up in Düsseldorf to support the, at the time, still very fictional Charley's Girls band. The fan club, however, developed into an association that was able to organise a few club nights in a space located at Sammonkatu 36, open to all ages, in Sorin Talo and in other restaurants and clubs. Safety Pins was active for just one year but provided the stage for the debut of many Tampere punk bands of the era and also attracted attention from outside the city limits (Karisaari 2017).

A participant explained,

> I really discovered punk through the Safety Pins Fan Club events. I was 13–14 years old, I went to *Sammonkatu*. There were plenty of Tampere garage bands, some of them were punk, some more *hämykamaa* [prog/hippie stuff] and some of them just interested in making noise. The event opened my young eyes about cultural activ-

ities in Finland at the time. *Safety Pins* was an event organised by young people themselves, which was an almost unknown happening in 1970s Tampere. If you were into youth activities, it was at the children's/youth department of a sport club, a political party, a congregation, the Martta etc. . . . The positive anarchy of Safety Pins provided a platform with no established order. It was new. (Hänninen 2015)

Despite the apparent spontaneity, Safety Pins had a clear and strict association structure, with a board, and issued membership cards, which could be obtained, for instance, from Epe's Music Shop. In 2018, the digitalised version of an old compilation cassette 'released' by the club circulated in the Safety Pins Fan Club Facebook group, which has currently about 220 members. The cassette featured songs from several local bands, in simple live recordings from gigs and some primitive demos. The sound is raw and the graphics are very basic, similar to what you would find in a grade-schooler's notebook, with a very limited use of punk newspaper cut-and-paste and no logos or stencils. In the group several photos of bands and scans from Safety Pins flyers also circulated, revealing the young age of its participants and the amateurish and spontaneous attitude they shared. A new generation of musicians entered the scene through this experience, and at the same time less educated and more working-class youth were able to discover punk and DIY as a means to express anger and frustration. Deindustrialisation also began taking effect in Tampere, and music did not stand still, with punk turning rawer and darker into hardcore punk.

FROM PUNK TO HARDCORE

Lättä, singer of Kohu-63, saw the step from punk to hardcore punk as a sort of continuum:

It all just changed overnight; punks used to wear jackets and ties with a shitload of safety pins on them, and then all the sudden everyone was wearing a studded leather jacket. The style changed. I didn't see it as a separate phenomenon but merely, as I said earlier, as a continuum. It wasn't the most radical change in the early eighties. The message maybe turned more aggressive.

For Bastards' Risto 'Rike' Jokela, whom I interviewed in Helsinki, August 17, 2011, the change was brought on by a generational hiatus, where the first wave of punk was an art-school, middle-class, London-created fashion that was immediately reabsorbed into pop music, while the second constituted a real upsurge of the white youth, caused by real genuine anger:

> The first punk scene died very quickly in Finland; it turned to new wave or pop—it was just '80–'81 when Eppu Normaali turned to pop and Pelle Miljoona turned to reggae . . . art . . . something not bad but different and all the first punk media . . . they were a little older guys and they said punk is dead, that's it and we were 'what the fuck? We've just started', and that's the reason why hardcore in Tampere became a big thing, because in Helsinki they stopped for a while. (interview, 2011)

Hardcore punk is the first genre that articulated itself in Tampere at the representational and material level, on the basis of deindustrialisation and crisis, in a very similar way to what happened in Torino. This had clear effects in the resonation of Tampere in the media on the European and global scale and also determined the survival of certain DIY practices in the city's cultural life.

Most significantly, hardcore punk broke the continuities, in terms of humour, domestication, and oddity, that were manifest in Manserock and in the first wave of punk. According to Rike (of Bastards),

> Especially in Tampere, music and rock music was always connected to humour, Eput [Eppu Normaali], Juice [Leskinen], and Popeda lyrics are very clever and suddenly we were not, we were absolutely serious and I like that it was something like 'no, this is not fun this is raw energy but no jokes', I know we sounded and looked ridiculous but still I think that it is easier to put yourself on stage and make jokes, but to be serious it means that you open yourself up and you don't hide . . . take it or leave it . . . it is something I liked a lot and there was this huge reaction no, you cannot do that so I think that the HC scene in Tampere was also a protest about this little bit conservative rock-and-roll scene where you have to go 'Hello nice to meet you' and we were like 'Where did you lose the danger? It doesn't go the same way like everything else' and that turned me on. (interview, 2011)

Basically, hardcore punk bands turned the carnivalesque function of music in a dull industrial city upside down. Carnival was no longer temporary and a mere mechanism to cope with production; it became perverse and menacing, with permanent status connected to deindustrialisation and other local historical traumas. Performing was no more about being humourous and became a very serious means to endanger the working everyday, first and foremost in terms of appearance. Manserock musicians and early punk bands were very commonly dressed, punks sometimes naively sporting a safety pin, sunglasses, or a ripped shirt; their style (just like their sound) did not overtly provoke. The hardcore punk look quickly took over as a uniform of military boots, studded leather jackets covered by patches and white paint writings, and spiky, dirty hair, often kept up by soap. The main colour was black. Hardcore punk musicians were also the first to adopt makeup for male members, with Jakke of Kaaos as one of the first mascara users, bending gender norms and values. Female members, who were already present during the Safety Pins years, continued working within the scenes; some wrote fanzines, and an all-female band, the Innocent Virgins, performed in a gig in 1982 with Kohu-63 and Riistetyt. In addition, drunkenness, having become a permanent status on and offstage, was exhibited and celebrated in lyrics. Hardcore punks were hanging out, drinking, and socialising in public spaces. Lahti and Lättä explain:

> Back in the days it was the centre where we all hang out and drank together. There were individual punk groups in neighbourhoods, and these groups met in the centre. Two most important spots were Old Church's front stairs or the park next to Library House. Of course, all the neighbourhood groups had their own drinking places in their own area.

The Finnish Public Order Act (*Järjestyslaki*) strictly regulates behaviour in public, forbidding noises, repeated threatening gestures, and object throwing. Drinking intoxicants in public places is legally forbidden, apart from a few exceptions. Hardcore punk resisted these laws and restrictions, not by resorting to humour but confronting them with dramatised chaos and disorder. This, of course, had consequences, according to Lahti and Lättä:

Lättä: Most problems were caused by one's outlook. You didn't have to be even drunk or anything, it could happen just after few beers, you would end up in police custody, that if you happened to look punk. They were trying to discourage people. And really it was even worse in Hervanta if you were outdoors after 11:00 p.m., you were always taken to drunk tank or on a forest road where they would beat you up. . . . From an ideological perspective it was really dull and boring time. It was shit. I'm trying to talk about people. They were more like looking 'what the fuck are they?'
Lahti: Yes, there was shitload of drunken guys ready to beat you up. 'Let's beat that peacock up. He has hair like that and so on'.
Lättä: Ready to attack. Yeah, but it was era of stagnation. Nothing new happened.

Photos from Tampere of this period, to be found online in DIY digital archives and in hardcore punk dedicated groups in social media, convey the striking contrast between the participants of this scene—in their sturdy outlook but also expressing subcultural enthusiasm and joy—and their social and spatial surroundings, which are uniform, bleak, and functionalist.

While Manserock band members were either from semi-rural villages in the Tampere region or resided in university dormitories in the city centre, hardcore punk bands had stronger connections with working-class, prefabricated residential areas (*lähiöt*) in suburban forests, such as Multisilta and Hervanta. Hervanta, in particular, has often been portrayed as a hotbed of social problems, 'the Bronx of Tampere', according to Rike (interview, 2011). The district was planned and constructed in the late 1960s as a quick solution to the increasing demand of housing, a consequence of the late urbanisation of the country (Nähri 1993). Lättä, of Kohu-63, grew up in the district:

Lättä: First apartment blocks were built there in the middle of forest. There was nothing.
Lahti: Not even a shop.
Lättä: Not even a shop van drove there. And a certain kind of people were put there to live.
Lahti: It was like a concentration camp of poor people.
Lättä: Yes, almost. At first they were planning on building a wall around it.

The two informants are aware of the urban ethos surrounding concrete
ghettos and their role in 'rock culture' (Cohen 2007a) to communicate
authenticity. Their portrayal of the housing area might be hyperbolic;
however, the district did work as a receptor for a certain kind of urban
rhetoric, even in a middle-sized Finnish town. The main point of terri-
torial localisation for Manserock was the country, to be understood both
as Finland as a whole and as its rural side; hardcore punk starts a new
kind of territorialisation based on the rhetoric of the ghetto/slum, which
is a clear reflection of deindustrialisation. Economic restructuring,
international geopolitical instability, and the slow demise of the working
class focused the public opinion on 'problem districts' and on their
inhabitants.

Rike, of Bastards, also implies that '[it] used to be a dangerous place
at that time because of the skinheads . . . they were an equal amount,
but much more terrifying, than punks' (interview, 2011). Lättä also
refers to the fact that 'when punks from Hervanta came to the centre,
everyone was afraid of them. They were rougher bunch of fuckers than
rest of the Tampere punks'. One anonymous informant (male, born in
1960, from Tampere-Hervanta, musician, fanzine writer, comic artist)
recalled in an interview:

> We lived in Hervanta, Tampere, which was the hardest place in the
> whole city at that time. We lived there from the beginning, in the
> blue house that was first built there. We went to school in the city;
> there wasn't even a grocery store, only stones and forest in Hervanta.
> Suddenly, the tall houses rose to the side, filling the whole area. The
> reputation of the northern half of the district began to be so hard
> that my friends outside the community did not dare to come down to
> the district, because in Hervanta you got almost certainly punched in
> the nose and they stole the valves from a bike, even if it was carried
> to the balcony on the fourth floor for safety. Yes, life was hard. The
> recession was on. There was a great mass of young people with noth-
> ing to do and bad roads were easy to find. Luckily, in addition to
> football, photography etc., we played music. That was a way out from
> doing bad things. Punk arrived right on time. (Hänninen 2015)

It is true that the district in the 1970s had a bigger concentration of
families than the rest of the city; as any other suburban development of
that time in Finland, it had its own facilities, such as schools and kinder-

garten. Local youth was therefore somehow proliferating in concrete spatial segregation, which, together with global economic downturn, caused social distress and increased stigmatisation.

DO IT YOURSELF!

All music from Tampere, from Manserock initiators to the early punk enactments, can be considered DIY in one way or another, especially in relation to recording technique, marketing strategies, and graphic design. This was mostly connected to Finnish cultural isolation, to Tampere's distance from the cultural capital Helsinki, and to the naive and spontaneous attitude of these bands. Hardcore punk bands broke from the past by implementing this production strategy in a two-folded way: on one hand, as a cultural tactic against the national record industry set in Helsinki, as a sort of self-activation, which had clear consequences in many individual careers and life choices; and on the other, as a reflection of a lack of economic means. Say Lahti and Lättä,

> You had to cope with the stuff you were able to get your hands on. You didn't go to a store to buy a distortion pedal back then. I remember some store selling an assembly kit that you could buy and make yourself a distortion pedal. I had a tube radio and a guitar, and my guitar had these old-fashioned microphones with magnets. I broke that magnet in three pieces and reassembled my guitar, and then I got some distortion to the sound. You had to come up with these kinds of solutions back then.

Most albums and EPs of these bands, even when released on proper independent record labels, contained self-made collages from newspapers (images of Reagan, clashes with the police) and history books (especially Nazi imagery), in a style deeply inspired by the work of British anarcho-punk pioneers Crass and by their graphic designer, Gee Vaucher. Fonts were also often cut out from newspapers, in a style made famous by Sex Pistols' graphic artist Jamie Reid, and sometimes they were even handwritten. In many ways, DIY was the only way to produce hardcore punk in such an isolated Nordic country, but it also offered the means to reach out first on the European and then on the global level to other bands, labels, and distributors. Finnish bands and distributors were actually quite active in this; for instance, one of the first Europe-wide compilation 7" (many cassette tapes were already available) was *Papi, Queens, Reichkanzlers and Presidennti* (*sic*), produced by Attack Punk Records in Bologna, Italy, in 1984. Seven bands were involved, each presenting one song: Irah (from Bologna), Total Chaos (from Tyne and Wear), Quinto Braccio (from Torino), Stromsperre (from West Berlin), Kaaos (from Tampere), Sottocultura (from Bologna), and Kollettivo (from Torino). The small DIY label from Bologna produced the EP, bands probably licensed the songs for free in exchange of a few copies, and all revenues were reinvested in future productions. Each band was given a space for lyrics (in this case, translated into English from the national language), addresses, political statements, lyrics explanations, and band logo. The cover is a simple single-colour drawing of a Bosch-inspired infernal animal/machine with the faces of Pope John Paul II, England's Queen Elizabeth II, Finnish president Koivisto, and German chancellor Schmidt attacked by a punk holding a broom. Running on one side of the cover is the statement 'do not pay more than 2000 lire/1 pound'. This is just one of the hundreds of 7" and tapes traded around the world that shared the above-mentioned features: cosmopolitanism, DIY, reinvestments of the profit in the scene, price-control, use of 33 rpm to extend possible playing time and include more songs, inclusion, in the cover folder, of a poster containing manifestos, lyrics, addresses, technical support for producing further music.

The fanzine *Disforia*, started by Takkop Farano (later Tax, from Negazione) in Torino, includes in its first issue a list of records and tapes on sale, in which Finnish band Terveet Kädet is featured with a live tape on a C-60, produced by Disforia Tapes itself (Farano 1983). It was common for bands to trade one copy of a tape, hoping to have it copied, released, and distributed locally. This strategy is also probably behind the enormous success that some Finnish hardcore punk bands received in Brazil (Ullvén 2016). For instance, Fábio, owner of Punk Rock Discos, a record shop in Sao Paolo and vocalist in many early hardcore punk bands, recalled:

> In 1982 Vote Vasko [a well-known member of the Finnish hardcore
> punk scene trading and distributing tapes] sent us a box of Finnish
> tapes and records. We played the tapes and not only got the Sao
> Paulo hardcore sound influenced by Finland but the whole Brazilian

scene. . . . More interesting—the Finns sung in Finnish—which taught us that you did not have sing in English. From there we all decided to sing in Portuguese. . . . I opened my record shop in Sao Paulo in 1979 and just a few years later I could, thanks to Vote, introduce hardcore from the entire world. They really opened my eyes—olho aberto!!! (Swedish Punk Fanzines n.d.)

DIY was also an important factor in the organisation of tours. For instance, according to Rike, Bastards left Tampere with train tickets and a list of contacts:

We were the first punk band in Finland that went abroad and we organised this tour and we travelled Europe by Interrail. We went to Italy, West Berlin and Denmark, the last gig would have been Madrid but we were so tired and we were already in Denmark so we went home we couldn't do it anymore and all the money was gone. (interview, 2011)

A few years later, Riistetyt joined Italian band Raw Power and other international bands in a long tour of the United States, culminating in a gig in the LA Grand Olympic Auditorium on August 10, 1984, headlined by Dead Kennedys.

Bastards were also the first band to produce an album of songs that were translated into English, aiming specifically at the international market. *Siberian Hardcore* (Rock-O-Rama Records, 1984) contains songs that were previously recorded in Finnish versions in *Järjetön Maailma* (insane world, Propaganda Records, 1983) and on previous EPs.

Of course photocopy machines, tapes, telephones, postal services, typing machines, electric music instruments (guitar, drums, bass), and mixing desks had been invented and were commonly available decades before the hardcore punk scene developed. Also, the idea of DIY cosmopolitanism is not new: sport clubs, religious associations, collectors' groups, political parties, and other music scenes were also widely networking at a European level, often using the same DIY instruments available to this particular scene: telephone, barter, and address lists. This was particularly common within an international network of industrial cities, framed by solidarity of workers across nations but also by competition. However, no other scene or interest group is so radically political in its independent choices and in maintaining them over time, regardless of spatial scales and economic growth; bands just consistently did it themselves. Moreover, the relevance of industrial cities in the hardcore punk world topography is striking; most European cultural centres were somehow irrelevant in the dense networking of this scene and allowed cities like Tampere, for instance, to acquire a strong, although merely underground, reputation. This was achieved once again by maintaining certain industrial city structural features, such as the attention to the material world of production, to the work ethic of the so-called industrial man, and to the mistrust for the cultural industries set in the capital city Helsinki.

SIBERIAN HARDCORE

Finnish lyrics and articulation completely abandoned Manserock crooning and diction to achieve a shouted, guttural howl. Finnish sounds are exotic to foreign ears; it has fewer consonants than English, and vowels can be howled to signify anger in a pretty effective way. Moreover, a lot of bands from Tampere were mixed with a lot of reverb on the voice, which increased the feeling of listening to an apocalyptic mayhem. Hardcore punk of the 1980s is also referred to as *Räkäpunk, räkä* meaning mucus:

> Lättä: Finnish punk is somewhat different. Maybe it's because of our language.
> Lahti: Finnish sounds angry.
> Lättä: And it is! We were (and still are) really angry because of issues we have been singing about. I think that emotion delivers well in Finnish. But the impact Finnish punk has had all over the globe, in Brazil, Japan, and the States.

Severi Helle (drummer of both Kohu-63 and Riistetyt in late-2000s formations), during an interview in Tampere, November 16, 2011, also suggested to me that

> it's maybe a linguistic thing that with figures of speech and the way we pronounce words different than in Helsinki and we have more

some letters like *R* [he emphasises the rolling sound of R] we are
from Tampe*R*e and this thing defines some of the sounds.

Lyrics were mostly connected to global politics and history with a stress
on dictatorships, Cold War issues, and police/state control. Song titles
referred a lot to warfare, revealing its geopolitical stress on Finland,
which relied on national service and a strong nationalist ideology to
overcome past traumas (the Winter War) and contemporary fears (nuclear war). There are also clear polemical takes on the police and on the
condition of living under constant surveillance. Local industrial-city issues are rarely touched upon, deindustrialisation is perceived hand in
hand with Cold War tension, nuclear annihilation, and political crises.
True, Tampere bands seem more inclined than bands from other cities
in Finland to articulate doom, desperation, and the no-future trope. In
particular Kaaos achieved a global subcultural status thanks to its ability
to perform an uncompromised dramatisation of crisis, especially in lyrics—via the voice of the singer Jakke—but also in the fast and confused
wall of sound. Jakke's 'grain of the voice' resonated with fans who could
not understand his lyrics but were captivated by his hopelessly sad
anger. Parallel to this, his early adoption of mascara and leopard-skin
patterns differentiated him from the rest of the masculine, studded-
leather punk image; his onstage antics, prompted by the abuse of alcohol, also contributed to his emanating a certain aura within the scene.

Kaaos's 'Työ tappaa' (work kills), released on the compilation *Yalta
Hi-Life* (Barabbas Records, 1984), is a clear stance against the eight-
hour working day and its effects on the life of workers, which can be
understood in connection to local industrial contingencies.

Bastards' 'Siberian Hardcore' (from *Siberian Hardcore*, Rock-O-
Rama Records, 1984) is among the first attempts to exploit Finnishness
as a market strategy by emphasising its oddity. This is achieved first and
foremost in textually equating Finland with Siberia, when after a refrain, the singer screams 'Suomi, sisu, sauna, Sibelius, perkele'; a list of
Finnish catchwords and stereotypes, known, and used to define Finland
from 'above'.

Kohu-63 recorded a straightforward song targeting local Tampere
politics in the title itself: 'Paavola', which appeared on *Pelimannimusaa*,
their debut 7" (Poko Records, 1981). The song was originally composed
and rehearsed by the Rash, the band of Hervanta where Lättä first sang

before joining Kohu-63. Pekka Paavola was mayor of Tampere between 1969 and 1985 and played a huge role in framing local policies, ranging from planning to cultural life. Lättä's inspiration for the song was connected to the '*200 vuotta kadulla*' (200 years on the street) demonstration, where the mayor called the police on the protesters (Saastamoinen 2007, 259–60).

It is only in the choice of some cover songs that we might find connections to the historical socialist heritage of Tampere. For instance, Bastards covered the Italian partisan song, 'Bella Ciao', and Kohu-63, the red civil war anthem, 'Punakaartilaisten Marssi'. Both were often sung in left-wing rallies, strikes, and union demonstrations. Bastards singer Lahti even sang an Italian original version of the song during their gigs in Italy:

> Lahti: Yes. That song ['Bella Ciao'] has been known in Finland for a long time but with Finnish words. But in Italy I sang it in Italian. Even today I'm not sure what I was singing but I had the lyrics written down on a piece of paper and the crowd had a blast.
> Lättä: At end of the day it's a partisan song.

Rike, who was playing guitar with Bastards, has an interesting anecdote about that:

> It was during the Bastards tour, there was this long train trip to Milano, I think, and there was this drunk, quite old Italian guy who drank with us and taught us the lyrics of 'Bella Ciao', and then he drank all our booze and our bass player was a bit pissed, and when the guy passed out, he cut his hair Mohawk-style, and then we played 'Bella Ciao' in those gigs, and it was quite a good success; we didn't know all the lyrics but who cares. (interview, 2011)

'Punakaartilaisten Marssi' also known as 'Puunakaartin Marssi' (red guards march) is a march based on German and Swedish folk melodies. The author of its Finnish lyrics is unknown, and the text was sung in several versions. It is among the best-known songs of the Red faction during the Finnish Civil War (1918), was sung by the red guards during marches, and became part of the Finnish working-class music tradition (Gronow 1973). Kohu-63 recorded it in a punk D-beat version for *Lisää Verta Historiaan* (more blood for history, Poko Records, 1982), their debut LP, as a sort of singalong drinking song. Lättä, Kohu-63 singer, considers it a tribute; he and Lahti opine that the Civil War is 'still a burden to Tampere', and the song lyrics still resonate with ongoing social inequities.

The cover of Bastards' debut album *Järjetön Maailma* (insane world, Propaganda Records, 1983), designed by Juho Juntunen, portrays the unmistakeable uniformed legs and bust (but not the head) of Carl Gustav Emil Mannerheim, the White guard military leader who defeated the Red side in the Finnish Civil War, who is depicted standing on top of a pile of corpses, prams, and toys. Mannerheim would later become commander in chief of the Finnish Army during the Winter War and Finnish president, and he is considered one of the most significant historical figures in the country, with monuments and streets carrying his name. This cover adopts and domesticates the punk choc aesthetics that were introduced, for instance, by the Sex Pistols on the cover of their 'God Save the Queen' single (Virgin Records, 1977), which features a collage by Jamie Reid defacing the queen (Worley 2017, 6). However, even in this case, there is a clear local echo on the role that Tampere played during the 1918 Civil War. The so-called Battle of Tampere was one of the largest battles that took place in a Nordic country and saw Mannerheim's White troupes sieging the city and defeating the Red faction:

> According to the estimates of the Finnish War Victims Project, the Red losses amounted to 1,100 killed, one-third of this figure resulting from reprisals and shootings immediately after the surrender. In addition, approximately 100 to 200 Russian soldiers were murdered by the White forces.
>
> The Whites took 11,000 Red prisoners, at least 290 of whom were executed after sentences by court martial. At least 1,400 prisoners died in the Tampere prison camp. All in all, eighty residential and forty-six industrial buildings were destroyed, and 504 families were left homeless. (Jalonen 2014)

Such a strong and fairly recent trauma in the life of the city was quickly sublimated by subsequent historical events (such as the Winter War) but surely left scars in individual family histories and in the internal image of Tampere and its inhabitants. The 'Tampere 1918' exhibition at the Vapriikki Museum displays pictures of the battle from both sides and reveals the horror and violence that took over the city over a few months. Warehouses and factories were often the last bastions of fierce Red resistance, and their bombed and destroyed ruins anticipated the future deindustrialised status of many of them.

NOTE

1. Direct quotes of Lahti, of Bastards, and Lättä, of Kohu-63 are from our interview, in Finnish, on November 16, 2011, in Tampere. Severi Helle supplied the translation.

7

INDUSTRIAL HERITAGES

The first time I set foot in Düsseldorf, I steadily walked the 450 metres from the railway station to the Mintropstrasse to spy inside an unassuming post-war courtyard at number 16. Behind a gate with an open shutter door, the courtyard revealed itself for what it was: an industrial space, functional for the loading and unloading of stuff from trucks into the building, away from the street. The courtyard also gives access to the rooms that Kraftwerk rented as a rehearsal space and where they set up their KlingKlang Studio from 1970 until the early 2000s. The door to the studio was, of course, shut, because the room has no formal use at the moment. There were no visible signs or plaques about the band in sight, just a traffic cone at the bottom of some concrete stairs, which is the band's icon, but it might have been there for some other reason. It was raining in the courtyard, but I still took a few pictures from the street, under the Elektro Müller sign on top of the shuttered door for my social media accounts. The sign simply refers to the electrical installation company, which shared the building with the band; however, 'Elektro' can also refer to a music genre, which Kraftwerk contributed in framing, while 'Müller' is one of the most common German surnames and it carries an umlaut. The sign is made of metal, common in industrial design and all over industrial cities. The font used for the company name is old-fashioned and slightly faded, calling for the reading of time in space. That sign might be the perfect object to exemplify the band's legacy, thanks to its German and industrial connotations, even if this association is actually based on misunderstanding and randomness. About a year later, thanks to Rudi Esch, I had the chance to visit the studio itself. The band had left their electricity plugs, a weird intercom receiver, and some sound-insulating panels; I clapped my hands to grasp a possible magic in the reverberation of the room, but it felt like nothing in particular, like a very short applause for an empty warehouse space. Books about the band and guidebooks about Düsseldorf music mention Mintropstrasse (Löding and Krohn 2018) and similarly, the Haçienda appears in every other story about music in Manchester; however, the Vanchiglia centro d'incontro in Torino and the room used by the Safety Pins Fan Club for some gigs in Tampere have followed a different destiny, disappearing through the mere passing of time, change in use or ownership, and redevelopment. It seems that the embodiment of popular music heritage in urban materiality is directly dependent on the relevance of individual bands in popular music history and canonisation. This has been the case since the very beginning; the Cavern, in Liverpool, where the Beatles played early in their career, might be the most celebrated and known example, although the club's history is not a straightforward one (Cohen 2007).

The four cities under investigation here applied very different strategies to handle their own industrial heritage and to encapsulate popular music in the process. Some policies and heritage processes were successful over time, others just for a period; some have provided a few jobs, and some have been disastrous and pricey failures.

Popular music has become one of the ingredients used in the individualisation of industrial cities and in the semiotic shifting of the industrial world from dull, grey reality towards aesthetic distinction and sensibility. It is very difficult to understand the concept of 'industrial chic' (Linkon 2018), without considering the role that music played as 'vanishing mediator' (Jameson 1973) during the period of deindustrialisation and as 'cultural catalyst' in the current times. However, to truly examine these processes, it is important to frame them within cultural heritage making in general.

CULTURAL HERITAGE AND THE BUILT ENVIRONMENT

First and foremost, heritage making is a process that paradoxically generates memory and oblivion at the same time. While electing something

as worth preserving, archiving, or restoring, we are also forgetting, erasing, obliterating something we consider not worth enough (Ricoeur
2004). Heritage making is also a practice and as such, it requires time,
curator skills, resources, and creative efforts. In industrial cities, heritage often celebrates architectures, while paying little attention to their
former function. This is, of course, just one specific kind of heritage, the
tangible one, made of materialities such as built landscapes, districts,
individual buildings, and other human-made architectures. Their role in
heritage making has not changed over time. Preservation of the material past in terms of buildings and their ruins represents the most relevant
form of heritage, shared by cultures all over the world, and it is the most
easily visible across the urban realm. The palimpsest metaphor (Bottà
2012; Huyssen 2003; Busà 2010) has been extensively used in references to the material layering of buildings, debris, and signs, pointing at
various eras and sociocultural constellations. Just like old parchments,
whose pages were scraped from old texts and rewritten, cities exhibit
the material and symbolic layering of their memory, embedded into
place.

Pierre Nora studies '*Lieux de Mémoire*' (realms of memory) and
their symbolic role in heritage making, memory, and history. In his
monumental analysis of French national memory, Nora first distinguishes immaterial, material, and ideal realms of memory and offers a
clear definition of these realms as

> any significant entity, whether material or nonmaterial in nature,
> which by dint of human will or the work of time has become a
> symbolic element of the memorial heritage of any community. (Nora
> 1996, xvii)

'Entity' is a fairly neutral term; however, the French historian uses
monuments, museums, children's books, mottoes, and other kinds of
sites, which work as material fixtures in space. He also defines memory
not as something that is fixed and immutable but as an entity that
historians can examine 'by way of its divisions, its real or imaginary
continuities, and its symbolic fixations' (Nora 1996, xviii). He also refers
to the fact that 'there are *lieux de mémoire*, sites of memory, because
there are no longer *milieux de mémoire*, real environments of memory'
(Nora 1989, 7), insisting therefore on the historical intentionality of
embodying memory into site. He underlines how 'there is no spontane-

ous memory' and therefore 'we must deliberately create archives, maintain anniversaries, organize celebrations, pronounce eulogies, and notarize bills because such activities no longer occur naturally' (Nora 1989, 12). This active and intentional attitude towards memory is a sign of our times and has caused a proliferation of archives and a sense of obligation towards maintaining the own individual or collective memory. It also fuelled an ineluctable distance and separation from the past. *Lieux de mémoire* are material, symbolic, and functional sites, where a community can build, negotiate, handle, and transmit its own memory, despite and outside history itself.

In reference to the temporality and its perception in heritage, Ricoeur conceptualises a 'third time', existing along the cosmological (cosmic, objective) and phenomenological (lived, subjective) one. This third time is not exclusively subjective or objective; it exists across these dimensions and it is able to symbolically mediate between them. Among the tools that the third time has at its disposal, we find 'archives, documents, monuments, and traces' (Fornäs 2016, 5215). These are tools that are able to mediate time and create links between cosmological and phenomenological time, they 'internalize cosmological temporalities in subjective experience while externalizing experiential flows in material audiovisual structures shared with others' (Fornäs 2016, 5219). By doing so, they provide means to perceive, structure, and process temporality.

Both popular music and empty industrial spaces are today understood and studied as cultural heritage. By looking at the evolution in definitions and actions of heritage-themed conventions, we can see both entering the field, roughly at the same time, which is unsurprisingly the same era when the post-industrial discourse arose.

The United Nations Educational, Scientific and Cultural Organization (UNESCO) established the World Heritage Convention in 1972, and its Article 1 states:

> For the purposes of this Convention, the following shall be considered as "cultural heritage":
> *monuments:* architectural works, works of monumental sculpture and painting, elements or structures of an archaeological nature, inscriptions, cave dwellings and combinations of features, which are of outstanding universal value from the point of view of history, art or science;

groups of buildings: groups of separate or connected buildings which, because of their architecture, their homogeneity or their place in the landscape, are of outstanding universal value from the point of view of history, art or science;

sites: works of man or the combined works of nature and man, and areas including archaeological sites which are of outstanding universal value from the historical, aesthetic, ethnological or anthropological point of view. (UNESCO 1972)

UNESCO initially defined culture along the natural heritage and framed it in material terms and under the recognition of a gatekeeper, such as history, art or science. This convention has so far brought about the recognition of 1,092 World Heritage sites across the world. Since the early 2000s, the list has included a growing number of industrial heritage sites, whose status is connected to deindustrialisation—for instance, the Welsh Blaenavon Industrial Landscape (since 2000), the German Coal Mine Industrial Complex in Essen Zollverein (since 2001), the English Cornwall and West Devon Mining Landscape (since 2006), and the Italian Ivrea, Industrial City of the 20th Century (since 2018) (UNESCO 1992–2019). These sites lost their original function in connection to deindustrialisation fairly recently in comparison to other buildings and monuments whose function did not change over time, as in the case of sacred architectures or historical centres, or that lost it centuries ago, as in the case of fortress and decorated caves. Their inclusion is justified in relation to their 'outstanding' architecture or as a testament to a cultural tradition that has disappeared.

The Faro Convention, issued by the Council of Europe (CoE) in 2005 and ratified by several European countries, defines cultural heritage as

a group of resources inherited from the past which people identify, independently of ownership, as a reflection and expression of their constantly evolving values, beliefs, knowledge and traditions. It includes all aspects of the environment resulting from the interaction between people and places through time. (Council of Europe 2005)

CoE's aim is to promote human rights and rule of law within Europe as a continent, and it has often mobilised cultural heritage in this direction, facilitating dialogue across cultural and ethnic borders in hotspots like Bosnia-Herzegovina or Cyprus. The definition provided in the convention is fairly wide but includes significant elements, such as the issue of ownership and the idea of culture as a process in evolution.

However, it is also deeply bound to the territory and to the physical reality of heritage. Its implementation includes the development of 'heritage walks' and other activities suited to activating communities and inter-European dialogues.

In 2003, UNESCO introduced the concept of 'intangible' cultural heritage, which

> means the practices, representations, expressions, knowledge, skills—as well as the instruments, objects, artefacts and cultural spaces associated therewith—that communities, groups and, in some cases, individuals recognize as part of their cultural heritage. (UNESCO 2003)

The idea of intangible cultural heritage responds to the will and at the same time to the need, already identified by Pierre Nora, to memorialise the past in all its forms and expressions, including symbolic ones and keeping with what UNESCO defines as cultural and natural heritages. It acknowledges a shift in *how* and *what* we consider worth preserving, celebrating, and memorialising and in *when* we think it is appropriate to do so. However, this convention also creates a divide between what is tangible and what is supposedly intangible because it exists only as idea, knowledge, or skill and, just like music, 'in the air'.

POPULAR MUSIC AS HERITAGE

The idea of an intangible cultural heritage has given rise to a growing corpus of research in relation to popular music, which is often limited to the so-called Anglosphere, both as canon and as geographical space. However, this kind of research provides interesting means to understand current dynamics in the promotion, memorialisation, and consumption of music. For instance, Sara Cohen (2007a; Cohen et al. 2015) questions the role that popular music plays at the urban level by revealing the continuous dialectical struggle between cosmopolitanism and insularity. Moreover, she always considers music making as a social practice, lived in everyday, invisible, and uneventful landmarks, such as rehearsal rooms and recording studios, but also bedrooms and corner shops (Cohen 2012). These intangible heritage sites are often the most at risk of oblivion and/or demolition, despite their centrality in lived music cultures, communities, and scenes (Cohen 2007b).

Sarah Baker (2010; Baker et al. 2018) has a different approach and considers popular music heritage not so much in relation to local memory building and lived cultures but much more in sociological terms, in relation to institutional and noninstitutional practices, sustainability, and activism.

Andy Bennett (2009) offers a third perspective and underlines how, for instance, rock music heritagisation is connected to baby boomers' generational legacy building and to the framing of a collective, although pluralistic and contested, cultural memory based on popular culture.

It seems that general approaches to cultural heritage and memory, such as the ones taken by Nora and Ricoeur and the ones targeting popular music as a specific subject of heritagisation diverge, at least with reference to temporal and spatial scales. Popular music studies seem to take for granted that music, as a product of late capitalism, operates in a flattened-out eternal present. This belief has been augmented by digitalisation, which turned music into data to be computed, classified, labelled, and charted into moods and atmospheres, which sometimes adopt time frames, just like in '1970s soul' or '1980s pop', but where these decades have no particular historical and temporal significance.

The transformation of music into heritage seems to happen in a historical vacuum, where the past is either intrinsically one-dimensional and superficial or perceived as such. Moreover, digitalisation has provided the means for everybody to create and share their own individual or collective music artefacts and archives online, bringing about an overflow of materials that were born as transient and ephemeral. Most importantly, heritagisation of music also has a clear connection to economic cycles, which have seen the collector value of popular music artefacts rise considerably over time. There is some bitter irony in seeing an old, battered 7", lined with a political 'pay no more than . . .' sum that simply covered the expenses, sell for hundreds of euros on Discogs or Ebay. For instance, Torino's band Declino's 1983 EP has been on sale for a median of 250 € on Discogs, with a visible 'non pagare più di

L. 1500' (do not pay more than 1.500 Italian lire, € 0,77) on the cover. Silvio, from that band, explained the upswing in the price like this:

> Collectors, on the one hand, try to buy back their youth, they are very often people who have established themselves professionally and to do so, they had to give up many things of their youth and now they try to gain accreditation after many years. The other trend is that of collectors tout court, you have to think that a few years ago, when the vinyl went into the attic, even the collectors that dealt with stuff like ceramics, started collecting vinyl, because the vinyl itself as a support became rare, it is a simple market phenomenon . . . and then there is a third aspect, in any case they were things that had a great artistic value, which at the time was not understood . . . after so many years, it is being recognised and therefore those records will always be worth more. (interview, 2011)

In the words of Silvio, it looks like the physical vanishing of music from deindustrialisation gave way to its return, as fetish, as object to be used in financial speculation. This is something I will explore in the next subchapter.

INDUSTRIAL CITIES AND MUSIC HERITAGES

As noted in chapter 1, the urgent relabelling of former industrial cities with the 'post-industrial' tag hinted at a new paradigm of development, putting places back on the map and attracting tourists, creating businesses, and reinvigorating communities. Sites of manufacturing and production became or were supposed to become sites of conservation, consumption, or both. Marketing strategies were implemented to make post-industrial cities appear as distinctive and cool places that were open for future business. All material elements, reminiscent of the industrial past, were either physically erased as toxic debris, sanitised as material cultural heritage, or reconverted into housing, service facilities, or performance spaces. Grey, industrial-city sameness was overcome by the imperative to stand out and be unique and different. These practices were institutionalised by the election of industrial cities as European Capitals of Culture (for instance, Glasgow in 1990, Liverpool in 2008, and the Ruhr in 2010) and by the establishment of a European

Route of Industrial Heritage. Even capital cities such as Dublin, Helsinki, and Berlin were affected because industrial areas with mixed
uses, commercial shorelines, and former industrial districts were reshaped to exhibit new forms of work and new modes of living, based on
smart services, information technology, education, and culture. These
processes fuelled inequalities: new inhabitants with new jobs often invaded the most appealing parts of towns, looking for authenticity and
industrial atmosphere, while less pleasant areas were abandoned or
segregated.

Popular music, which had vanished from industrial cities, in terms of
discourse and 'urban ethos' at least, came back as a strong element of
local individualisation and place pride. In *Paris: Capital of Modernity*,
David Harvey (2003) examines modern Paris and the formation of the
urban bourgeoisie in the nineteenth century, through literary representations of the time, Balzac's novels in particular. Harvey identifies how
the fetish dominates the modern city and describes it as 'the human
habit of attributing to mere things (in this case the city) magical, mys-
terious, and usually hidden powers to shape and transform the world
around us, and thereby to intervene directly in or even determine our
lives' (Harvey 2003, 53). According to him, nineteenth-century Parisian
literature was able to peel away the fetish and reveal how greed and
economic gain lay at the foundation of capitalist urbanisation. In nineteenth-century Paris, at least according to Harvey, literature was an
emergent force, able to shape alternative and anti-hegemonic understandings of the city. The function of literature changed over time and
today Balzac belongs to a canon of writers, including Victor Hugo and
Charles Baudelaire, that supposedly celebrated Paris and defined the
city's magic and mystery, corroborating its fetishisation. These authors
represent the literary heritage of the city, and their memory is pre-
served in guided tours, toponyms, monuments, guidebooks, and
plaques all over the city.

The same happened to industrial city music from the time of
deindustrialisation. Especially since the early 2000s, concomitant with
the inclusion of recent industrial architecture in the World Heritage
list, we find the meaning and function of music changing drastically and
becoming a heritage-making force, which catalysed the so-called industrial chic as new fetish.

By looking at popular music heritage in four industrial cities after deindustrialisation, I would like to reveal a shift in the function of music in them towards heritage making. As I will show in chapter 8, music worked as a sonic vanishing mediator, as something intangible and transient. Only lately has it resurfaced as a cultural catalyst towards the redevelopment or preservation of certain material buildings, monuments, and districts, or as a main ingredient in whole city brands. This shift from transient and intangible to static and tangible commodifies popular music: museums and tourist marketing strategies, local policies and global attitudes, digitalisation and media operate with music as commodity, regardless of its previous function as social practice.

The four cities under examination provide very different contemporary uses of music produced in them under deindustrialisation, and they developed different heritage-making strategies. For instance, the popular music from Manchester under investigation in this book has been the subject of feature films and documentaries, memoirs, and historical studies. The history of Factory Records was fictionalised into *24 Hour Party People* (Winterbottom 2002), while *Control* (Corbijn 2007) is based on the life of Ian Curtis. Joy Division was dissected in oral histories (Savage 2019) and documentaries (Gee 2007), while all three remaining members of the band published individual memoirs (Hook 2012; Sumner 2014; Morris 2019). Morrissey's youth was fictionalised into the biopic *England Is Mine* (Gill 2017) and turned into a graphic novel (Chrisoulis 2018), while the Smiths' singer himself (Morrissey 2013) and guitar player Johnny Marr (2016) penned autobiographies. Innumerable other books have been written about the Manchester music scene in general and about individual bands and musicians, ranging from oral histories to academic essays, from encyclopaedias to photo books. All these examples can be gathered around two main typologies, the first being fictionalisation, the attempt to memorialise music through fictional works such as biopics, graphic novels, and novels. This strategy has been very successful in creating a codified Manchester myth as 'heteronormative and male-oriented' (Brunow 2019). The second is connected to a more factual and archival attitude towards music, with credibly authentic reconstructions of 'what really happened' in documentaries, oral histories, essays, and memoirs. At the basis of both, there is the attempt to construct a coherent structure, a narrative strategy, and therefore I gather them into a single typology.

Another strategy consists in embedding music into place. This happens mostly in connection with tourism and the commercial mobilisation of heritage. For instance, the North Rhein Westfalia tourism board published in 2018 a new social media campaign under the label #*urbanana*, the urban jungle of western Germany. The campaign is based on experiential tourism and offers heterogeneous activities and experiences around the region. 'Sound of #urbanana', for instance, works as an app, enhancing the city exploration of Cologne, Düsseldorf, and the Ruhr Area, through music landmarks. The 'Pop Trail Düsseldorf' encompasses twenty-one spots in a walking route of approximately two and a half to three hours. Most of these are connected to Düsseldorf's music past and include the Ratinger Hof, the Kunstakademie, and Mintropstrasse 16 but also morbid locations, like the place where electronic musician Wolfgang Riechmann was murdered in 1978. Contemporary or recently closed music clubs are also included, like the Salon des Amateurs and Unique, but they play an ancillary role, in favour of the ones with a more clearly defined heritage status. Limited mostly in the city centre and in the *Altstadt* in particular, the route does not engage with uneventful and repetitive music landmarks described by Cohen, such as rehearsal spaces, bedrooms, youth centres, and recording studios. The tour territorialises music into its most spectacular and eventful spots. Some of these can only be understood as *lieux de mémoire*, activated by the pop trail and by its digital storytelling and otherwise consisting of anonymous closed doors in urban settings, despite their glorious past. A similar approach is Manchester Music Tours, a private tourism enterprise started by the late Craig Gill (former drummer for Inspiral Carpets), which involve coach and walking tours ranging from general ones to specific 'The Smiths/Morrissey', 'Joy Division', 'The Hollies', 'Oasis', 'Factory Records', 'Happy Mondays', and 'The Stone Roses' tours in and around Manchester. These tours feature blue plaque sites but also underpasses and bridges that are connected to certain song lyrics, former recording studios, rehearsal spaces, and birthplaces. They rely less on walkability or location and more on offering a totalising experience to music fans, probably inspired by the consolidated success of the 'Magical Mystery Tour' in neighbouring Liverpool. In this case it is not an app but tourist guides themselves who temporarily activate certain spots into *lieux de mémoire*, through their stories and through embodying an authentic connection to the scene.

For instance, John Robb, music writer and leader of the Membranes, has recently guided some of 'The Smiths/Morrissey' tours. This second typology of music heritage making can be defined as material embodiment, as an attempt to impregnate real urban spots with past music memories, be they connected to music content, production, consumption, or musicians' lives.

A third strategy consists in branding new developments or redevelopments through local music heritage, making music instrumental to these processes. Increasingly, twentieth-century popular music is playing a role in people's housing, working, and travelling choices. For instance, in Manchester the Haçienda Apartments are a housing complex developed on the former site of the Haçienda club. Music heritage becomes an asset; it might positively influence the real estate value of properties during the renewal of the former club site. In Tampere, the *Solo Sokos Hotel Torni* is an eighty-eight metre, twenty-five-storey-tall hotel completed in 2014. It is the first of a series of skyscrapers that are going to transform the area surrounding the main railway station into the so-called Tampere Travel and Service Centre. The hotel has two bars, Moro Sky Bar, on the twenty-fifth floor with an amazing view of the city, and Paja Bar, at street level. Both bars are adorned with photos from local musicians; the Paja Bar is completely Manserock-themed, with original clothes, instruments, and LPs adorning the red brick walls, in a similar fashion to the Hard Rock Café chain, and at the entrance a life-size cardboard cut-out of Popeda's Pate Mustajärvi now invites guests to have beer and a burger. In each room of the hotel, guests find alongside the usual gadgets a CD compilation of Manserock band on sale, produced by Paja Bar and with liner notes by Poko Records' Epe Helenius. The CD includes punk initiators Sensuuri, Kollaa Kestää, and Karanteeni, along with the expected Juice Leskinen, Popeda, and Eppu Normaali.

In all the cities considered, there is also another form of embodied music heritage that takes two different paths. The first consists in bands' reunions or revamping through touring, with the release of new material or the reissuing of old material. Bands from all the mentioned cities have been actively doing this. Bands from Tampere, such as Rattus, Riistetyt, and Kohu-63 eventually reached Brazil, Japan, and the United States in new formations that sometimes included musicians who were not yet born at the time of their first releases; Bastards,

Tampere SS, and Holy Dolls re-formed temporarily for a single gig or for some dates in summer festivals. Peter Hook from Joy Division and New Order has been touring under the moniker Peter Hook and the Light and playing his old band albums in their entirety. The discography of Negazione has been reissued in a collector box by Contempo Records, while several unreleased live recordings are currently available for download on the band's Bandcamp account, while F.O.A.D. Records reissued all of Declino recordings in one LP. In Düsseldorf, the Lieblingsplatte Festival invites German bands to perform their most important album. On December 8, 2018, Male played each song of *Zensur und Zensur*, their 1979 debut album in front of an audience that included the city mayor among a crowd of nostalgic fans and former punk colleagues (Kühlem 2018). These re-formations and reissues are, of course, still intrinsically music; at the same time, they exist only in relation to their previous existence as authentic expression of a certain structure of feeling, the one of deindustrialisation, so therefore they can be understood as heritage, although an embodied and performative one. There is, however, a second related embodiment, which is the one inspiring social activism and DIY activities in and outside mere music performance. For instance, in Tampere, for a short period of time, a group of bands was able to claim for themselves Keltainen Talo, a wooden house, which was built in proximity to the railway station and was supposed to be demolished to make space for the above-mentioned Tampere Travel and Service Centre. Rented to Maria Mattila temporarily, the house provided a performance space, a gallery, housing, workshops, barter clothes shop, and a recording studio, without any hierarchy or control and in absolute, militant DIY style, which allowed the Tampere alternative music scene to flourish and develop (Jansson 2017). This experience has continued since 2018 with the Romu & Random kiosk. *The Guardian* featured an interesting article concerning the DIY skate parks developed by Kaarikoirat, a local Tampere collective (King 2019). The article underlines the current appeal of DIY-led regeneration and its social role, especially in a city that has yet to reinvent itself after deindustrialisation, in the face of depopulation and unemployment. The article doesn't mention possible continuities with the 1980s DIY, hardcore punk music scene, despite a picture featuring a skateboarder with a Kaaos patch on his jeans jacket. Vastavirta is a consolidated institution within the Tampere music scene. The venue opened in the Pispala district, a picturesque district of wooden houses, formally inhabited by working-class families, that is undergoing gentrification. It has a packed weekly program of shows from international and local touring bands and functions as a significant gathering spot for the whole Finnish punk scene. Pispala is also the site of Hirvitalo, another wooden house transformed into a DIY social center with art galleries, a recording studio, and a bike-repair shop.

Torino also has a long history of squats and DIY spaces scattered around the city's industrial wasteland; they all evolved after but are clearly linked to the initial hardcore punk scene. For instance, in 1987 a collective of activists and punk squatted El Paso Occupato, which is still today one of the most active *centri sociali occupati autogestiti* in Italy and plays a significant role in archiving and preserving independent musical and nonmusical heritage, for instance, through its self-run publishing house Nautilus. Nautilus is responsible for *1983/85—Storia & Memoria*, the Contrazione book and CD anthology, and for the book *Franti. Perché era lì. Antistorie da una band non classificata*. However, El Paso's radical political stance has also caused some conflicts. Marco (of Negazione), for instance, referred to the fact that Negazione used to play both in El Paso and in the legal and licensed commercial live music venue Hiroshima Mon Amour and this 'created a fracture with the most intransigent scene of the Torino anarchopunks', but the band justified this as 'individual choice, we always believed a lot in individual choices' (interview, 2011).

In Düsseldorf, Olivia, from Östro 430, sees this embodied heritage in social activism and work, especially in the ecologically conscious kind:

> There is the Nilsson, a small club/café near here and I think the oldest project that the city left the youth to run autonomously, then they continued with the Kiefernstrasse and there was the Salzmann-bau, a huge squatted factory . . . one of the biggest projects, that has celebrated its thirtieth anniversary, this or last year, is the Ökotop Heerdt in Heerdt . . . that is urban gardening; when they founded it 'urban gardening' did not exist, and they were growing stuff organically and freely, not like in the normal allotment gardens . . . there was only one rule, not to use pesticides and genetically modified stuff. (interview, 2018)

A last kind of heritage making is very much connected to the writing of this book. Over the years I have downloaded and collected a vast archive of digitalised books, fanzines, c-cassettes, vinyl records, leaflets, letters, stickers, and pictures. Some of these are pdfs and mp3s that gave me direct access to a copy of physical material I could have never laid my hands upon otherwise because it was extremely expensive, out of reach, existing in a few copies only, damaged, erased, broken, forgotten, or lost. Baker and Huber (2015) refer to 'rubbish' archives with regard to existing DIY archives and museums run by activists and the collection of popular music artefacts that would otherwise be disposed of. The authors document the anxiety of some of these vernacular archivists and collectors in relation to the 'disposability' of popular music and the ease by which it turns into trash. Baker and Huber also reveal an interesting in-between state, where past popular music artefacts are stored 'under the bed', until collectors discover them or they are donated to them. Digitalisation offers an alternative, which might be seen as more democratic and at the same time more dangerous than the preservation of physical artefacts. On one hand, a researcher with the adequate tacit knowledge of the field is able to discover and acquire innumerable amounts of material available online. On the other, the lack of adequate archiving knowledge, together with digital amateurism, net piracy, malware and the financial costs of maintaining and updating digital platforms can generate electronic waste and digital rubbish and put into question the authenticity of what is found. There are plenty of blogs and social media groups devoted to music under consideration in this book, and many former scene participants and witnesses actively participate in creating, curating, and discussing online the digitalised material they kept stored 'under their bed' for years.

To sum up, there are five significant typologies of heritage making in relation to popular music in industrial cities (Table 7.1):

Table 7.1.

Heritage Typology	Examples	Function of Music
Mediated/narrated	Films, memoirs, documentaries	Score
Embedded	Music-themed tourism	Spatiality
Instrumental	Music-themed redevelopments	Enhancement, stimulus, brand, curation
Embodied	Live music; alternative and emergent activism	Performed and lived phenomena
Digitalised	Archives, blogs, collections	Data

8

FROM VANISHING MEDIATOR TO CULTURAL CATALYST

Music, Space, and Place

The highly organised material interaction of capital and labour in man-ufacturing shaped Manchester, Düsseldorf, Torino, and Tampere. Manchester is the first city in the world that organised and planned itself through industrial production, with material layers going back to the first industrial revolution, dominated by red brick architectures, canals, and chimneys but also by monuments, museums, and buildings representing the Commonwealth and the British Empire. Düsseldorf is a city ambivalent towards its industrial surroundings and the luxury derived from them; it is a functional German city, organised by social democracy and welfare, with a central area dominated by art museums and galleries, shopping streets, and a well-known nightlife mile. Torino is a one-company town, where the automobile industry dominated the urban realm, but also a former state capital and Olympic site. Tampere is a small town that was developed by the intuition of a Scottish busi-nessman into a textile and paper industry centre but nowadays is also a media, business, and entertainment hub. Today, all four cities are also educational centres, with research universities and universities of ap-plied sciences. Strong football teams dominate their respective national and international leagues and championships. As shown in the previous chapter, music has also partly been implemented as a cultural catalyst and as a heritage strategy of some kind.

However, walking around these cities made me wonder many times where exactly the music went, apart from the souvenir shop and the guided tour. This chapter takes a look at music as a 'vanishing mediator', which was able to articulate itself in place, enabling the transition from the industrial to the post-industrial condition, but disappearing once the post-industrial discourse, so to say, 'won'. In this chapter I also clarify further the reduction of music to 'culture' and the effects this has in shaping places and our understanding of them.

MUSIC AS VANISHING MEDIATOR

Vanishing mediator is a beautiful and productive metaphor, referring to something on the verge of disappearing but still able to work as intermediary between two conflicting concepts. It looks like the condition itself of mediator ignites the process of vanishing, conveying heroism and self-sacrifice. This is the way, for instance, uprisings are examined in historical and political research and where, for instance, Bey (1991), among others, finds their potential. The concept also reflects how much we can gain by looking at a process of change as a relational and dialectical field. This is, for instance, the way Doreen Massey (2005) conceived space, as a product of interrelations, where distinct trajectories coexist, collide, get closer, and separate.

Frederic Jameson (1973) first conceived and used the concept of vanishing mediator in an article focused on Max Weber and on his idea of *Wertfreiheit*. This article is very much a product of its time, and Jameson seems preoccupied with looking critically at Weber's sociology from a Marxist and at the same time Freudian standpoint, inspired, for instance, by the work of Marcuse. Its main aim is to contrast the 'vulgar Marxism' and 'economism' views, which reduced Weber's thought as anti-Marxist, especially in relation to *The Protestant Ethic and the Spirit of Capitalism*, which was seen as antithetic to the base-superstructure Marxist simplification. Jameson claims that Weber's work can be actually considered as a contribution to historical materialism.

According to Jameson, Weber's thinking is narratively organised and dominated by pairs of binary oppositions: 'bureaucracy versus *Charisma*, but also: asceticism versus mysticism, *Berufmensch* versus *Fachmensch*, *Realpolitik* versus ethics, politics versus science, and so forth'

(Jameson 1973, 63). To sort out the basic elements of Weber's thinking, Jameson adopts Greimas's semantic rectangle. This rectangle is able to expand our understanding of conceptual oppositions, generating additional elements from the initial basic binary structure. Jameson goes on to analyse several typologies of Weber's sociological thinking with this scheme; however, he also criticises the fact that when dealing with the analysis of historical change and narrative structures, the mind tends to reduce the diachronic 'in what are essentially synchronic or static and systematic terms' (Jameson 1973, 69). To deal with Weber's thinking related to historical transformation, Jameson adopts the formula that Lévi-Strauss developed as ultimate reduction of every myth and tests it in relation to the main thesis behind *The Protestant Ethic and the Spirit of Capitalism*. According to Jameson, this book shows how Protestantism prepared the conditions for the rise of capitalism, thereby inverting the vulgar Marxism idea of base (the economic sphere) always determining the superstructure (religion, worldviews). Protestantism was able to ignite the step towards modernity, by universalising feudal beliefs and making everyday life more religious, thereby unchaining the feudal beliefs from the mere religious sphere. By doing so, it also vanished. Once rationalisation was completed, Protestantism had no more reason to exist in that function.

Comparing Lévi-Strauss's formula with Greimas's rectangle, Jameson claims that the first is more suited to convey the 'irreversible character of narrative and historical change' (Jameson 1973, 75), but the second puts forward 'the hypothesis of some central mediatory figure or institution which can account for the passage from one temporal and historical state to another' (Jameson 1973, 75). Jameson's aim, however, is to achieve a more thorough reading of Weber's thinking able to express both the presence of a mediation and at the same time convey the idea of a diachronic process. He achieves this by devising a 'notation', which is able to show the presence of a 'catalytic agent, which permits an exchange of energies between two otherwise mutually exclusive terms' (Jameson 1973, 78) and that 'serves as a bearer of change and social transformation, only to be forgotten once that change has ratified the reality of the institutions' (Jameson 1973, 80).

Applying this simple notation to the main idea of this book would result in something like Table 8.1:

Table 8.1.

	Industrial City	Music	Post-Industrial Cities
Material production	[+]	+	
Symbolic consumption		+	+

Music played a significant intermediary role, in the narrative and historical step of deindustrialisation, from industrial to post-industrial cities. Music maintained and expanded the idea of industrial city as merely a city shaped by the highly organised material interaction of capital and labour in manufacturing. The scenes featured in this book rarely focused their attention towards the industrial city as a place. However, they maintained an aesthetic fascination towards industrial spaces and sounds. They took production and materiality for granted and adopted a certain work ethic, which focused on 'getting things done' in DIY fashion but also relying on tacit knowledge and on a radical redefinition of the role of an industrial citizen. By using industrial imaginaries in the production of musicscapes and in celebrating an industrial 'structure of feeling', they were able to consolidate their belonging into industrial societies and sometimes emphasised to the point of exaggeration their belonging to the working class. In addition, these scenes removed the brackets from the idea that material production could only happen in highly organised, monofunctional settings and exclusively in relation to heavy production. Music anticipated the flexible organisation of work and the 'creative' reindustrialisation that, for instance, Stahl associates with post-1989 Berlin, 'even if only in an incipient and localized sense' (Stahl 2008, 306).

However, industrial city music scenes also introduced symbolic consumption; they showed how places can be mediated and consumed, how atmospheres and emotional bonds to places can be implemented in various ways, ranging from the political to the more hedonist, from the art-related to the carnivalesque. Different paradigms of development and different solutions arose from this. However, they all shared a common narrative, with the industrial paradigm becoming old and unsustainable. Paraphrasing Jameson, music scenes didn't deindustrialise the city, they turned the whole world into a factory.

Once the post-industrial transition was over, a new economic swing hit European cities on the basis of flexible services, diversification of businesses, and entrepreneurialism. This is when music and the social/

economic spheres became, in the words of Simon Reynolds, 'uncoupled' (see Introduction) and industrial city music disappeared or mutated completely.

For instance, historian Owen Hatherley has often pinpointed Tony Wilson's role in implementing a vision for post-industrial Manchester based on capitalist greed and on real estate speculation, and built on Wilson's status as music visionary (Hatherley 2010b; Mule 2011; Brooks 2018). In particular, in *A Guide to the New Ruins in Great Britain*, he states how in a fairly recent documentary, *Joy Division* (Gee 2007),

> Wilson reflected on how Manchester had gone from being the first industrial city in the early nineteenth century to what is today: Britain's first successful post-industrial city. After the blight of the 1970s it is now a modern metropolis once again, this time based on media and property rather than something so unseemly as industrial production. The old entrepreneurs built the mills where workers toiled at twelve-hour shifts and died before they were forty; the new entrepreneurs sold the same mills to young urban professionals as industrial-aesthetic luxury housing. Wilson squarely credited Joy Division and Factory Records with a leading role in this transformation, but he was by no means alone in doing so. Nick Johnson, one of the directors of Urban Splash, has given presentations in which he dates the beginnings of his company to the Sex Pistols' gig at the Free Trade Hall. (Hatherley 2010a, 120)

Hatherley seems to imply that music should be a force of resistance against property redevelopment, gentrification, and post-industrial Manchester, but Tony Wilson's entrepreneurial spirit somehow corrupted the 'oppositional, independent pop music' (Hatherley 2010a, 117) and this is why the city hasn't produced anything interesting since the post-punk days (Hatherley 2010a, 120).

Music can, of course, be in the oppositional field and can have a clear political inclination in particular times and under specific circumstances; however, Hatherley sees this function in what Jameson would call synchronic and static ways. Music has played a particular role in deindustrialisation, and the fact that Tony Wilson at a certain point went from being an independent record company owner to a post-industrial/creative city believer makes us wonder: Where did the music go in this process? Once its function as mediator of a social and economic transformation ceased to be viable, it disappeared. This happened in different ways in the four considered cities and under slightly different circumstances, but the result was the same. Music was a significant barometer for urban transformation, a social practice able to mediate radical transformations in space, work, life, and economy, which vanished and came back later as something radically different. Slavoj Žižek (1991) in his analysis of Hegelian dialectics reflects on the structuralism idea of 'determination-by-absence', where he distinguishes between 'immediate presence' and 'historical mediation', revealing how something stays the same in form to be able to change and become its contrary, its negation (Žižek 1991, 181–82). Žižek also identifies how the vanishing mediator takes up its role because of a gap between form and content (1991, 185), where the first mediating step concerns content, which is changing inside an old form, while the second step is a formal change. This last step is the one that brings the vanishing mediator to the drop-off point.

MUSIC TODAY: CULTURAL CATALYST

Jameson, at the end of his article, problematises this dialectic narrative further and gives a final reading of Weber's work as a 'series of progressive and cumulative negations, each of which projects the previous material as it were onto a different thematic level while at the same time preserving its fundamental unity' (Jameson 1973, 88). Just like Protestantism, music did not vanish; it just radically changed its function, turning from a mediator involved with radical changes at the level of content and form, or in Marxist materialist terms, of base and superstructure, to a cultural catalyst instrumental to post-industrial place making. I am using the term *cultural catalyst* because on one hand, I would like to stress the 'reduction to culture'; on the other hand, I am interested in revealing the instrumental activating role that music plays in relation to places.

Increasingly, academic research has cornered 'culture' into three main paradigms. The first paradigm assigns to culture an ancillary and commodified function, in exclusive relation to capitalist production. For instance, research about cultural industries (Scott 2001; Hesmondhalgh 2007) aimed at differentiating cultural industries from other forms of production, for instance, by stressing the role that the symbolic level plays in the production and in the consumption of cultural industries products and services, ranging from the record industry to internet content production. However, the end result was very different. Scott, for instance talks about 'commodified symbolic forms' as

> products of capitalist enterprise that cater to demands for goods and services that serve as instruments of entertainment, communication, self-cultivation (however conceived), ornamentation, social position-ality, and so on, and they exist in both 'pure' distillations, as exem-plified by film or music, or in combination with more utilitarian functions, as exemplified by furniture or clothing. (Scott 2001, 12)

According to Scott, basically any industry can be considered a cultural industry because all goods and services are, in the end, symbolic forms, and regardless of their utilitarian function, they belong in the category of culture. Moreover, culture seems to be understood only in instru-mental and ancillary relation to the economy.

Similarly, urban planning and place-making theory has focused on cultural districts or quarters, trying to assess their role in contemporary urban revitalisation (Roodhouse 2010; Montgomery 2003; Banks and O'Connor 2017). There are various definitions of cultural districts, but central areas, touristic zones, cultural hubs, heritage sites, and creative industry headquarters are always mentioned; abundant are also refer-ences to cafés and restaurants, food parlours and entertainment miles, revealing the assumption that culture must be understood, in anthropo-logical and sociological terms, as a whole way of life or as a lifestyle.

At the beginning of the twenty-first century, Richard Florida has had a key role in defining the relation between culture and urban space, capitalism, and society as a whole. His writings popularised the idea that cultural and creative spaces were the keys to innovation and the notion that culture and its measurement and indexing are ancillary to econom-ic development and success. His definition of creative class also corrob-orated the idea that with deindustrialisation, the working class also ceased to exist and what cities needed especially were people with degrees.

The above-described notion of culture is inflated to occupy the whole symbolic realm and, therefore, it can be adopted to describe basically any kind of contemporary industry and any kind of contempo-

rary urban development, as long as they are products of capitalist enterprise. Basically, it excludes any form of cultural activity or creative industriousness that falls outside the capitalist box and that cannot be
measured or quantified in terms of economic gain. In addition, it pola-
rises city spaces into cultural and noncultural ones, therefore increasing
inequalities.

The second paradigm is even more embedded into the anthropological definition of culture as a whole way of life. For instance, in social
theory, the notion of 'culture of poverty' implies that unequal conditions, such as stigmatisation, spatial segregation, displacement, and
marginalisation are connected to a system of values, beliefs, and norms
that are perpetuated within families as a proper cultural formation. By
using it in reference to poverty, researchers tend to deny the material
forces that are at the basis of any lived experience and operationalise
culture as lifestyle as the cause for inequality. Instead of focusing on
structural economic changes, just like the ongoing erosion of welfare
states, researchers focus on so-called cultural factors, which marginal
groups are supposed to perpetuate over generations (Small, Harding,
and Lamont 2010). This idea is vulgarised in right-wing populist discourse, where culture equals a monolithic and conservative system of
values embedded into a lifestyle to be defended from the attacks of
other monolithic lifestyle cultures, defined in terms of ethnicity, religion, politics, sexuality, race, language, and nation (Waisbord 2019).

A third paradigm is cultural quantification. Increasingly, 'culture' in
general and music in particular are understood as data and therefore
measured, rendered, and analysed through quantitative methods. These
methods allow us to visualise and interpret sets of data about tastes,
genres, gender, and identity, but they fail to provide means to detect
nonrepresentational elements and affect. There is also a growing number of studies in medical and biological sciences that address 'culture'.
Tracking brain activity and examining genes seem to provide valid scientific answers to cultural matters, ranging from music preferences
among twins (Microsoft Team 2009) to bullyism (Jha 2007).

Reducing music to 'culture' means taming the former's social and
political connotations and the role it played as vanishing mediator during deindustrialisation. It means subordinating it to its capitalist-
organised structures, like the music industry; relegating it to specific
'places' and to the sphere of everyday leisure or lifestyle; and quantify-

ing it in playlists and charts (Stahl and Bottà 2019). It also means constraining it into intangible cultural heritage, as shown in chapter 7.

Industrial city music never really vanished, just like the industrial city itself. Its presence in contemporary music production has never been so strong, with a myriad of acts duly reproducing the sparse and tense musicscapes of post-punk and early electronic, as if they were coming from 1980s Manchester or Düsseldorf. Quantitative studies also suggest that sadness and desperation have risen in the charts, traced through 'moods' (Interiano et al. 2018) and lyrics (DeWall et al. 2011). Music videos have often paralleled this 'new bleak' by readopting industrial and brutalist architecture as settings.

This aesthetic trend has a clear beginning, as far as the internet is concerned, with 'Rust Belt chic'. This label gathers blogs and online discussions surrounding industrial ruins across the United States, to be traced back, for instance, to the work of Detroit artist Lowell Boileau's *Fabulous Ruins of Detroit*, John Slanina's *I Will Shout Youngstown* blog and Richey Piiparinen and Anne Trubek's *Belt Magazine* (Linkon 2018, 131–34). These initiatives fuelled discussions on activism, local community work, and civic engagement, which sometimes materialised in participative planning and preservation and the reactivation of empty buildings through collaborative projects. However, 'Rust Belt chic is also rife with contradictions. It is at once idealistic and cynical, nostalgic and strategic' (Linkon 2018, 132). Linkon's analysis of Rust Belt chic focuses on four main points. This form of deindustrialisation literature engages in place remaking and aims at shifting narratives and reputations from negative to 'chic', thanks to the real engagement of local writers and by claiming ownership of local stories. In doing so it also adapts 'the values and culture of the past as resources for responding to the challenges of the present' (Linkon 2018, 143), therefore developing a Rust Belt aesthetic, which is partly based on local civic spirit and the activation of DIY practices and partly a marketing tool for economic development. This brings into the forefront a claim for authenticity, which can be defined as a cultural construct with contradictory meanings (Peterson 2005; Zukin 2009, 2010). Linkon suggests that authenticity in the realm of industrial cities has a tangible dimension in the material presence of history as empty industrial architecture, which is able to define a subjective place identity. This has consequences in terms of place consumption, which has been steadily looking for real experiences, atmospheres, and histories as marketable attributes. More-over, Rust Belt chic re-creates an industrial working-class past, which is solely white, erasing and ignoring racial conflicts and the intersection of race and class in Rust Belt history.

There have been other labels in the anglosphere to refer to similar phenomena taking place not exclusively on the internet but being am-plified there, such as 'ruin porn' and 'smokestack nostalgia' and 'indus-trial cool'. These terms are sometimes used to point a finger to external unauthentic appropriations of the industrial heritage, although what these criticisms reveal is complexity of dealing with the past(s) and their different resonance in different contexts (Strangleman 2013).

As I showed in my analysis of Detroit's heritage in the 2011 Chrysler Superbowl ad (Bottà 2015), popular music plays a significant role in 'curating' the industrial past and in fetishising decline, especially be-cause it provides 'atmospheric triggers' to catalyse attention towards former industrial cities, certain areas, and individual buildings. More-over, it can become an instrument to whitewash the negative sides of ongoing urbanisation processes by working on memory and heritage. The connection between industrial city music and the gentrification that many industrial cities are facing cannot be underestimated.

MUSIC AND PLACE

Mobilising Linkon's analysis of Rust Belt chic towards music, we are facing similar contradictions. Lately, for instance, the 'sonic hauntology' has been increasingly and uncritically used in writings about music making in industrial cities.

Hantologie is a neologism that Jacques Derrida invented as a combi-nation of *hanter*, to haunt and *ontologie*, ontology. He used it in refer-ence to Marxism in a short text from 1993 entitled *Spectres de Marx* and translated into English in 1994 with the title *Spectres of Marx, the State of the Debt, the Work of Mourning, & the New International*. This text took up the famous spectral beginning of the *Communist Manifesto* and combined it with a short quote from *Hamlet* about time being out of joint to examine the role that communism has played in post-1989 global terms. This is enough to stimulate the wit of two bloggers and music journalists from England: Mark Fisher and Simon Reynolds, who started fiddling with the concept in connection to recent memory and lost futures in contemporary electronic music. Fisher consolidated his understanding of the term on his blog *K-Punk* and later in *Ghosts of My Life* (2014), while Reynolds uses it in *Retromania* (2011). Fisher, for instance, wrote about the 2006 LP by London electronic musician Burial in these terms:

> Burial is haunted by what once was, what could have been, and—most keeningly—what could still happen. . . . Audio hallucinations transform the city's rhythms into inorganic beings, more dejected than malign. You see faces in the clouds and hear voices in the crackle. What you momentarily thought was muffled bass turns out only to be the rumbling of tube trains. (Fisher 2014, 122)

His writing is rich in metaphors and tropes referring to a sound, which seems to generate organically from post-apocalyptic and natural disaster–ridden South-London, a layered imaginary space of failed experiments, false memories, and never realised expectations, where pasts and futures collide. Consistently, in his short and intense blog posts he creates a collection of hauntological music and artists, with a corollary of visual references, in obscure films, series, and artworks.

Reynolds historicises Fisher's and his adoption of the term by referring to 2005, when they used it to refer to a loose collective of British electronic music artists, mostly on the Ghost Box label. These musicians and crate diggers sample forgotten analogue and digital sounds from old records and tapes and mix them with drones, soundscapes, spoken word, and noise (Reynolds 2011, 328). Reynolds seems to be very preoccupied by curating a pure British hauntologist canon, although as far as possible alien to nationalist ideology; a paradoxical attempt, when for instance he refers to accents as being 'bound up with a sense of nationality' in a 'matrix of collective character' (Reynolds 2011, 337).

The temptation to give a hauntological read to industrial city music and to its relation to the industrial past in times of deindustrialisation is very strong; especially in relation to bands I grew up with, such as Joy Division, Negazione, Franti, and Fehlbarben, and I am aware of the risks involved in doing this.

The first risk is connected to nostalgia, the unclear and undistinguished longing for something that is in an undetermined temporal or spatial elsewhere. Popular music is the perfect trigger for the evocation of 'elsewhere', for instance, distant places, certain periods of our life, persons we lost, and emotions we once felt. David Hesmondhalgh states that music matters because it *often feels intensely and emotionally linked to the private self* and it is *often the basis of collective, public experiences'* (Hesmondhalgh 2013, 1–2). The affective dimension of music plays a significant role in relation to place. It creates a 'privatised auditory bubble' (Bull 2005) that allows us to get by in our everyday life of work (I am writing this with headphones on, my laptop pumping out music from Spotify while it registers my typing), leisure, commuting, and falling asleep. It makes routine bearable and tweaks our visual place perception into a cinematic experience. As 'imaginative practice' music invests in place 'as an organizing principle of playlists, but also as a mnemonic-symbolic tool to engage with or retreat from the landscapes travelled through' (Boldermann and Reijnders 2019, 17). *Listening* to music connects us to places on an affective and imaginative level, however it also does it in ways, we are partly aware and in control of. Theodor W. Adorno explained this in materialist terms: popular music is standardised and evokes standardised reactions to standardised forms (Adorno 1941). Listening to Joy Division on headphones while travelling through landscapes of deindustrialisation, dancing to techno in an abandoned warehouse, going to a punk gig under a railway arch are emotional experiences that are soaked in nostalgia, as sound seems to emanate directly and without mediation from history, from the *haunted* rusty and faded place textures, and from the sensuous *ghosts* of its past industriousness.

This emotional trigger is something we expect, something we are in control of and willing to invest in. Moreover, it is something we perceive as authentic, as naturally emanating from places, as 'culture'.

This book's case studies reveal that music making was not exclusively connected to a *spectral* understanding of place and to gloom as a vehicle of authenticity. In fact, if we compare scenes and sounds in the four case studies, we find a much more relational and nuanced understanding of place and of the 'place of music' in deindustrialisation; in addition, we can also critically address the definition of what industrial city music might be, something that I leave to the conclusion.

CONCLUSION

This book tells stories of hope and resilience, of industriousness and creative energy taking place in bad times and wrong places under distressed circumstances. Through interviews, I was able to participate in making sense and reflecting on what Harry Rag called *'pure Freude'* (interview, 2018), the pure, unconditioned joy of music making, which was at the bottom of these scenes and their creative endeavours. Music is first and foremost a social practice, a way to learn, to perform, and to communicate with others, and an immense means of pleasure, both to performers and listeners.

This book also tells of a loss, of the uncoupling of music and the socio-economic realm, which happened exactly because of deindustrialisation. The whole world was affected by this paradigm change, but industrial cities suffered the most in the process. This was due partly to their peculiar built environment, which abounded in buildings specifically built for industrial production, and to planning, which was mainly instrumental to facilitating production. The crisis became visible in industrial cities, through the sudden emptying of warehouses, sealing of buildings, stopping of machines, and shrinking. Its effects were also very much visible on its citizens, who became unemployed, had to redirect their education and expertise, downsize their aspirations and dreams, and become flexible, whatever that meant.

Music had played a significant role in industrial cities from the very beginning. Industrial folk, Chicago blues, Motown soul, early German electro, and English glam were born in industrial cities, and they all

share common structural features, such as originating from a displacement of sort, creatively using repetition and noise, and articulating
work. They reflect a material disposition towards producing something
tangible and, paradoxically, they are also able to point affectively at
something else—a dream, aspiration, feeling, or will—located outside
the mere industrial settings. They are able to articulate love, revolution,
laziness, hedonism, escape, and abandonment. In short, the 'industrial'
in music cannot be reduced to the avant-garde adoption of industrial
noise; it is a wider carnivalesque celebration of life, in the presence of
but also in spite of the industry. Football and music are so determinant
in industrial city culture and life because they both implicitly point at an
escape: footballers and rock stars lift themselves up from the anonymous mass and are able to leave it all behind.

In punk and 'post-punk' there are several continuities with industrial
city music; however, what deindustrialisation brought about was a complete repositioning of music as social practice. Industrial city music
used to absorb certain features of the industrial city and make them
tolerable; with punk and 'post-punk' this doesn't happen. With deindustrialisation, music started dramatising uprooting, crisis, and the sudden
loss of direction. It dealt with negative feelings without making them
more tolerable; on the contrary, it embraced them as inspiring forces
and learnt to pogo dance to them.

However, music during deindustrialisation also created pockets of
publicity from below, 'proletarian spaces', where the symbols of decay,
waste, pollution were renegotiated into something positive, exciting,
and somehow joyful. Music became a way to be together, to create a
sociability not embedded in production or political resistance but in
residual activities and in local and discontinuous reindustrialisation.

Moreover, this was not happening only in contexts where music was
able to raise you from the masses and make you a star—like, for instance, the United Kingdom. It was happening in all industrial cities
around the world where deindustrialisation was taking place.

The origins of punk can be traced back to New York City and London, cities whose financial and cultural power operates on a global
basis; the mutation into 'post-punk', on the other hand, encompasses a
surprising kaleidoscope of genres, aesthetics, and music styles, across
national cultures, languages, and racial, class, and gender divides while
maintaining, however, a strong connection with industrial cities, both as

atmosphere and as place of origin. In many countries, capital cities and their urban palimpsests were deeply embedded into national history, tradition, and cosmopolitan high culture, but industrial cities were places whose roots were immersed in anonymous concrete and steel, similar in design, population, and rhythms to one another and at the same time relegated to low culture and localism. This is why industrial 'sounds' travelled, echoed, and resonated across music scenes, from Tampere to Torino, from Düsseldorf to Manchester, and back again.

Deindustrialisation reconfigured the music map of the world and with it the power and social relations embedded in space. It made school kids from Torino feel that they played a role in defining how they wanted to live, laugh, and play, and what they wanted their city to be known for. Deindustrialisation brought about the chance to see 'the public' as a place to grow organic vegetables and to organise a concert, to get drunk and to perform art. In this process, however, music slowly lost importance and 'vanished'. Music worked as a generator of possible translations of the industrial city into the post-industrial. In relation to this, it is possible to see different approaches in the four cities under examination in this book.

Manchester, for instance, maintained the most connections to previous industrial city cultures; at least in lyrics and in musicians' self-representation, the city adhered to the humanist paradigm and to the influence of social realism. It also built the most continuities between deindustrialisation and post-industrial music or, put differently, between 'post-punk' and house music. Post-industrial music genres such as techno and house developed in Manchester and increased the feeling of accelerating towards a possible future. Düsseldorf articulated a solid though temporary affinity between popular music and art. It was also a forerunner in relation to synthetic sounds and to understanding the creative chances of digitalisation and technology. Torino showed how continuities in political struggle provided spaces for the articulation of dissent in musical terms. The scene also allowed the formation of a new publicity from below, which was emergent and alternative. Tampere exposed how the industrial city carnivalesque provided only a partial antidote to boredom and dullness, while aggression and noise better articulated the presence of past historical traumas and anticipated future distresses.

In all cities, deindustrialisation music worked as an emancipatory force on a variety of levels. At the individual dimension, it provided informal learning that led to 'DIY careers' (Bennett 2018) and other forms of professionalisation, although with some important differences. To begin with, social policies and legislations, ranging from family to welfare, from unemployment benefits to the status of students, were very different within 1980s Europe, and a DIY professionalism could be achieved only under the very favourable circumstances of social democracies. Many informants quoted Amsterdam and West Berlin as havens and heavens for post-punk action across Europe. Surely, music making involved a huge amount of clerical work based on fax machines, stamped letters and telephone bills, and logistic expertise in relation to organising and travelling on tour. Several informants told me about an 'own approach' to their contemporary or past professions. The industrial city 'habitus' based on industriousness and on 'getting things done', together with the hands-on approach of DIY survived music and was translated by them into a variety of professions, ranging from university professor to film director, from physiotherapist to finance analyst, from record stall seller to permaculture farmer.

At the same time, the 'structure of feeling' of deindustrialisation also created links and networks, which projected individual lives beyond and above the limits imposed by national borders and mother tongue, creating for the first time some kind of a European identity (Bottà 2018).

At the urban level, deindustrialisation music liberated territories and spaces for creative work from below and for what I referred to as 'squatting/occupying space with noise'. The willingness to invest time in empty industrial spaces led to their later election into the field of cultural heritage, at the local, national, and supranational level. Music making paralleled the awakening of purely visual and aesthetic interests for industrial ruins that led to the development of the industrial fetish. Both music and these purely visual interests also anticipated and gave way to the renewal and reactivation of former industrial spaces into 'creative quarters' within the service economy. Despite this, certain forms of political resistance and activism survived music and are to be found in the practice of squatting, in social centres and in permaculture, across the cities under consideration in this book.

Deindustrialisation also distorted our common understanding of music making and musical ability. Presenting a paper on the theme of this book in a small seminar in the industrial Finnish city of Pori, I received an interesting comment from a jazz musician, who told me that it is self-evident that punk kids wanted to make noise like a freight train or a chainsaw; it is the easiest thing to do when you cannot play. Once you learn how to play properly, you move on. This comment was based on a classic understanding of music as a language to be learnt, according to which only mastering a musical instrument allows for properly communicating real meanings. Some of my informants were onstage weeks after they formed a band and got an instrument in their hands, putting this understanding of music as communication into question.

Deindustrialisation is an in-between moment where meanings temporarily failed and where time and space felt 'out of joint'. Music anticipated and accompanied this disruption by dealing extensively with noise, most of the time in subconscious and intuitive ways and partly according to the imitation and hybridisation of musical influences. The direct translation of the industrial soundscape into music is not straightforward; it involves mismatches, assonances, mistakes, and randomness, yet it plays a great role as narrative and self-mythologisation. Today, several bands introduced in this book belong to the canon in the construction of the 'sound' of a particular city. This operation constrains a social practice into a fictional locale and into an artificial and curated canon, built on erasures. Music mediated a fundamental step in contemporary societies and then vanished, to come back as local folklore, to be formalised, celebrated, archived, digitalised, and turned into heritage. After the accomplishment of the post-industrial shift, or at least after its discursive took over, music mutated into a deterritorialised force, another flexible and faceless expression of the post-industrial society.

Deindustrialisation music was rediscovered, 'culturalised', and reterritorialised as an instrument to promote and enhance contemporary neoliberal urbanisation, in short, for profit. This is connected in part to its augmented or 'amplified' authenticity. Real people made 'deindustrialisation music' through 'true work' in shared rehearsal spaces and on low stages in overcrowded bars, often obtained from vacant industrial spaces. This music re-created the lost industriousness and 'buzz' of these spaces, emptied in the name of economic restructuring. Currently, the very same music is repurposed to do the same for the newly reconverted industrial spaces or for the new developments mimicking them.

However, not all the music considered in this chapter faced the same destiny as cultural catalyst. There has been a clear erasure of certain music cultures, of certain individual artists, or of certain genres. This has happened, for instance, in relation to gender, where female artists, bands, and contributions to music have been either diminished or altogether excluded from history, with the rare chance of being 're-discovered' later on the basis of a contemporary need for 'female quota'. Pre-existing gender gaps and the basic rock male orientation lingered on, but deindustrialisation music gave way to female creative effort and to embracing gender equality. More research work is definitely needed to achieve a fuller understanding of this.

Hardcore punk has also been partly forgotten in the contemporary deindustrialisation music canon. Its harshness and uncompromising at-titude towards mainstream society has often been problematic, inside and outside this particular scene itself. Problems like violence in and outside gigs, alcoholism, and drug abuse dramatised the crisis a step further than the punk carnivalesque and a city might tolerate. It is rare today to see these bands, especially in Torino and Tampere, get the recognition that is accorded to other more cerebral and organic forms of 'post-punk', such as synth-pop. Sometimes industrial music has been preferred due to its isolationist approach in production and consump-tion despite sharing with hardcore punk an extreme noise agency.

In addition, industrial cities have also been sites of displacement and migration, in relation to national, continental, and colonial histories. Some of my informants showed this in accents, attitudes, and self-representations. The example of Manchester reveals that the influence of black music played a significant role in forging 'post-punk' and in the slow shift towards electronica and dance music; however, the possible African American origin of *Motorik* and of certain industrial aesthetics has often been downplayed. Black music connections might go beyond the obvious ones in electronic dance music and the British context, and this definitely calls for further studies.

My fascination for industrial cities under deindustrialisation, their music production, and the memories and traces left by both is still here, approximately ten years after having started working on these issues and thirty years after having witnessed a German artist banging on some rebar art. I still enjoy exploring industrial cities and sometimes I am awestruck by experiencing unexpectedly the 'pure joy' of being in a run-down room listening to noisy guitar or synth sounds, shouts in an unknown language, and repetitive drum patterns. There are always ways to keep music viable as a means for resistance and to experience it as a social practice.

REFERENCES

Abbott, Erik. 2014. *Cologne Carnival "Alternative" Stunksitzung: Carnivalization? Meta-Carnival? Or Bakhtinian Restoration?* New York: CUNY Academic Works.

Adorno, Theodor W. 1941. "On Popular Music." In *Studies in Philosophy and Social Science*, by Theodor W. Adorno, 9:17–48. New York: Institute of Social Research.

Akbar, Ahmed. 2018. "Heimat, Volk and Contemporary Germanic Music." In *Journey into Europe: Islam, Immigration and Identity*, by Ahmed Akbar, 63–64. Washington, DC: Brookings Institution Press.

Albiez, Sean. 2006. "Print the Truth, Not the Legend: Sex Pistols, Lesser Free Trade Hall, Manchester 7 June 1976." In *Performance and Popular Music: History, Place and Time*, edited by Ian Inglis, 92–106. Abingdon, UK: Ashgate.

Albiez, Sean, and David Pattie. 2011. *Kraftwerk: Music Non Stop*. New York: Continuum.

Allen, Robert C. 2009. *The British Industrial Revolution in Global Perspective*. Cambridge: Cambridge University Press.

Antonelli, Carlo. 2006. "Cara Vecchia Italia Sei un Paese nei Guai." *Rolling Stone*, April 30, 2006, 137.

Arrighi, Giovanni. 1994. *The Long Twentieth Century: Money, Power and the Origins of Our Times*. London: Verso.

Aunola, Manu. 2009. "Patrons and Pahtfinders: Two Tales of Successful Strategic Evolution in the Finnish Music Industry." Licentiate thesis, University of Tampere.

Badham, Richard. 1986. *Theories of Industrial Society*. London: Routledge.

Baker, Sarah. 2010. *Community Custodians of Popular Music's Past: A DIY Approach to Heritage*. New York: Routledge.

Baker, Sarah, and Alison Huber. 2015. "Saving 'Rubbish': Preserving Popular Music's Material Culture in Amateur Archives and Museums." In *Sites of Popular Music Heritage: Memories, Histories, Places*, edited by by Sara Cohen, Robert Knifton, Marion Leonard, and Les Roberts, 112–24. New York: Routledge.

Baker, Sarah, Catherine Strong, Lauren Istvandity, and Zelmarie Cantillon. 2018. *The Routledge Companion to Popular Music History and Heritage*. New York: Routledge.

Bakhtin, Mikhail. 1984. *Problems of Dostoevsky's Poetics*. Minneapolis: University of Minnesota Press.

Bangs, Lester. 1995. "Kraftwerkfeature." In *The Faber Book of Pop*, edited by Hanif Kureishi and Jon Savage, 481–86. London: Faber & Faber.

Banks, Mark, and Justin O'Connor. 2017. "Inside the Whale (and How to Get Out of There). Moving On from Two Decades of Creative Industry Research." *European Journal of Cultural Studies* 20 (6): 637–54.

Barr, Tim. 1998. *Kraftwerk. From Düsseldorf to the Future (with Love)*. London: Ebury.

Barthes, Roland. 1957. *Mythologies*. Paris: Edition du Soleil.

Bartos, Karl. 2017. *Der Klang der Machine*. Cologne: Eichborn.

baukunst-nrw. 2008 (last modified). "Mannesmann-Hochhaus." Accessed March 5, 2018. https://www.baukunst-nrw.de/objekte/Mannesmann-Hochhaus--250.htm.

Beauchamp, Dan E. 1981. "The Paradox of Alcohol Policy: The Case of the 1969 Alcohol Act in Finland." In *Alcohol and Public Policy: Beyond the Shadow of Prohibition*, edited by Mark H. Moore and Dean R. Gerstein, 225–54. Washington, DC: National Academies Press.

Becker, Howard. 1982. *Art Worlds*. Berkeley: University of California Press.

Belgiojoso, Ricciarda. 2014. *Constructing Urban Space with Sounds and Music*. Farnham, UK: Ashgate.

Benjamin, Walter. 1963. *Das Kunstwerk im Zeitalter seiner technischen Reproduzierbarkeit*. Frankfurt am Main: Suhrkamp.

Bennett, Andy. 2009. "'Heritage Rock': Rock Music, Representation and the Heritage Discourse." *Poetics*, no. 37, 474–89.

Bennett, Andy. 2004. "Consolidating the Music Scene Perspective." *Poetics*, no. 32, 223–34.

Bennett, Andy. 2018. "Youth, Music and DIY Careers." *Cultural Sociology* 12 (2): 133–39.

Bennett, Andy, and Keith Kahn Harris. 2004. *After Subculture: Critical Studies in Contemporary Youth Culture*. Basingstoke, UK: Palgrave, 2004.

Bennett, Andy, and Richard A. Peterson. 2004. *Music Scenes: Local, Translocal, and Virtual*. Nashville: Vanderbilt University Press.

Bernelli, Silvio. 2009. *I Ragazzi del Mucchio*. Milan: Sironi.

Bey, Hakim. 1991. *Temporary Autonomous Zones*. New York: Autonomedia.

Bielmeier, Franz. 1978. "Punk in Deutschland." *The Ostrich*, July/August 1978.

Bielmeier, Franz. 2013. "charley's girls—prima probe! mai 1978 im ratinger hof (keller)." YouTube, October 26, 2013. https://www.youtube.com/watch?v=S4VDIg4dbDY&feature=youtu.be.

Bielmeier, Franz. 2014. "charley's girls 1978 (live in new orleans)." YouTube, December 18, 2014. https://www.youtube.com/watch?v=JDJVQAm_iAE&feature=youtu.be.

Bijsterveld, Karin. 2008. *Mechanical Sound. Technology, Culture and Public Problems of Noise in the 20th Century*. Cambridge, MA: MIT Press.

Bilton, Chris. 2013. "Playing to the Gallery. Myth, Method and Complexity in the Creative Process." In *Handbook of Research on Creativity*, edited by Kerry Thomas and Chan Janet, 125–37. Cheltenham, UK: Elgar.

Blum, Alan. 2001. "Scenes." *Public*, no. 22-23, 7–35.

Blumer, Herbert. 1986. *Symbolic Interactionism*. Berkeley: University of California Press.

Böhme, Gernot. 1993. "Atmosphere as the Fundamental Concept of a New Aesthetics." *Thesis Eleven* 36: 113–36.

Bohn, Chris. 1981. "A Computer Date with a Showroom Dummy." *New Musical Express* (June): 31–33.

Boldermann, Leonieke, and Stijn Reijnders. 2019. "Sharing Songs on Hirakata Square: On Playlists and Place Attachment in Contemporary Music Listening." *European Journal of Cultural Studies* (May): 1–17.

Booth, Robert. 2009. "Artists' Creative Use of Vacant Shops Brings Life to Desolate High Streets." *The Guardian*, February 18, 2009.

Bottà, Giacomo. 2009. "The City That Was Creative and Did Not Know: Manchester and Popular Music, 1976–1997." *European Journal of Cultural Studies* 12 (3): 349–65.

Bottà, Giacomo. 2012. "Berlin as Urban Palimpsest." In *Villes invisibles et écritures de la Modernité*, edited by Aurelie Choné, 43–54. Mulhouse, France: Orizons.

Bottà, Giacomo. 2015. "Dead Industrial Atmopshere: Popular Music, Cultural Heritage and Industrial Cities." *Journal of Urban Cultural Studies*, no. 1-2, 107–20.

Bottà, Giacomo. 2018. "Trying to Find a Clue Trying to Find a Way to Get Out! The European Imaginary of Joy Division." In *Heart And Soul: Critical Essays On Joy Division*, edited by Martin J. Power, Eoin Devereux, and Aileen Dillane, 33–46. London: Rowman & Littlefield International.

Bottà, Giacomo, and Ferruccio Quercetti. 2019. "Brigade Rosse. The Clash, Bologna and Italian Punx." In *Working for the Clampdown: The Clash, the Dawn of Neoliberalism and the Political Promise of Punk*, edited by Colin Coulter, 209–22. Manchester: Manchester University Press.

Botte, Marie-Claire, and René Chocholle. 1984. *Le Bruit*. Paris: Presses Universitaires de France.

Boym, Svetlana. 2008. *Architecture of the Off-Modernity*. New York: Princeton Architectural Press.

Braun, Hans Joachim. 1999. "Themen der Technik in der Musik des 20. Jahrhunderts." In *Technik zwischen Akzeptanz und Widerstand*, edited by Gerhard Stadler and Anita Kuisle, 167–89. Münster: Waxmann.

Brocken, Michael. 2003. *The British Folk Revival 1944–2002*. London: Routledge.

Brooks, Michael. 2018. "Europe Endless: Owen Hatherley on the Lost Continent." *The Quietus*, July 1, 2018. https://thequietus.com/articles/24887-trans-europe-express-owen-hatherley-interview.

Brown, Adam, Justin O'Connor, and Sara Cohen. 2000. "Local Music Policies within a Global Music Industry: Cultural Quarters in Manchester and Sheffield." *Geoforum* 31 (4): 437–51.

Brunow, Dagmar. 2019. "Manchester's Post-Punk Heritage: Mobilising and Contesting Transcultural Memory in the Context of Urban Regeneration." *Culture Unbound. Journal of Current Cultural Research* 11 (1): 9–29.

Buckley, David. 2012. *Kraftwerk Publikation*. London: Omnibus Press.

Bull, Michael. 2005. "No Dead Air! The Ipod and the Culture of Mobile Listening." *Leisure Studies* 24, no. 4 (October): 343–55.

Busà, Alessandro. 2010. "City of Memory." In *Encyclopaedia of Urban Studies*, edited by Ray Hutchison, 158. Thousand Oaks, CA: SAGE.

Bussy, Pascal. 2001. *Kraftwerk, Man, Machine and Music*. London: SAF.

Byrne, David. 2002. "Industrial Culture in a Post-Industrial World: The Case of the North East of England." *City*, no. 6, 279–89.

Camagni, Roberto. 1991. *Innovative Networks: Spatial Perspectives*. Hoboken, NJ: John Wiley & Sons.

Chrisoulis, Con. 2018. *Tales of the Smiths*. London: Omnibus Press.

Clark, Peter. 2009. *European Cities and Towns: 400–2000*. Oxford: Oxford University Press.

Cohen, Sara. 2007a. *Decline, Renewal and the City in Popular Music Culture: Beyond the Beatles*. Aldershot, UK: Ashgate.

Cohen, Sara. 2007b. "'Rock Landmark at Risk': Popular Music, Urban Regeneration, and the Built Environment." *Journal of Popular Music Studies* 19 (1): 3–25.

Cohen, Sara. 2012. "Bubbles, Tracks, Borders and Lines: Mapping Music and Urban Landscape." *Journal of the Royal Musical Association* 137 (1): 135–70.

Cohen, Sara, Robert Knifton, Marion Leonard, and Les Roberts. 2015. *Sites of Popular Music Heritage: Memories, Histories, Places*. New York: Routledge.

Coney, Brian. 2018. '40 Years On: Pere Ubu's The Modern Dance Revisited'. The Quietus, January 22, 2018. https://thequietus.com/articles/23892-pere-ubu-the-modern-dance-review-anniversary.

Contrazione. 1983. *Yeti Punkzine*.

Contrazione. 2006. *1983/85 Storia e Memoria*. Torino: Nautilus.

Corbijn, Anton, dir. 2007. *Control*.

Coulthard, Jim, and Marie-Louise Coulthard, dirs. 1972. *Sheffield: City on the Move*.

Council of Europe. 2005. *Convention on the Value of Cultural Heritage for Society*. Faro, Portugal.

Cowie, Jefferson, and Joseph Heathcott. 2003. *Beyond the Ruins: the Meanings of Deindustrialization*. Ithaca, NY: Cornell University Press.

Crossley, Nick. 2015. *Networks of Sound, Style and Subversion: The Punk and Post-Punk Worlds of Manchester, London, Liverpool and Sheffield, 1975–1980*. Manchester: Manchester University Press.

Cummins, Kevin. 2012. *Manchester: Looking at the Light through the Pouring Rain*. London: Faber & Faber.

Danto, Arthur. 1964. "The Art World." *Journal of Philosophy*, no. 61, 571–84.

Davies, Jim K. 2011. "B1—Buzzcocks." *BandLogoJukeBox*, November 30, 2011.

Dee, Michael. 1998. "Interview with Klaus Dinger from Pop Magazine." Dingerland, October 1998. https://www.dingerland.de/pop_int.html.

De Sario, Beppe. 2009. *Resistenze Innaturali*. Milano: Agenzia X.

De Tocqueville, Alexis. (1835) 1958. *Journeys to England and Ireland*. New Haven, CT: Yale University Press.

Devereux, Eoin, and Melissa Hidalgo. 2015. "'You're Gonna Need Someone on Your Side': Morrissey's Latino/a and Chicano/a Fans." *Participations: Journal of Audience and Reception Studies* 12 (2): 197–217.

DeWall, C. Nathan, Richard S. Pond, W. Keith Campbell, and Jean M. Twenge. 2011. "Tuning in to Psychological Change: Linguistic Markers of Psychological Traits and Emotions over Time in Popular U.S. Song Lyrics." *Psychology of Aesthetics, Creativity and the Arts* 5 (3): 200–207.

Dicker, Holly. 2018. "Join in the Chant: Inside the Cult of EBM." Resident Advisor, August 21, 2018. https://www.residentadvisor.net/features/3311.

Dreyer, Sven-André, and Michael Wenzel. 2018. *Keine Atempause: Musik aus Düsseldorf*. Düsseldorf: Droste.

Drucker, Peter F. 2007. *The Future of the Industrial Man*. New York: Routledge.

Dubin, Robert. 1987. *The World of Work. Industrial Society and Human Relations*. New York: Garland.

Emery, Jay. 2019. "Geographies of Deindustrialization and the Working Class: Industrial Ruination, Legacies and Affect." *Geography Compass*, no. 13, e12417.

Engels, Friedrich. (1845) 1969. *The Condition of the Working Class in England*. n.p.: Panther.

Epstein, Josh. 2014. *Sublime Noise. Musical Culture and the Modernist Writer*. Baltimore: Johns Hopkins University Press.

Esch, Rüdiger. 2014. *Electri_City. Elektronische Musik aus Düsseldorf*. Berlin: Suhrkamp.

Evans, Edwin. 1930. "The Liege Festival." *Musical Times* 71, no. 1052 (October): 898–902.

Evans, Karen, Penny Fraser, and Ian Taylor. 1996. *A Tale of Two Cities: A Study in Manchester and Sheffield*. London: Routledge.

Farano, Roberto. 1983. "Produzione / Distribuzione." *Disforia* (fanzine), November 19, 1983.

Felski, Rita. 1999. "The Invention of Everyday Life." *New Formations*, no. 39, 13–31.

Fisher, Mark. 2014. *Ghosts of My Life. Writings on Depression, Hauntology and Lost Futures*. Winchester, UK: Zer0 Books.

Florida, Richard. 2002. *The Rise of the Creative Class*. New York: Perseus.

Flür, Wolfgang. 2017. *I Was a Robot*. London: Omnibus.

Foot, John. 2001. *Milan since the Miracle: City, Culture and Identity*. Oxford: Berg.

Fornäs, Johan. 2016. "The Mediatization of Third Time Tools: Culturalizing and Historicizing Temporality." *International Journal of Communication* 10:5213–32.

Fraser, Nancy. 1990. "Rethinking the Public Sphere: A Contribution to the Critique of Actually Existing Democracy." *Social Text* 25/26:56–80.

Gee, Grant, dir. 2007. *Joy Division*.

Gelder, Ken. 2007. *Subcultures: Cultural Histories and Social Practice*. Oxon, UK: Routledge.

Gill, Andy. 1997. "Kraftwerk." *Mojo*, April 1, 1997.

Gill, Mark, dir. 2017. *England Is Mine*.

gleim, ar/gee. 2016. *German Punk: The Early Years*. Cologne: Artbookers.

Goddard, Michael, Benjamin Halligan, and Nicola Spleman. 2013. *Resonances: Noise and Contemporary Music*. New York: Bloomsbury.

Goldblatt, David. 2008. *The Ball Is Round: A Global History of Soccer*. New York: Riverhead.

Gould, Peter, and Rodney White. 1974. *Mental Maps*. London: Penguin.

Goven, Jennifer. 2005. "From the Delta to Chicago: Muddy Water's Downhome Blues and the Shaping of African-American Identity in Post World War II Chicago." *McNair Scholars Journal* 8 (1): 62–69.

Gronow, Pekka. 1973. *Laulukirja: Työväenlauluja kahdeksalta vuosikymmeneltä*. Helsinki: Tammi.

Gunn, Simon. 2013. "Beyond Coketown: The Industrial City in the Twentieth Century." In *Industrial Cities: History and Future*, edited by Clemens Zimmermann, 29–45. Frankfurt: Campus.

Habermas, Jürgen, Sara Lennox, and Frank Lennox. 1974. "The Public Sphere: An Encyclopedia Article." *New German Critique*, no. 3, 49–55.

Hänninen, Juho. 2015. "Mihin jäi punk?" Oranssi ry, accessed February 20, 2019. http://www.oranssi.net/pienlehdet/mihinjaipunk.html.

Hall, Peter. 1975. *Urban and Regional Planning*. Middlesex, UK: Penguin.

Hall, Stuart. 1987. *Representations: Cultural Representations and Signifying Practices*. London: Sage.

Hall, Stuart, and Tony Jefferson. 2003. *Resistance through Rituals: Youth Subcultures in Post-War Britain*. London: Taylor & Francis.

Hartmann, Elke. 2003. "Die futuristischen Vier." *Focus*, September 11, 2003.

Harvey, David. 1989. *The Condition of Postmodernity: An Inquiry into the Conditions of Cultural Change*. London: Wiley.

Harvey, David. 2003. *Paris: Capital of Modernity*. New York: Routledge.

Harvey, David. 2005. *A Brief History of Neoliberalism*. Oxford: Oxford University Press.

Harvey, David. 2010. *The Enigma of Capital and the Crises of Capitalism*. Oxford: Oxford University Press.

Haslam, David. 2000. *Manchester, England: The Story of the Pop Cult City*. London: Harper Collins.

Hatherley, Owen. 2010a. *A Guide to the New Ruins of Great Britain*. London: Verso.

Hatherley, Owen. 2010b. "The Situationists and the City. Ed. Tom McDonough (Verso, London, 2009)." Critic's Guides. *Frieze*, April 1, 2010. https://frieze.com/article/situationists-and-city.

Hebdige, Dick. 1979. *Subculture: The Meaning of Style*. London: Routledge.

Hesmondhalgh, David. 1998. "Post-Punk's Attempt to Democratise the Music Industry: The Success and Failure of Rough Trade." *Popular Music* 16 (3): 255–74.

Hesmondhalgh, David. 2005. "Subcultures, Scenes or Neotribes? None of the Above." *Journal of Youth Studies* 8 (1): 21–40.

Hesmondhalgh, David. 2007. *The Cultural Industries. 2nd Edition*. London: Routledge.

Hesmondhalgh, David. 2013. *Why Music Matters*. Chichester, UK: Wiley Blackwell.

Hietala, Mariatta, and Mervi Kaarninen. 2005. "The Foundation of an Information City: Education and Culture in the Development of tampere." In *e-city: Analysing Efforts to Generate Local Dynamism in the City of Tampere*, edited by Antti Kasvio and Ari-Veikko Anttiroiko, 183–218. Tampere: Tampere University Press.

Higson, Andrew. 1996. "Space, Place, Spectacle: Landscape and Townscape in 'Kitchen Sink' Films." In *Dissolving Views: Key Writings on British Cinema*, by Andrew Higson, 133–56. London: Cassell.

Hilsberg, Alfred. 1978. "Krautpunk: Rodenkirchen is Burning." *Sounds*, March 1978, 20–24.

Hook, Peter. 2009. *The Hacienda: How Not To Run A Club*. London: Simon & Schuster.

Hook, Peter. 2012. *Unknown Pleasures: Inside Joy Division*. London: Simon & Schuster.

Hornberger, Barbara. 2011. *Geschichte wird gemacht. Die Neue Deutsche Welle: Eine Epoche Deustcher Popmusik*. Würzburg, Germany: Königshausen & Neumann.

Huyssen, Andreas. 2003. *Present Pasts: Urban Palimpsests and the Politics of Memory*. Stanford, CA: Stanford University Press.

Huyssen, Andreas. 2006. "Nostalgia for Ruins." *Grey Room* (Spring): 6–21.

Interiano, Myra, Kamyar Kazemi, Lijia Wang, Jienian Yang, Zhaoxia Yu, and Natalia L. Komarova. 2018. "Musical Trends and Predictability of Success in Contemporary Songs in and out of the Top Charts." *Royal Society Open Science* 5, no. 171274, 1–16.

Jalonen, Jussi. 2014. "Battle of Tampere." In *International Encyclopaedia of the First World War*, edited by Ute Daniel et al. Berlin: Freie Universität Berlin.

Jameson, Fredric. 1973. "The Vanishing Mediator: Narrative Structure in Max Weber." *New German Critique*, no. 1, 52–89.

Jansson, Panu. 2017. "Maria Mattila ja unelma Keltaisesta talosta." *City*, February 20, 2017.

Jha, Alok. 2007. "Bullying Is in the Genes, Study Suggests." *The Guardian*, December 27, 2007.

Justman, Paul, dir. 2002. *Standing in the Shadow of Motown*.

Karisaari, Juho. 2017. "Punkkarin Tampere. Paikallisuus punkkareiden muistelukerronnassa." Master's thesis, University of Tampere.

Keitel, Wilhelm, and Dominik Neuner. 1992. *Gioachino Rossini*. Munich: Knaus.

Kiechle, Melanie. 2016. "Navigating by Nose: Fresh Air, Stench Nuisance, and the Urban Environment, 1840–1880." *Journal of Urban History* 42 (4): 753–71.

King, Alex. 2019. "Upward Slope: How Skateboarding Transformed 'the Manchester of Finland'." *The Guardian*, April 16, 2019.

Klüver, Reymer. 2008. "Tod am laufenden Band." *GeoEpoche. Die Industrielle Revolution* 20 (March): 152–62.

Kneif, Timor. 1982. *Rockmusik: Ein Handbuch zum kritischen Verständnis*. Reinbek bei Hamburg: Rowholt.

Kohn, Margaret. 2009. "Dreamworlds of Deindustrialization." *Theory and Event* 12, no. 4.

Korczynski, Marek. 2007. "Music and Meaning on the Factory Floor." *Work and Occupations* 34 (3): 253–89.

Korczynski, Marek. 2014. *Songs of the Factory: Pop Music, Culture and Resistance*. Ithaca, NY: Cornell University Press.

Koskela, Hille. 2006. "'The Other Side of Surveillance': Webcams, Power and Agency." In *Theorizing Surveillance: The Panopticon and Beyond*, edited by D. Lyon, 163–81. Cullompton, UK: Willan.

Koskela, Hille. 2010. *Fear and Its Others: Social Geographies*. London: Sage.

Krakauer, Siegfried. 1996. *The Mass Ornament. Weimar Essays*. Cambridge, MA: Harvard University Press.

Krause, Monica. 2006. "The Production of Counter-Publics and the Counter-Publics of Production: An Interview with Oskar Negt." *European Journal of Social Theory* 9 (1): 119–28.

Krims, Adam. 2007. *Music and Urban Geography*. New York: Routledge.

Kühlem, Max Florian. 2018. "Campino als Überraschungsgast bei Male auf der Bühne." *Rheinische Post*, December 11, 2018.

Laf, Ernst. 1954. "Deutschland: Vom Beginn des 20. Jahrhunderts bis zum Gegenwart." In *Die Musik in Geschichte und Gegenwart*, by Ernst Laf, 344–58. Kassel: Bärenreiter.

Lash, Scott, and John Urry. 1987. *The End of Organized Capitalism*. Madison: University of Wisconsin Press.

Lehtovuori, Panu. 2010. *Experience and Conflict: The Production of Urban Space*. Farnham, UK: Ashgate, 2010.

Leigh, Thomas. 2012. "Dying Steel Sector Takes Big Role in French Politics." *New York Times*, February 22, 2012, 17.

Lerner, Gad. 2010. *Operai: Viaggio all'Interno della FIAT—La Vita, le Case, le Fabbriche di una Classe che Non C'è Più*. 2nd ed. Milano: Feltrinelli.

Levra, Umberto. 2001. *Storia di Torino. Volume 7: Da Capitale Politica a Capitale Industriale*. Torino: Einaudi.

Lindner, Rolf. 2004. *Walks on the Wild Side: Eine Geschichte der Stadtforschung*. Frankfurt am Main: Campus.

Lindner, Rolf. 2006. "The Cultural Texture of the City." In *The ESF-Liu Conference Cities and Media: Cultural Perspectives on Urban Identities in a Mediatized World*, edited by Johan Fornäs. Linköping, Sweden: Linköping University Electronic Press.

Linkon, Sherry Lee. 2018. *The Half-Life of Deindustrialization: Working-Class Writing about Economic Restructuring*. Ann Arbor: University of Michigan Press.

Linn, Allison. 2009. "Recession Works Way into Pop Culture." MSNBC, July 23, 2009.

Lipietz, Alain. 1992. *Towards a New Economic Order*. Oxford: Oxford University Press.

Lipsitz, George. 2007. *Footsteps in the Dark. The Hidden Histories of Popular Music*. Minneapolis: University of Minnesota Press.

Löding, Ole, and Philipp Krohn. 2018. *Sound of #Urbanana: A Journey through the Pop History of Cologne, Düsseldorf and the Ruhr Area*. Düsseldorf, Germany: Tourismus NRW.

Lynch, Kein. 1960. *The Image of the City*. Cambridge, MA: Harvard University Press.

MacColl, Ewan, ed. 1954. *The Shuttle and Cage: Industrial Folk Ballads*. London: Workers Music Association.

Makanowitsky, Barbara. 1965. "Music to Serve the State." *Russian Review* 24 (3): 266–77.

Manchester Digital Music Archive. 2016. "Dr. CP Lee on The Squat, Manchester University, 1971–1982." October 2, 2016. https://www.youtube.com/watch?v=XLEXavzMb9o.

Marketing Sheffield. 2018. "Welcome to Sheffield." Accessed October 9, 2018, http://www.welcometosheffield.co.uk.

Marr, Johnny. 2016. *Set The Boy Free*. London: Century.

Marx, Karl. 1977. *A Contribution to the Critique of Political Economy*. Moscow: Progress.

Massey, Doreen. 1984. *Spatial Divisions of Labour: Social Structures and the Geography of Production*. Basingstoke, UK: Macmillan.

Massey, Doreen. 2005. *For Space*. London: SAGE.

Mauser, Siegried. 2007. "Expressionismus und neue Sachlichkeit in den zwanziger Jahren." In *Hindemith Interpretationen: Hindemith und die zwanziger Jahren*, edited by Sackmann Dominik, 12. Bern: Peter Lang.

McRobbie, Angela. 1989. *Zoot Suites and Second-Hand Dresses*. London: Macmillan.

McVeigh, Tracy. 2012. "Posh Punk: Fashion Turns the Clock Back to 1977." *Observer Fashion*, January 7, 2012.

Mele, Christopher. 2000. *Selling the Lower East Side: Real Estate, Culture and Resistance in New York City*. Minneapolis: University of Minnesota Press.

Microsoft Devices Team. 2009. "Nokia Music Study Shows We Can't Help Loving Pop." *Microsoft Windows Blog*, November 16, 2009. https://blogs.windows.com/devices/2009/11/16/nokia-music-study-shows-we-cant-help-loving-pop.

Milestone, Katie. 1996. "Regional Variations. Northerness and New Urban Economies of Hedonism." In *From the Margins to the Centre. Cultural Production and Consumption in the Post-Industrial City*, edited by Justin Wynne and Derek O'Connor, 91–116. London: Routledge.

Mitchell, Don. 2003. *The Right to the City: Social Justice and the Fight for Public Space*. New York: Guilford.

Mitchell, Gillian. 2007. *The North American Folk Music Revival: Nation and Identity in the United States and Canada 1945–1980*. Aldershot, UK: Ashgate.

Mitchell, Tony. 2009. "Sigur Rós's Heima: An Icelandic Psychogeography." *Transforming Cultures eJournal* 4 (1): 172–98.

Mittagspause, comp.. 1982. *Punk Macht Dicken Arsch*.

Montgomery, John. 2003. "Cultural Quarters as Mechanisms for Urban Regeneration, Part 1: Conceptualising Cultural Quarters." *Planning, Practice & Research* 18 (4): 293–306.

Moore, Michael, dir. 1988. *Roger and Me*.

Moretti, Franco. 1998. *Atlas of the European Novel 1800–1900*. London: Verso.

Morgenstern, Ulrich. 2015. "Folk Music Research in Austria and Germany. Notes on Terminology, Interdisciplinarity and the Early History of Volksmusikforschung and Vergleichende Musikwissenschaft." *Musicologia Austriaca—Journal for Austrian Music Studies*, September 2015. http://www.musau.org/parts/neue-article-page/view/17.

Morris, Stephen. 2019. *Record, Play, Pause*. London: Constable.

Morrissey. 2013. *Autobiography*. London: Penguin.

Muggleton, David, and David Weinzierl. 2003. *The Post-Subcultures Reader*. Oxford: Berg.

Mule. 2011. "Featured Interview: MULE Speaks to Owen Hatherley (Part 2)." *Mule*, March 9, 2011.

Muscha, and Trini Trimpop, dirs. 1977. *Blitzkrieg Bop*.

Nähri, Mikko. 1993. *Hervanta, vuorenpeikkojen maa*. Tampere, Finland: City of Tampere.

Negt, Oskar, and Alexander Kluge. 1993. *Public Sphere and Experience: Towards and Analysis of the Bourgeois and Proletarian Public Sphere*. Minneapolis: University of Minnesota Press.

Nettleingham, David. 2019. "Beyond the Heartlands: Deindustrialization, Naturalization and the Meaning of an 'Industrial' Tradition." *The British Journal of Sociology* 70 (2): 610–26.

Nevarez, Leonard. 2013. "How Joy Division Came to Sound Like Manchester: Myths and Ways of Listening in the Neoliberal City." *Journal of Popular Music Studies* 25 (1): 56–76.

Nolan, David. 2006. *I Swear I Was There: The Gig That Changed The World*. Shropshire, UK: Independent Music Press.

Nora, Pierre. 1989. "Between Memory and History: Les Lieux de Mémoire." *Representations* (26): 7–24.

Nora, Pierre. 1996. "From Lieux de Mémoire to Realms of Memory." In *Realms of Memory: The Construction of the French Past*, by Pierre Nora, xv–xxiv. New York: Columbia University Press.

Numminen, Mikko. 2013. "Juhlaviikoilla esiintyvä Thurston Moore: 'Helsinki on suosikkini'." *Suomen Kuvalehti*, August 16, 2013.

O'Connor, Justin. 1999. "Popular Culture, Reflexivity and Urban Change." In *Creative Cities: Cultural Industries, Urban Development and the Information Society*, edited by Jan Verwijnen and Panu Lehtovuori, 76–100. Jyväskylä, Finland: UIAH.

Orchestre Symphonique de Paris. 2013. "Iron Foundry." *A Young Person's Guide to the Avant-Garde*. Cond. Julius Ehrlich. Comp. Alexander Mosolov.

Oswalt, Philipp. 2004. *Shrinking Cities Working Papers II: Manchester/Liverpool*. Berlin: Kulturstiftung des Bundes.

Parent-Duchâtelet, Alexandre-Jean-Baptiste. 1824. *Essai sur les Cloaques ou Égouts de la Ville de Paris*. Paris: Crevot.

Payer, Peter. 2007. "The Age of Noise. Early Reactions in Vienna 1870–1914." *Journal of Urban History* 33 (5): 773–93.

Peck, Jamie, and Kevin Ward. *City of Revolution. Restructuring Manchester*. Manchester: Manchester University Press, 2002.

Peterson, Richard A. 2005. "In Search of Authenticity." *Journal of Management Studies* 42, no. 5 (July): 1083–98.

Petridis, Alexis. 2008. "Things Really Must Be Bad: AC/DC Are No 1 Again." *The Guardian*, October 27, 2008.

Picciuolo, Vanni 'Franti'. 1994. "Radio Interview." By Sergio Tosato. Translated from Italian by Giacomo Bottà. *Estamos en Todas Partes* (CD).

Preston, Peter. 1994. "Manchester and Milton-Northern." In *Writing the City: Eden, Babylon and the New Jerusalem*, edited by Peter Preston and Paul Simpson-Housley, 31–57. London: Routledge.

Quilley, Stephen. 1999. "Entrepreneurial Manchester: The Genesis of Elite Consensus." *Antipode*, 185–211.

Quilley, Stephen. 2000. "Manchester First: From Municipal Socialism to the Entrepreneurial City." *International Journal of Urban and regional Research* 23 (4): 601–15.

Quispel, Chris. 2005. "Detroit, City of Cars, City of Music." *Built Environment* 31 (3): 226–36.

Raine, Sarah. 2019. "'In the Pitch Black Dark': Searching for a 'Proper Nighter' in the Current Northern Soul Scene." In *Nocturnes: Popular Music and the Night*, edited by by Geoff Stahl and Giacomo Bottà, 21–34. London: Palgrave Macmillan.

Rexroth, Dieter. 2005. *Beethovens Symphonien: ein musikalischer Werkführer*. Munich: Beck.

Reynolds, Simon. 2006. *Rip It Up and Start Again: Postpunk 1978–1984*. London: Penguin.

Reynolds, Simon. 2009. "'Cession Musicians?" *FACT Magazine*, February 21, 2009.

Reynolds, Simon. 2011. *Retromania: Pop Culture's Addiction to Its Own Past*. London: Faber & Faber.

Reynolds, Simon. 2016. *Shock and Awe: Glam Rock and Its Legacy*. London: Faber & Faber.

Reynolds, Simon. 2018. "The First Sensitive Punk: Remembering Buzzcocks' Pete Shelley." *Pitchfork*, December 8, 2018.

Richters, Denisa. 2015. "Bald Flüchtinge in Ex-Vodafone-Bauten." *Rheinische Post*, September 23, 2015.
Ricoeur, Paul. 2004. *Memory, History, Forgetting*. Chicago: University of Chicago Press.
Rietveld, Hillegonda C. 2014. "Voodoo Rage: Blacktronica from the North." In *Black Popular Music in Britain Sincen 1945*, edited by by Jon Stratton and Nabeel Zuberi, 153–68. Farnham, UK: Ashgate, 2014.
Robb, John. 2009. *The North Will Rise Again: Manchester Music City 1976–1996*. London: Aurum.
Roodhouse, Simon. 2010. *Cultural Quarters. Principles and Practice*. 2nd ed. Bristol: Intellect.
Russolo, Luigi. 1967. *The Art of Noise*. New York: Something Else Press.
Saastamoinen, Mika. 2007. *Parasta lapsille: Suomipunk 1977–1984*. Helsinki: Johnny Kniga.
Savage, Jon. 1991. *England's Dreaming: Sex Pistols and Punk Rock*. London: Faber.
Savage, Jon. 2019. *This Searing Light, the Sun and Everyhing Else: Joy Division, the Oral History*. London: Faber & Faber.
Schütte, Uwe. 2017. *German Pop Music: A Companion*. Berlin: De Gruyter.
Schaefer, Murray R. 1977. *The Soundscape: Our Sonic Environment and the Tuning of the World*. New York: Knopf.
Schumpeter, Joseph. 1942. *Capitalism, Socialism and Democracy*. New York: Harper and Brothers.
Schwabe, Oliver, dir. 2016. *Keine Atempause: Düsseldorf, der Ratinger Hof und die neue Musik*. Produced by WDR.
Scott, Allen J. 2001. "Capitalism, Cities, and the Production of Symbolic Forms." *Transactions of the Institute of British Geographers* 26 (1): 11–23.
Senior, Jennifer. 2009. "Recession Culture." *New Yorker*, May 10, 2009.
Shaw, Hollie. 2009. "Doh! The Recession has Gone Pop." *National Post*, June 19, 2009.
Sheffield Libraries Archives and Information. 2005. *Sources for the Study of Sheffield's Battle for Clean Air*. Sheffield: Sheffield City Council.
Shields, Rob. 1991. *Places on the Margin: Alternatives Geographies of Modernity*. London: Routledge.
Simmel, Georg. 2007. "Die Ruine: ein ästhetischer Versuch." *Der Tag*, February 22, 1907.
Simpson, Dave. 2017. "How Buzzcocks Invented Indie (with help from the Sex Pistols, a Renault and the Quo)." *The Guardian*, January 12, 2017.
Skaniakos, Terhi. 2010. *Discoursing Finnish Rock: Articulations of Identities in the Saimaa-ilmiö Rock Documentary*. Jyväskylä, Finland: University of Jyväskylä.
Small, Mario Luis, David J. Harding, and Michele Lamont. 2010. "Reconsidering Culture and Poverty." *Annals of the American Academy of Political and Social Sciences* 629 (1): 6–27.
Smith, Suzanne E. 1999. *Dancing in the Street: Motown and the Cultural Politics of Detroit*. Cambridge, MA: Harvard University Press.
Springer, Johannes, Christian Steinbrink, and Christian Werthschulte. 2008. *Echt! Pop-Protokolle aus dem Ruhrgebiet*. Duisburg, Germany: Salon Alter Hammer.
Stahl, Geoff. 2008. "Cowboy Capitalism. The Art of Ping Pong Country in the New Berlin." *Space and Culture* 11 (4): 300–324.
Stahl, Geoff, and Giacomo Bottà. 2019. "Introduction: Because the Night. . . ." In *Nocturnes: Popular Music and the Night*, edited by Geoff Stahl and Giacomo Bottà, 1–18. London: Palgrave Macmillan.
Stokes, Martin. 1997. *Ethnicity, Identity and Music: The Musical Construction of Place*. Oxford: Berg.
Strangleman, Tim. 2013. "'Smokestack Nostalgia', 'Ruin Porn' or Working Class Obituary: The Role and Meaning of Deindustrial Representation." *International Labour and Working Class History* 84 (Fall): 23–37.
Strangleman, Tim, James Rhodes, and Sherry Linkon. 2013. "Introduction to Crumbling Cultures: Deindustrialization, Class, and Memory." *International Labour and Working-Class History*, no. 84, 7–22.

Straw, Will. 1991. "Systems of Articulation, Logics of Change: Communities and Scenes in Popular Music." *Cultural Studies* 53:368–88.
Straw, Will. 2001. "Scenes and Sensibilities." *Public*, no. 22-23, 245–57.
Stubbs, David. 2014a. *Future Days: Krautrock and the Building of Modern Germany*. London: Faber & Faber.
Stubbs, David. 2014b. "How Motorik Infected the Mainstream, by Future Days Author David Stubbs." The Quietus, August 7, 2014. https://thequietus.com/articles/15929-david-stubbs-krautrock-motorik.
Sumner, Bernard. 2014. *Chapter and Verse: New Order, Joy Division and Me*. London: Random House.
Swedish Punk Fanzines. n.d. "The 20 Most Essential HardcoreRreleases in the Nordic Countries." Accessed April 9, 2019. http://www.swedishpunkfanzines.com/?page_id=12096.
Teipel, Jürgen. 2001. *Verschwende deine Jugend*. Frankfurt am Main: Suhrkamp.
Tickell, Adam, and Jamie Peck. 1996. "The Return of the Manchester Men: Men's Words and Men's Deeds in the Remaking of the Local State." *Transactions of the Institute of British Geographers* 21 (4): 595–616.
Topelius, Zacharias. (1873) 2013. *En Resa i Finland*. Helsinki: SLS.
Townsend, Mark. 2010. "Return of Underground Rave Culture Is Fuelled by the Recession and Facebook." *The Guardian*, November 10, 2010.
Tranfaglia, Nicola. 1999. *Storia di Torino. Volume 9: Gli Anni della Repubblica*. Torino: Einaudi.
Ullvén, Lasse. 2016. "The Curious Cultural Exchanges between Finnish and Brazilian Punks: 'A Contribucao milionária de todos os erros.'" Master's thesis, University of Malta.
UNESCO. 1972. *Convention Concerning the Protection of the World Cultural and Natural Heritage*. Stockholm.
UNESCO. 1992–2019. "World Heritage List." World Heritage Centre, accessed May 23, 2019. https://whc.unesco.org/en/list.
UNESCO. 2003. *Convention for the Safeguarding of the Intangible Cultural Heritage*. Paris, France.
Van Paassen, Pierre. 1936. "Durruti Dumange, José Buenaventura: 2,000,000 Anarchists Fight for Revolution Says Spanish Leader." *Toronto Daily Star*, August 18, 1936, 1–5.
Vicari Haddock, Serena. 2004. *La Città Contemporanea*. Bologna: Il Mulino.
Von Moltke, Johannes. 2005. *No Place like Home: Locations of Heimat in German Cinema*. Berkeley: University of California Press.
Waisbord, Silvio. 2019. "Populism as Media and Communication Phenomenon." In *Routledge Handbook of Global Populism*, edited by Claudio de la Torre, 221–34. Abingdon, UK: Routledge.
Waitt, Albert R., III. 2009. "Best Songs for the Recession." The Hangover, March 13, 2009. https://thehangover.wordpress.com/?s=best+songs+for+the+recession&submit=Search.
Wessel, Horst A. 1990. *Kontinuität im Wandel. 100 Jahre Mannesmann AG 1890–1990*. Düsseldorf: Mannesmann AG.
Wicke, Peter. 1992. "Populäre Musik als theoretisches Konzept." *PopScriptum* (Forschunszentrum Populäre Musik der Humboldt-Universität zu Berlin), no. 1.
Williams, Raymond. 1977. *Marxism and Literature*. Oxford: Oxford University Press.
Williams, Raymond. 1980. *Culture and Materialism*. London: Verso.
Winterbottom, Michael, dir. 2002. *24 Hour Party People*.
Woods, Bret D. 2007. *Industrial Music for Industrial People*. Tallahassee: Florida State University Press, 2007.
Worley, Matthew. 2017. *No Future: Punk, Politics and British Youth Culture 1976–1984*. Cambridge: Cambridge University Press.
Wynn, Jonathan R. 2015. *Music/City: American Festivals and Placemaking in Austin, Nashville and Newport*. Chicago: University of Chicago Press.
Zimmermann, Clemens, ed. 2013. *Industrial Cities: History and Futures*. Frankfurt: Campus.
Žižek, Slavoj. 1991. *For They Know Not What They Do*. London: Verso.

Zukin, Sharon. 2009. "Changing Landscapes of Power: Opulence and the Urge for Authenticity." *International Journal of Urban and Regional Research* 33, no. 2 (June): 543–53.
Zukin, Sharon. *Naked City: The Death and Life of Authentic Urban Places*. Oxford: Oxford University Press, 2010.

INDEX

24/7 city, 85–86

AC/DC, 3
Agnelli, Gianni (a.k.a. L'avvocato), 131–132
Agnelli, Giovanni, 111
Altstadt (Düsseldorf), 90
anni di piombo, 114
Arrighi, Giovanni, 30
art world, 8
Avraamov, Arseny, 47

Bastards, 15, 148, 154, 156, 158, 172
Battle of Tampere, 158
'Bella Ciao', 157
Benjamin, Walter, 49
Bernelli, Silvio, 119
Bertotti, Marzio (a.k.a. Mungo), 123
Beuys, Joseph, 92
Bielemeier, Frank (a.k.a. Mary Lou Monroe), 95
Blatto, Maurizio, 131
Blitzkrieg Bop (film), 94
Blue Vomit, 129
Braatz, Peter (a.k.a. Harry Rag), 98, 101, 102
Brigate Rosse, 114
Buzzcocks, 72

Caberlin, Mara, 118
Can, 104, 107

Capra, Gianpiero, 123, 126, 127, 132
carnevalesque, 142
carnival, 90
Carsch-Haus Festival, 100
Cavalera, Max, 137
Centre for Contemporary Cultural Studies (CCCS), 7
centri d'incontro, 117
Charley's Girls, 95
Chicago blues, 54–55
Chicago School of Sociology, 7, 134
Cinotto, Simone, 112
civil rights movement, 50
Collettivo Punx Anarchici, 122–124
Condannati a Morte nel Vostro Quieto Vivere, 133
Contrazione, 118
Council of Europe, 165
Crass, 125
creative destruction, 29
creative milieu, 68, 75
crisis: automobile industry, 114; capitalism, and, 30; decay, and, 39; economic, 4; financial, 2; oil, 114
Crossley, Nick, 8
cultural sensibility, 39
Curtis, Ian, 170

'Dancing in the Street', 57
De Rossi, Antonio, 119
De Tocqueville, Alexis, 24

ABOUT THE AUTHOR

Giacomo Bottà is a part-time lecturer with the title of docent in urban studies at the University of Helsinki. He received a PhD in comparative studies from the Libera Università di Lingue e Comunicazione IULM Milan.

www.ingramcontent.com/pod-product-compliance
Lightning Source LLC
Chambersburg PA
CBHW030649270326
41929CB00007B/273